Praise for *The Intelligent Ledger*

'Forty years of banking transformation compressed into a single, urgent thesis. The Intelligent Ledger isn't a prediction – it's already being built. Read this now and find out how.'

—Joseph Edwin, *Sr. Partner, Bain & Company*

'Part biopic, part call to arms: this is a fantastic read for anyone reflecting on the journey the banking industry has gone on to date... and what comes next.'

—Leda Glyptis, *Chair of the Board, Bourn AI*

'Easy to read and impossible to put down, Intelligent Ledger shows how AI is an opportunity rather than a threat. An essential read for anyone participating in the future of banking.'

—Tom Shen, *Board Member, tyfone, inc., CSI, ZSuite Technologies*

'Dharmesh Mistry's boots are made for walkin' and they're walking banking straight into Quanvergence – the new era shaped by the nexus of four interconnected forces acting simultaneously.'

—Dr. Efi Pylarinou, *Founder, Growfin*

'I have been at Dharmesh's side for the past 30 years, watching him lead at the coal face as a true visionary, digitally enabling financial services. When he talks about the future, he speaks from a position of knowledge and experience. He knows what he is talking about.'

—Dave Wallace, *CEO, NMD +, and Co-host of Dave and Dharm Demystify* Podcast

The Intelligent Ledger

Dharmesh Mistry with Louis R. Carlozo

The Intelligent Ledger

How Agentic AI, Quantum Computing, Data, and Tokenisation Are Transforming Banking

palgrave
macmillan

Dharmesh Mistry
Reading, UK

Louis R. Carlozo
Qwoted
Chicago, IL, USA

ISBN 978-3-032-32841-0 ISBN 978-3-032-32842-7 (eBook)
https://doi.org/10.1007/978-3-032-32842-7

Cover Credit: mhibyusuf16.

This Palgrave Macmillan imprint is published by the registered company Springer Nature Switzerland AG
The registered company address is: Gewerbestrasse 11, 6330 Cham, Switzerland

For Amy

Always there, come rain or come shine . . . Lou Carlozo

Dedicated to my dad, Vasanbhai Gopal Mistry (1939–1992)

The greatest gift a father can give is the learning that comes from watching him work hard, build something successful, and then have it snatched away through a technology shift that was completely out of his control. His story deeply shaped my path, kept me looking ahead, and contributed entirely to my success. I am certain he is looking over me today, and so I dedicate this book, and the future it anticipates, to him . . . Dharmesh Mistry

Foreword

I've had the good fortune to be a guest on *Dave and Dharm Demystify* twice. Both times, he asked versions of the same question: What does it feel like to build a bank from scratch? It always sparks the question – if you're going to do it all from scratch, how do you avoid falling into the trap of building a copy of what already exists?

The truth is that when you have no legacy infrastructure to protect, no existing customer base to cannibalise, and no organisational immune system defending last decade's business model, the way to do things better can be surprisingly clear. After all, you do not need to predict the future. You just need to be honest about the present.

That's what this book is.

Griffin is, by Dharmesh's taxonomy, a pipe bank. Deliberately. We hold a full UK banking licence, we've built core infrastructure from the ground up, and we provide it to fintechs and platforms building modern, tech-led financial products.

Unlike most of the pipe banks Dharmesh looks at, though, our gross margins are around 90%. That's not an accident – it's what happens when you make an unambiguous strategic choice and build everything around it. We've never wanted to own the customer journey – and in giving that up, we've been ruthlessly efficient about building valuable infrastructure. We want to be the best possible foundation for the companies that build on top of us.

But! I'm not here to talk about us as a case study. It's more to make the point . . . it's okay to be a pipe bank or a platform bank. The danger lies in thinking you're one when you're really the other.

The banks that will stagnate over the next decade will be the ones that refuse to choose at all – those that try desperately to keep one foot in economics and the other in aspiration, and wound up the structural economics of neither.

Banks, partly by design, and partly by accident, are not known to make decisive strategic decisions when confronted with an evolving technological and cultural landscape. The banker's mentality is to avoid loss, not to embrace potential.

The question this book really asks is not so much about one technology or another as much as about the culture and strategy of banks. It's whether the people running the financial institutions of today will be able to see clearly enough, and act decisively enough, given everything that's institutionally arrayed against both.

Dharmesh ends with what he calls the Monday Morning Question: Who, in your organisation, is accountable – by name, with a budget, and a timeline – for building the Intelligent Ledger capability this book describes?

It's the right question. And the fact that most readers will find it difficult to answer is precisely the point.

David Jarvis
Co-founder and CEO, Griffin Bank

Foreword

For the past forty years we have repeatedly convinced ourselves that each new technology wave was revolutionary. We computerised branches, built ATM networks, launched internet banking, embraced mobile apps, migrated to the cloud and opened our systems through APIs. Each step made banking faster, cheaper, and more convenient. Yet none fundamentally changed what a bank actually is.

In fact, one of the biggest mistakes the banking industry makes is confusing digitisation with transformation whilst, beneath every innovation, sits the same truth which is that financial institutions are built around the very same principles that have existed since the Medici a millennium ago. What are they? Maintaining a ledger of financial transactions.

The problem is that a ledger is designed to remember the past, whilst customers increasingly need help navigating the future.

Nobody wakes up in the morning wondering what happened to their money yesterday. They worry about their money tomorrow. They worry about whether they can afford a home; whether they are saving enough for retirement; whether changing jobs is financially sensible; whether their children will be secure in an uncertain world; whether they can afford tomorrow.

Today's banking systems are extraordinarily good at recording what has already happened, but remarkably poor at helping people decide what should happen next.

That is why this book is not really about artificial intelligence, quantum computing, tokenisation or digital twins, even though all of those technologies feature prominently in the pages ahead. It is about what happens when these technologies converge.

History rarely changes because of a single invention. It changes when several technologies mature simultaneously and reinforce one another. The smartphone did not transform the world because of a touchscreen. It transformed the world because mobile broadband, processors, batteries, cloud computing and app ecosystems all arrived together. Banking is now approaching its own moment of convergence, and the consequences are likely to be every bit as significant.

The Intelligent Ledger is all about moving from a passive record of financial history to become an active participant in our financial lives. It understands context rather than simply transactions. It anticipates needs rather than waiting for instructions. It simulates outcomes before decisions are made and increasingly executes those decisions on our behalf. In other words, the intelligent ledger evolves from recording money to understanding people.

That idea challenges almost every assumption upon which modern banking has been built.

For decades, banks have competed by manufacturing and distributing financial products. In the decades ahead, they are far more likely to compete by providing intelligence. The institutions that understand their customers best will create the greatest value, whilst those that continue measuring success through the number of products sold will discover that the products themselves have become commodities.

This is also why I believe many readers will initially disagree with parts of this book. They should. Books about the future are not valuable because every prediction proves correct. They are valuable because they force us to rethink assumptions that have become so familiar we no longer question them.

Whether every forecast made here unfolds exactly as described is almost irrelevant. What matters is that the direction of travel is becoming increasingly clear. Artificial intelligence is becoming infrastructure. Money is becoming programmable. Financial advice is becoming autonomous. Banking is moving from a world of transactions to one of continuous intelligence.

If that sounds ambitious, it should.

Every major technological revolution has sounded ambitious until, with hindsight, it became obvious. Looking back, the internet feels inevitable. Smartphones feel inevitable. Cloud computing feels inevitable. None of them felt inevitable at the time. *The Intelligent Ledger* is another of those ideas that, a decade from now, leaves us wondering why we ever imagined banking could work any other way.

The real question, therefore, is not whether this transformation will happen. It is who will lead it. Funnily enough, I recently added a cartoon to my presentations on this theme.

Change management is the life of our world. It is the core of what makes success and failure. Those who change succeed. Those who do not fail.

This is critical thinking as some institutions will recognise that the future belongs to those who understand customers rather than products. Others will continue optimising twentieth-century business models with twenty-first-century technology. History suggests those are not the organisations that define the future.

This book is not simply a prediction about where banking is heading. It is a challenge to everyone responsible for building it.

The Intelligent Ledger will not give you answers, but it will help you think about adapting to change and, if nothing else, that's a good thing.

'It is not the most intellectual of the species that survives; it is not the strongest that survives; but the species that survives is the one that is able best to adapt and adjust to the changing environment in which it finds itself.' Charles Darwin, The Origin of Species

Chris Skinner
Author of Intelligent Money and Intelligent Bank, CEO, The Finanser

CHRIS SKINNER
MAKING FINANCE FUN AND EASY TO UNDERSTAND
DIARY OF A PONZI SCHEME
FOR EVERYONE
A THRILLING STORY.
EASY TO READ.
HARD TO FORGET.
INTELLIGENT BANK
FOR PROFESSIONALS
DEEP INSIGHTS.
STRATEGIC THINKING.
FUTURE READY.
DIARY OF A PONZI SCHEME
CHRIS SKINNER
INTELLIGENT BANK
CHRIS SKINNER
A FINANCIAL THRILLER INSPIRED BY TRUE EVENTS
THE FUTURE OF FINANCE IS INTELLIGENT
REAL PEOPLE. REAL GREED. REAL CONSEQUENCES.
LOVE. LIES. MONEY. POWER.
A STORY THAT WILL STAY WITH YOU LONG AFTER THE LAST PAGE.
PERFECT FOR FANS OF FINANCIAL THRILLERS AND TRUE STORIES.
I EXPLAIN FINANCE THROUGH STORYTELLING. BECAUSE EVERYONE DESERVES TO UNDERSTAND MONEY.
Chris Skinner
THE NEXT FINANCIAL REVOLUTION.
STRATEGIES FOR BANKS, FINTECHS AND FINANCIAL INSTITUTIONS.
WRITTEN FOR LEADERS WHO WANT TO STAY AHEAD OF THE CURVE.
ESSENTIAL READING FOR FINANCIAL LEADERS AND INNOVATORS.
TWO BOOKS. ONE MISSION.
FINANCIAL FREEDOM FOR ALL.
AVAILABLE WORLDWIDE
amazon
WATERSTONES
BARNES&NOBLE
audible
Apple Books

Preface

When it comes to breakthrough technology, divining the future is a very risky business.

The fortune-telling falls neatly into two distinct categories: Overblown cynicism and unchecked enthusiasm. Maybe the naysayers and breathless dreamers just want to draw attention to themselves. Regardless, anyone who lays claim to the metaphorical crystal ball might as well drill three holes in it, call it a bowling ball and heave it down the Silicon Alley in hopes of landing that elusive 7–10 split.

In terms of the cynics, even the esteemed newspaper of record, The New York Times, has got it wrong. Horribly wrong. On numerous occasions.

In 1903, the Times declared that 'it might be assumed that the flying machine which will really fly might be evolved by the combined and continuous efforts of mathematicians and mechanics in from one million to ten million years.' That was on 9 October. Not even 40 days later, Wilbur and Orville Wright pulled off the feat on 17 December. Five times, in fact.

Ditto for rocket travel. On 13 January 1920, the paper blasted the ideas of rocketing pioneer Robert H. Goddard thus: 'Professor Goddard . . . does not know the relation of action to reaction, and of the need to have something better than a vacuum against which to react. . . . Of course he only seems to lack the knowledge ladled out daily in high schools.'

It took half a century, and the Apollo 11 moon landing, for the Times to issue a correction.

As for the opposite end of the tech blather spectrum, examples of exuberance riding off the rails are legion. Think about the forecast of a helicopter in every driveway, made just after World War II. (You can actually see a 'commuter' model, built by United Helicopters, Inc., at the Hiller Aviation Museum in San Carlos, Calif.)

Or how about ... household nuclear-powered vacuums? Yup. (We shall avoid the obvious pun involving 'suck' here.) That prediction came in the 1950s as the future seers informed us these devices would become homefront staples within ten years. Perhaps the fear of meltdown, from the device itself and/or the anxious user trying to tame it, cut that prophecy short.

Some tech titans only get it half right. While Microsoft co-founder Bill Gates helped bring personal computing to the masses, his vision of a PC in every home did not include a smartphone in every hand. He miscalculated the growth rate of cellphones, which allowed Android to claim the spot as the standard non-iPhone platform. Reflecting on this in 2019, Gates said: 'The greatest mistake of all time is the mismanagement I engaged in that caused Microsoft not to be what Android is.'

Even today, we're not immune to seeing the future through rose-coloured glasses, literally. Google Glass 'smartglasses' and the Oculus Rift virtual reality headset inspired much fanfare in 2014 and 2016 respectively. People went gaga over the 'eyewear visions' these two exotic devices inspired. Today, they rank as footnotes with a niche user base: Barely seen, you might say.

So why write a book that makes bold (or foolish) predictions about the future of financial technology taken to an unprecedented level? We've even attached a specific year to it: 2032. By that time, banks as we've known them for generations will be supplanted by the very first financial 'platforms'. Imagine your health or household data, updated in real time, enabling agentic AI and digital twins to guide your every financial decision.

It's enough to make banks obsolete. Perhaps even irrelevant. And we explain how.

Have Dharm and Lou gone round the bend?

Or are they looking around the bend to spy a glimpse of what's next?

As discussed in this book, it's no small matter to place two industry reputations on the line. Dharm ranks as a pioneering technologist with 40 years' experience. Mobile and online banking as we know them owe a great debt to him. I possess far less mileage as a banking podcaster (about ten years), though I've become a regular presence and session host at Money2020 US, one of the world's largest banking conventions. Along the way, I've interviewed hundreds of banking executives to understand technology's impact on finance and get a take on what these people think, not what marketing departments trumpet.

Dharm – who takes the lead in everything you're about to read – acknowledges that many factors may keep the Intelligent Ledger, from which this book takes its name, from reaching fruition. Potential players have appeared not just in digital banking but also in fields such as utilities. But none has emerged with a clear vision or stated intention of creating something beyond a bank.

Make no mistake, though: Quantum computing, which will make financial platforms possible because of its immense calculating power, already exists. Google, Amazon, Microsoft, and IBM have launched it. Their machines are up and running, available to use on the cloud on a pay-per-use basis, though the technology still requires time to mature. It is not yet foolproof.

Secondly, sensible ways to portray the future rest on past predictions that held water. Back in 1965, Intel co-founder Gordon Moore did not predict computers would lead to some superhuman sci-fi invention coated in 3D fairy dust. Instead, he posited Moore's Law: The observation that the number of transistors on a microchip doubles approximately every two years, while the cost of computers halves.

Moore was right. In 1965, computers had 50 to 60 transistors. Today, a classical (non-quantum) computer might boast more than 100 billion in a single CPU. As mentioned in this book, Dharm began his adult computing adventures around 1990 by purchasing an Intel 386SX machine. It cost the equivalent of £9,000 in today's money. Today, that computer with its 80 MB hard drive would serve well as a paperweight or conversation piece but that's about it. Any smartphone brandishes more power by multitudes. As for 80 MB, you cannot find a USB drive available at such a miserly capacity, though you can buy one that holds 4 GB for about £4.

So technology's on the march. Great. But where's it marching to? The heart of this book does not concern the many ways that fintech and computer technology change before us. Each gadget, capability or LLM could be likened to one of a thousand stars in an evening sky.

Rather, what we seek to elucidate – draw, even – is a constellation. We start with all the bright points of tech: Agentic AI, quantum, digital twins, stablecoins and the live utilisation of dynamic data, always changing and building. You can connect those dots to reveal a clear portrait of banking's future.

This is not a commuter helicopter landing in your lap. These component parts add up to create an entirely new system – the financial platform – that embraces a complete aspect of how you run your finances. Dharm offers a fine example through his experiences creating AskHomey, which sought to put every financial variable or decision for the homeowner in one place.

He recognised, in a way banks could not, how utilities, mortgage rates, contractor rates and much more operated in their own unique ecosystem. The platform would chug away to reveal and execute on smart financial opportunities that could save money and improve efficiency. Customers would become customers for life – all of them – because the process of porting their data to a competitor would prove too high a mountain to scale. Brilliant!

Except that the timing was wrong. COVID-19 hit, contractors retreated and computer firepower was not up to the task. (Dharm does not shy from discussing the five times he misread 'revolutionary silo' technology changes. He's the furthest thing from a self-promoting, self-styled prophet you will ever meet.)

Now: An old newsroom jape from my Chicago Tribune days held that all you have to do is connect three points, and voila, you have a trend. So how do we know the constellation here is not just arbitrary, a sophisticated intellectual game of connect the dots?

Two more stars here involve coalescence, the place where technology meets human needs. At $600 USD at the time of its release, the Oculus Rift made for a pretty nifty toy that you could file under 'be the first kid on your block'. But at best, it qualified as a 'nice to have,' not a need to have. People did not require one any more than a vacuum powered by uranium.

Meanwhile, the hunger for a financial platform that can help people execute savvy financial moves has never been greater. By and large, banks have a limited ability to do this, and much more incentive to sell you a loan product or a new credit card. Does that make sense? Bottom line-wise, yes. But in terms of their clientele and their true needs, it amounts to a contradiction.

A 2024 survey by Discover found that four in five Americans reported anxiety about their financial situation, with 34% experiencing moderate or severe anxiety. Debt made the list as a top stressor. On which side do the overwhelming majority of banks stand? You know the answer.

That brings us to the final star cluster: Convergence. Like Moore's Law, this phenomenon is firmly rooted in history. You only have to look back to 2007 and the advent of the iPhone. Sexy as this smartphone was, the breakthrough was not just about the device. Reliable 3G networks, touch interfaces, cheap and expansive storage, and expanded battery life all hit the mark at the same time. Five technologies. Each one alone would have been incremental. Together, they created a fundamentally different apparatus that made everything before it obsolete.

Pre-iPhone, commuters on the tube read newspapers, then watched TV at home and shook their heads in interminably long bank lines. (You got to the front and the 'next teller please' sign always popped up. Dark magic.) Well, where are those papers now? As for the banking and video watching, along with music playing, email checking and a whole lot more, those riders do that right from their seats. Look at them go!

This is what the oncoming convergence looks like in 2026. Digital twin technology has matured. APIs are available. Integration is possible. Privacy frameworks exist. You can build a complete picture of a customer across six layers – physical, environmental, social, emotional, cognitive, and financial – with tech available today, not ten years from now.

So where does that leave us and what does that mean for the forecasts contained in this book? The constellation lines that connect all the stars could also be viewed as extrapolated lines on a graph. And while extrapolation never amounts to 100 percent certainty, we see all signs pointing to 2032.

Something else: Platforms hold the potential to democratise access to financial strategy like nothing else before them. Assuming an affordable point of entry – likely since customers become customers for life, allowing platform operators to make a volume play – they can help everyday people advance their financial lives, no matter their state. We introduce you to two such folks in this book, Clyde and Amara, a hypothetical white-collar worker and a single mother respectively.

If you're rolling your eyes at this point, we get it. Perhaps you know at a far deeper level than we do just how much divining the future of technology is very risky business indeed.

But choosing to close our eyes to what lies right before us is riskier still. Bankers and banks that take such a stance in 2026 will find themselves inching ever closer to irrelevance. Those who choose to adopt now, internal politics and shareholder pressure be damned, stand the chance to realise success beyond their wildest dreams.

Huh? How?

That thesis informs the core of this book. In reading it, we invite you to keep your eyes and minds open, and dare to change your view of what comes next.

Chicago, IL, USA Louis R. Carlozo
24 April 2026

Author's Note: As This Book Went to Press

Books that argue for a five-year window face a structural problem: The window starts moving the moment the manuscript is filed. Between the day I sent the last chapter to my editor and the day this book reached your hands, the world I describe in it kept turning. Three developments are worth flagging here, not because they disturb the argument that follows, but because they sharpen it.

On 15 May 2026, OpenAI launched a personal finance preview inside ChatGPT Pro, connecting US subscribers' bank accounts, credit cards and investment portfolios directly to the chatbot via a Plaid integration covering more than 12,000 institutions. The product runs on a new GPT-5.5 Thinking model, with Intuit integration to follow. In the launch post, OpenAI disclosed that more than 200 million people were already asking ChatGPT financial questions every month *before* the product existed. Chapter 13 anticipated this. The 'AI platform as primary financial relationship' is no longer a chapter heading. It is in the sidebar of an app that more people use weekly than use most banks.

On the regulatory side, the US Digital Asset Market Clarity Act reached Senate Banking Committee markup in mid-May 2026, building on the GENIUS Act passed by the Senate the previous July. Whether the full legislation lands in 2026 or slips to 2027 changes the *date* of stablecoin regulatory clarity, not the *direction*.

In quantum computing, HSBC and Vanguard each disclosed late-2025 results from collaborations with IBM that bring retail banking and asset management into a conversation previously dominated by investment banks. JPMorgan's joint work with Quantinuum on quantum speedup, announced in May 2025, sits alongside them. IBM is now publicly targeting 'quantum advantage', a calculation done more accurately, cheaply or efficiently than classically, by the end of 2026.

None of these change the argument that follows. All of them make it harder to dismiss. The window is still open. It just got narrower.

Reading (UK) Dharmesh Mistry
25 May 2026

Acknowledgements

Books like this one do not get written alone, and this one less than most.

Lou Carlozo has been more than an editor. He has been a collaborator, a sounding board, and the person I could rely on to tell me when what I had written made perfect sense to me and almost none to anyone else. The readability of this book is substantially his doing; any remaining lapses are entirely mine. He has been a true partner: Honest, direct and the source of much-needed interjection of humour when things got tough.

I first started writing about technology for Computing magazine over 20 years ago, and have Mike Simons to thank for that. Then after a short break thanks to Tanya Andreasyan of FinTech Futures, I got back into it, this time focused on core and digital banking. Through Tanya I also met Leda Glyptis and Theodora Lau who really encouraged me to move on to writing a book and have supported me through the journey and helped me to believe that what I had to say was worth saying at length. They say that writing is only a small part of publishing a book and boy are they not wrong. So huge gratitude to Tula Weiss (and the Palgrave Macmillan team) for her kind patience (I asked a lot of questions) and expert guidance in getting us to the finish line. In an industry that produces a great deal of noise, the four of them have always known the difference between signal and performance. Their advice shaped this book in ways that do not show up in any specific paragraph but are present throughout.

Tarne Westcott and Dave Wallace have been thinking partners across more conversations than either of us can count, and their fingerprints are on the ideas in this book even where their names are not. Both of them and Lewis Hyam, Andy Maguire, and Jason Watkins have been colleagues and friends across different chapters of a long career. Each has inspired and contributed more than they probably realise, in the way that the best professional relationships always do: Through challenge, through candour, and through the occasional well-timed reminder that the customer is the point of all of this.

And then there is my family. A career in banking, the kind that spans forty years, multiple continents, boardrooms and start-ups, late nights and early flights. This is not something a person sustains without people at home who hold everything together while you are away. My wife, Kirti, and my kids: Vishal and Jade, did that, repeatedly and without complaint, for longer than was fair to ask. Jade is also the amazing creative talent behind the pictures that summarise each chapter. This book is dedicated, with more gratitude and love than I know how to express properly, to them.

Last but not least, I'd like to acknowledge my AI of choice, Claude, for assisting with the research, fact-checking, and on my grammar, spelling, and editing though a little sycophantic at times.

Contents

1

Forty Years of Revolution: Why This Time Is Different

1.1 The Lesson, Driven Home by a Blue Ford Escort

Though primitive on the level of stone tablets and chisels by today's standards, the computers of 1981 provided business leaders and laymen alike with powerful, revolutionary tools, the stuff of science fiction made everyday fact. And for the teenage son of a TV repairman, they were more compelling than any futuristic programme on the BBC Doctor Who and his time-travelling TARDIS? Kids' stuff. The future had in fact arrived via floppy discs shaped like flying saucers and motherboards straight from the brain of a mysterious mothership.

IBM introduced its first PC, the 5150, with an Intel processor that clocked in just short of 5 MHz. Microsoft's revolutionary disk operating system, MS-DOS, lit up the black screens with characters in a green, boxy pixel font. Macs existed only as prototypes and pencil sketches, a part of Apple's 'Macintosh Project,' but the Apple II was already a big hit in computer classes; you could even expand its RAM to an astounding 48 KB.

The technology was less powerful than the cheapest of cheap smartphones today. But for a 14 year old, it was enough to get me hopelessly addicted to computing, especially when I saw how far a little bit of tech savvy could take an ordinary guy like my computer science teacher.

D. Mistry, L. R. Carlozo, *The Intelligent Ledger*,
https://doi.org/10.1007/978-3-032-32842-7_1

Before the computer age, Mr. Neilson might as well have driven to our school in a no-frills Ford Cortina, headed for a staff car park full of bangers. But soon after selling Spectroids, a game he'd written for a new 8-bit home computer system known as ZX Spectrum, he bought a new Ford Escort. It was not cheap for anyone on a schoolteacher's salary. He paid somewhere around £14,000 for it (roughly $19,000) in today's money.

I stared at its bright navy blue paint job – glimmering in a sea of rust and tired, dented panels – and thought, 'Wow. Writing code can make you some serious money.'

Though cars and driving were still years away for me, the sight of that blue Escort changed everything. It showed me that this thing I loved to do, writing code, was not just a hobby or an obsession. I was not just messing around. I was training for something real, my future.

Back then, I coded in the computer room from 7:30 a.m. until school started; stayed after school another 90 minutes, spent my summers hunched over a keyboard. Meanwhile, another car stayed top of mind, but for much different reasons.

My dad drove an old white Cortina. He ran a television repair shop, fixing TVs with glass valves and vacuum tubes. Then transistors came. Then integrated circuits. The technology shifted beneath him, and he did not shift with it. In 1985, his business went bankrupt. I was 18, had just finished college and passed computer science with an A. I failed maths, but there was a good reason for it: I was too busy writing code to attend class.

Now the maths of our family finances emerged front and centre. When Dad's business died, the bankruptcy hit us hard. I hunted for my first job and the £4,500 salary I landed at Lloyds Bank would cover our mortgage. Now my dad never knew I'd turned down double that from Royal Bank of Scotland to work in their data centre managing mainframes. But some numbers do not add up where a calling is concerned. I chose programming at Lloyds over £9,000 at RBS because I wanted to write code, not manage machines.

I've pondered that choice a lot over the past four decades: Passion over pay. But I've also thought about my dad's TV repair shop, about how you can be excellent at what you do, work hard, have loyal customers, and still die when technology shifts.

His business died not for lack of effort or energy but because his job stopped mattering.

As you read this sentence, the same story is unfolding in financial services, all the way from the boots-on-the-ground, customer-facing side up to the penthouse C-suite. In a manner of speaking, there will be no TVs to repair. The evidence, irrefutable and indelible, surrounds us.

Banking as we know it is falling by the wayside. The digital die is cast. Banking as we know it is about to change forever.

****

This time is different because the model of banking is changing.

I do not say this because I'm smarter now than at 20 but because I've finally learnt to recognise the pattern of technology shifts that actually matter versus those that just change how things work. This chapter tells the story of that journey, a story of being wrong, repeatedly, about what would transform banking. Of building what I thought was revolutionary in a single tech silo only to realise it was incremental. Of seeing banks ignore obvious transformations until crisis forced action. (Large institutions often resist change until the business is at stake.)

And I see why convergence is happening right now: With digital twins, quantum computing, agentic AI, platform economics and tokenisation. *This marks banking's TV valve-to-transistor moment.*

I first proposed what I now call Platform Banking in 1996; the response from four UK bank CEOs set the template for everything this book argues. The full story is told in Chapter 4, but the short version is this: I was right, nobody listened, and Royal Bank of Scotland (RBS) proved the model by doing what NatWest Bank declined to do. My dad did not see his technology shift coming until too late. I'm writing this book so you can avoid, and transcend, a similar fate.

1.2 1981–1986: Coding Cracks the Career Code

The Texas Instruments TI-99/4A that my dad bought me in 1981 had 16KB of RAM. (The cheapest computer you can buy today boasts 250,000 times as much.) It stored programs on magnetic cassettes. I can still hear the high-pitched screech as the tape drive loaded code, hours of work that might or might not load come crunch time. I spent every possible moment in the school computer room, three hours a day on average. While it was not on the order of a new-car sum, my skills were already paying off. I made pocket money writing computer science homework for my classmates. I helped Mr. Neilson test his games. I wrote my own, including a game based on the 1980s TV show 'Play Your Cards Right' that a coding magazine published. One summer holiday I researched and wrote about the history of computers, from Charles Babbage's Difference Engine, to room-sized mainframes, to personal computers in just over a century. My teacher scored it A++. I still have that paper somewhere.

At 14, I already noticed the pattern that would define my career. Technology does not just get better; it gets more accessible and accessibility changes everything. By college only two things interested me, coding (which I loved) and money (which I needed), not necessarily in that order. Aside from arithmetic I could not see the point of all the other aspects of maths, which explains why I failed my A-levels. Meanwhile, my computing tutors were not very good, so I stopped attending lectures and essentially taught myself and wrote code. My final year project was a cross-assembler for the 6502 processor that ran the BBC Micro. The college only had two BBC Micros for a class of 12 students, but we had 15 PCs. So, I created a programme that let students write and assemble 6502 machine code on the PCs, which meant they only needed the BBC Micro briefly to test their programs. It birthed an approach I would use throughout my career. Solve the constraint, make the resource more accessible, and enable more people to do better work.

By 1986, at age 18, I had three job offers. The shoe shop where I worked part-time offered me a trainee management role. I felt tempted as I eyed up the manager's BMW company car (even better than the Escort and checking off the 'money, which I needed' box).

Why would I take a job with Lloyds Bank when RBS offered twice as much and the BMW's gleam had caught my eye? Simply put, I could continue coding and still cover the family mortgage with my salary of £4,500. This decision came to define my career: choosing work I believed in over money. It did not always work out, though sometimes it did brilliantly. Regardless, I've never regretted following the tech first, even though money always mattered at some level. Growing up poor shapes you.

But the fear of ending up like my dad, achieving excellence that crumbled into irrelevance, I translated into something beyond a dwindling bank account balance. I stayed hungry to keep ahead of the digital changes, though as I set off in 1986 I did not realise how often I'd mistake new channels for real transformation.

* * *

1.3 1986–1994: Lloyds Bank and the First Revolution That Was Not

Walking into Lloyds Bank in September 1986 felt like walking into college with much smarter tutors. We were taught mainframe development in PL/1 using Jackson Structured Programming, where I first learnt the power of code reuse: patterns that could be applied repeatedly rather than writing everything from scratch. My first project was for BIT, Branch Information Technology. The goal was nothing less than to automate branches. The goal for my team was to digitise forms that branch staff previously completed by hand. The project would roll out to more than 2,000 branches with more than 45,000 PCs, networked using Token Ring (later Ethernet) and connected to mainframes via telecoms with a maximum bandwidth of 55K.

I sat behind smoked glass screens in user experience labs, watching branch staff struggle to use a mouse for the first time. Most had never touched a computer. We were teaching 45,000 people to use PCs and Windows software while simultaneously digitising their entire workflow. It was massive. It felt revolutionary.

It was not.

It added up to automation – better, faster, more efficient automation – but fundamentally the same paper processes migrated to digital. In my youthful ardour I missed a crucial distinction: I thought we were transforming *banking* whilst we were actually just transforming *channels*. Even in this first project we used two-digit year fields to save on storage, always assuming these systems would be replaced by the time Y2K became an issue (some were not).

Later, I bought my own PC, an Intel 386SX, for £2,500, a huge outlay then, roughly £9,000 today (and about the same price as a top-flight 2026 Mac desktop with an M3 Ultra chip and 16TB of SSD storage). The bank would not initially retrain me for PC/Windows development, so I trained myself. I worked on Lloyds' huge investment to centralise operational customer data: name, age, address, salary, etc. Product data still sat in separate core systems.

In 1992, I joined a team led by Andy Maguire to help the bank retain its top customers. Lloyds had done analysis that showed approximately 5% of customers earned 80% of the bank's profits and keeping that 5% was hugely important. Andy was a graduate line manager going places; he later led BCG's banking practice and became Global COO at HSBC. He taught me so much about management and business, and introduced me to Charles Handy's 'The Empty Raincoat', a book about meaning and purpose in work I'd return to decades later. Most importantly, he showed me that data was not just a record of facts. Data equals intelligence. The application I helped write in Microsoft Visual Basic allowed branch managers to interrogate data about their most profitable customers by using indexed files (ISAM) because we lacked a proper database. Basic stuff by today's standards but revelatory in 1992.

The business sponsor was Peter Harvey, a renowned expert in credit risk who understood that data could be leveraged for more than just assessing loan applications. Working day-to-day was Lewis Hyam, who learnt much from Peter but brought his own innovative ideas; Lewis later became Lloyds Bank's first Chief Data Officer before retiring. Years later I actually brought Lewis into Temenos (where I served from 2012 to 2019) as a consultant to help me understand his 'single brain' concept for our digital engagement solution. Working with Andy, Peter, and Lewis opened my eyes. Data was not just about records. It revealed patterns. It was intelligence and prediction. For the first time, I started to think about what else we could do if we had more data, better data, connected data.

Another mentor from this period, Steve Kirby, introduced me to Rapid Application Development, a very early precursor to Agile (an iterative, flexible approach to project management and software engineering). While everyone else followed rigid waterfall methodologies with 18-month development cycles, Steve proved that you could build, test, learn and iterate quickly. That philosophy served me well from then on out. After the customer profitability project, I joined a new bank program focused on Business Process Re-engineering. Teams of business specialists and branch staff worked together with shared pools of expertise for compliance, HR, and technology. There were six business streams and having worked across them, I saw something no one else seemed to notice: The inefficiencies *between* silos were greater than the inefficiencies *within* them. We were not looking at the problem broadly enough.

In my own time, I created a prototype that demonstrated the power of a 'Single Customer View'. I got a demo directly to the Head of Retail Banking by waiting until his personal assistant had gone home and . . . I just showed up. Bold? Naïve? I was 26 and did not know better. He peppered me with questions: Who are you? How did you come to this view? How quickly could this be developed?

The demo showcased concepts that would become commonplace 20 years later but stood out as revolutionary in 1994. Workflow management with shared workloads and prioritised work queues, role-based access, navigation through hyperlinks in summary data, and even the concept of a natural language navigation system. The bank already had 30 Windows applications with plans to implement at least another 30. Aligning functionality and data was becoming impossible but my natural language navigator solved that problem.

News broke of my audacious visit. I distributed more demos across the head office. Eventually I was asked to present at the bank's regional heads conference. Nobody from IT had presented there before. It was quite an honour but did not go down well in my department in technology. They felt I had misled the business about what tech could deliver. My concept did not come from the R&D team. It was an idea without a home, without a sponsor, without a place in the hierarchy. I became the person who 'set expectations beyond what IT can deliver', a sin in banking IT.

Sensing that the grass might be greener elsewhere, I left Lloyds Bank in August 1994. For any feelings of being misunderstood, I know now that I'd been blind to a misunderstanding of my own. That is, I'd built a vision of unified customer intelligence, but only using banking data. Transactions. Products. Balances. The same 10% of customer data banks had always had, just presented better. I thought unifying that 10% was revolutionary. But it was just a step, not a revolution.

In later years Lloyds did follow up on some concepts behind the Single Customer View, spending hundreds of millions leveraging data to create insights about customer behaviour, when customers might leave, which would become profitable, what product recommendations to make to whom through which channel and when. They even spotted economic trends via customer data that turned out more accurate than the UK government's own figures. Still, this rested on financial data alone. The other 90% of what drove customer behaviour? Banks did not have it, and still do not, most of them.

In 1994, I did not even know that 90% existed. I just knew I needed to see more of the technology world than on the inside of one bank.

* * *

1.4 1994–2001: Building the Internet When Nobody Believed in It

In August 1994 I joined CentreFile, a technology subsidiary of NatWest Bank. There I led client-server projects, the latest thing at the time, moving from monolithic mainframes to distributed systems. Soon after in 1995 I was promoted into the main bank to head strategy and architecture for NatWest Cards. Here I first proposed what I now call Platform Banking.

While studying for an Open University MBA in the evenings, I came up with an idea I called 'Franchising Banks', essentially white-labelling banking to brands. The rationale was simple: A bank could broaden its customer base and a brand could deepen its customer relationships if you separated the two. The bank provides regulated infrastructure; the brand owns the customer relationship. I wrote to the CEOs of four major UK banks to put the idea to them. Two said, 'Thanks but no thanks'; one reply contained four words I have never forgotten: 'We own our customers.' Not 'serve'. Own.

RBS replied that this did not align with their strategy; NatWest found it interesting as they were already white-labelling credit cards extensively but did not want to pursue it either. Then about a year later, NatWest's COO asked me to contribute to the business justification for a white-label banking deal with Tesco. I did. The NatWest board declined: too much cannibalisation risk, not the right time. RBS took the deal. Tesco Bank launched in 1997, backed by RBS infrastructure, and served millions of customers for more than two decades. The model worked exactly as I had described it. It just was not NatWest that proved it. The irony now is that NatWest Boxed delivers on this exact concept.

Lesson learnt? The right idea at the wrong time is just a memo nobody acts on. I would learn that lesson at least three more times over my career.

* * *

At NatWest I held a good position and enjoyed my role. I learnt about distributed systems, strategy and architecture at scale. But something much bigger was shaking the world outside the walls of the banking IT department. The internet, now teamed with a graphical browser, was set to change everything. In April 1997, I joined a start-up called Entranet and this is where things got interesting. I met and befriended Dave Wallace, today the co-host of my 'Demystify' fintech podcast. Everything I have learnt about customer experience, journeys and branding is down to years of interaction and education from Dave. It was Dave who taught me the differences between user interface, customer experience and customer journeys. I first met Tarne Westcott there, too; today he serves as an executive director at UBS.

At Entranet, we delivered some of the very first online banking solutions, not just websites with product listings but actual transactional banking over the internet. Beyond this, we built for whatever devices customers had and used: web, mobile, kiosks, digital TV set-top boxes, even Microsoft Money integration. Tarne and I anchored our first major project for Co-op Bank. It was the UK's first internet bank built on Java, delivered on the web, on the first Windows CE device *and* on a kiosk for branches. All in 1997. One codebase, multiple user interfaces; build once, deploy everywhere; meet customers on their devices rather than force them onto yours.

In parallel I delivered EagleStar insurance, the world's first insurance policy sold online. Not quotes, not information, but actual policy purchase fully transacted online. *First. In. The. World.* Then we delivered Woolwich Building Society, the UK's first mobile banking application in 1999. Three years before smartphones, on WAP browsers and feature phones. And because nobody quite believed any of this was possible, I also appeared on BBC's 'Tomorrow's World' to demonstrate online voting running simultaneously on a digital set-top TV box, games console, mobile phone, Java screen phone, the web, and a kiosk. Six different devices, one codebase. The future in 1999, before the 21st century arrived and eight years ahead of the first iPhone.

* * *

1.5 1999: A Retail Platform Vision That Banking Lacked

Close to $1 billion. At the crest of the dot-com boom, that was the value of an online sports retailer called Kitbag, formed by two people I knew well. Chris Gibson had left Entranet to start Kitbag, a company headed up by a good friend of mine, Jason Watkins.

When I visited Jason in 1999, he gave me a demo of Kitbag's back-office system. His team had built it entirely from scratch and it worked like nothing I'd ever seen. This was before Shopify, before e-commerce platforms, before anyone had figured out how to build online retail at scale. Jason understood something fundamental: You need to control the whole process. So, his team built *everything*: the storefront, the analytics, inventory management, logistics integration, and payment processing. He'd automated and connected everything in a data-driven juggernaut. Jason could tell you when the last Liverpool FC shirt was sold, its size, the postage to deliver it and its destination. It represented complete operational intelligence across every dimension of the business.

But Jason was not just framing out a retail operation. He was building a platform. He quickly adapted the Kitbag system to provide white-label shops for F1 Racing, Wimbledon, Reebok, Manchester United, PSG, and more. Each looked different, branded for the club or organisation, but the same platform, intelligence and operational excellence drove each retail site. Jason understood platform economics in 1999: Build it once, deploy it many times. Each new customer adds data that makes the platform smarter; each integration makes the network more valuable; the business compounds.

I was floored. I walked away thinking, 'This is what transformation actually looks like.' Then it occurred to me that at some future point, Jason could step completely outside the operation and let some digital intelligence run this business: a single brain that would not only track everything but decide it as well. From the day we met, I recognised Jason as a true visionary. His thinking about business and technology has consistently stayed ahead of the curve and his creation was one of the few that stood after the dot-com bubble burst.

Kitbag, which changed hands several times, was acquired by Fanatics in 2016 and turned over more than $6.2 billion in 2025. The vision Jason brought to life in 1999 blossomed into a multi-billion dollar platform business.

It's hard to argue with success like that, or the persuasion of the person behind it. Jason later inspired me to run the Marathon des Sables, a 250 km ultramarathon through the Moroccan Sahara Desert, considered the toughest footrace on Earth. Hence, it was Jason who also taught me to challenge what I thought was possible, physically and mentally.

* * *

Meanwhile, the banking industry was more or less running on the spot.

They celebrated how customers could check balances online. And there I was, delivering 'revolutionary' internet and mobile banking applications. But retail had already figured out complete operational intelligence *and* platform economics. I did not fully appreciate the depth of what I saw at Kitbag in 1999. I thought the lesson stemmed from operational intelligence, better data, better systems, better visibility. I did not yet understand the deeper meaning.

Kitbag's intelligence was simpler than what banking needed. They tracked objects, physical things that move through predictable processes, while banking needs to track humans with complex, contextual, multi-domain data about people's lives. Platform economics beats product economics; Jason understood this in 1999, while banks in 2026 still think in terms of *product* sales. Yet you must control the whole process or become irrelevant. Jason built everything because owning the complete customer experience was the only way to build a defensible business, while banks outsource the customer experience to aggregators and comparison sites. The question for banks in 2027 and beyond is this: Will they learn from retail's 28-year head start?

Banks have all the advantages Jason lacked in 1999: customer trust, regulatory licences, capital, brand, existing relationships. They just need the vision to see what Jason saw when he started Kitbag.

We did not transform things platform-wise. But I was so engrossed in the technology, so excited by what we were building, that I could not see the distinction. *The future of access did not equal the future of banking.* That realisation would take me another decade and company tenure to understand in full.

* * *

1.6 2001–2012: Building the Platform Nobody Wanted (Yet)

In 2001, I left Entranet to start edgeIPK with my business partner Mike Williams. At the time, building digital banking solutions had grown complex. Every bank wanted multi-channel, but building for web, mobile, kiosk or whatever new device came next required massive amounts of duplicated effort. Different codebases. Different teams. Different release cycles. We had a clear vision when we built edgeConnect: create a no-code/low-code platform specifically for financial services. Design once, deploy everywhere. Help them move thousands of green screens and Windows apps to the browser. Build customer journeys visually, not through thousands of lines of code. Enable business people to design experiences without waiting for technology backlogs.

Talk about an ultramarathon. We spent 11 years building and refining edgeConnect. Eleven years learning what financial services institutions actually needed versus what they said they needed. Eleven years of sales conversations where banks said, 'This looks amazing' and then did not buy because their IT departments said, 'We can build this ourselves' (they could not) or 'This does not fit our architecture' when their architecture was the real problem. As it turns out, we built the right thing at too early a time, before generative AI.

Low/no-code platforms later grew extensively and launched a massive industry. Our roadmap even had a long-term vision of evolving the platform to Voice-Driven Development. Tell our platform what you want and it will generate it. For 2011, it was way ahead of its time. Every bank wants to enable business users to design customer experiences without writing code and from 2001 through 2012, they *said* they wanted it. But they were not ready to buy it.

So those 11 years trudging through the no-code/low-code Sahara taught me something crucial: Customer experience itself matters, but customer experience platforms do not if the underlying banking model does not change. You can make the interface beautiful. You can make the journey frictionless. But if the products underneath still sit atop the same siloed mess of fragmented data and manual decision-making, the pretty interface does not matter. We were still building better channels for the same old banking.

Then in 2012, Temenos acquired edgeIPK. While it was not a massive exit or unicorn sale, it validated that we'd built something valuable, even if the market was not quite ready for it. More importantly, the Temenos acquisition gave me the newfound ability to influence hundreds of banks simultaneously. Temenos served more than 1,000 banks globally. If I could get Temenos to build something, those institutions would use it. At last, I had the platform to try building what I'd envisioned 18 years earlier in that prototype demo at Lloyds: a single brain that understood customers completely and made intelligent decisions in real time. Finally, I could attempt to actually transform banking, not just digitise it. In time, I'd learn that even having the platform, customers and technology was not enough if the fundamental business model did not change.

* * *

1.7 2012–2019: A Single Brain, Half Aware

After I joined Temenos as Product Director, I was promoted a year later to Chief Digital Officer with a mandate to create their global digital banking strategy. This was my shot!

After all those years building channels and platforms, I finally had the scale to build what I'd envisioned for close to 20 years: a unified intelligence system that could understand customers completely and make real-time decisions about how to serve them. I pulled in the brilliant Lewis Hyam from Lloyds Bank, leveraging his three decades of working with banking data to create an engagement platform. At the core of this platform sat an intelligence engine, which Lewis envisioned and named the 'single brain'.

The concept was straightforward. Instead of using siloed systems to make isolated decisions – one each for mortgage offers, credit card offers, and investment recommendations, to name a few – we would create a unified intelligence that understood the complete customer relationship and made coordinated decisions about what to advise or action when. Break down the product silos. Unify the data. Create centralised rules that optimise for customer lifetime value, not individual product sales. Enable real-time personalisation based on complete banking context. Make the bank smarter about each customer than any individual product team could possibly be.

And we built it.

We realised real-time customer decisioning across all products, personalised offers based on complete banking relationships, a unified rules engine that determined what to offer whom and when. Although our initial focus rested on sales, the goal was to create a data-driven brain for all customer decisions across the bank to replace hard-coded business rules.

I presented this to bank CEOs across the globe from 2013 to 2015. Those who understood it loved it: 'This is so powerful, it's the future,' they said. 'We've been talking about breaking down silos for years,' they said. 'This could increase our product sales by 20 to 30%,' they said. And they were right. The single brain did all that as it enabled personalisation at scale. But . . .

It failed to transform banking.

The single brain had the same limitation I missed in 1994. It only knew banking data. It knew your complete financial relationship with the bank and could make sophisticated decisions about the timing and type of product offers.

But it did not know whether you were pregnant.

Or how your commute was killing you.

It did not know your parents were ageing and would need care.

It was blind to your relationship struggles.

It had no idea your job was about to relocate you.

And none of its reams and reams of data could tell this single brain a single thing about the life context that drives every major financial decision, yours and mine.

To be sure, the single brain marked a massive leap forward from siloed systems. It was necessary. It worked. Banks that implemented it saw real benefits. But the paradigm shift, if there was one, merely amounted to better product pushing: More sophisticated, coordinated and personalised, but product pushing nonetheless. Pushing products *to* customers rather than understanding what customers actually needed *for* their financial lives. I'd unified 10% of customer data and thought that equalled 'complete understanding.' I'd built a brain that only saw financial behaviour and thought that was 'intelligence'. I even envisioned that the single brain would replace rules-based decisions with AI more than a decade before large language models leapt into public consciousness.

But I also knew that was not the only thing that had to change. I wanted banks to recognise that they needed to go beyond banking data entirely: *To see it, literally*. So, in 2016, I created a video called 'The Bank of Me'.

In it, I depicted what banking's future would look like. Conversational AI would help customers across their complete financial lives, not just banking products, but integrated services that spanned beyond traditional banking boundaries. Again, nobody believed this was possible with the available technology and it was not, but the vision was clear. You can still find the video today on YouTube if you search for 'The Bank of Me'.

Again, I was too early, this time by eight years.

The conversational AI of 2016 could not handle the complexity. I did not fully see this limitation until I left Temenos in 2019, posting on LinkedIn on 31 October that it was just 'time for the next chapter'. But the vision was right. And today, LLMs of many flavours – GPT-4, Claude, Perplexity and Gemini, to name a few – are proving that what folks saw in my 2016 demonstration is finally buildable.

* * *

1.8 2019–2023: Too Early (Again!): How AskHomey Proved Journey Ownership but Still Fell Short

After I sold edgeIPK to Temenos, I cleared my debts and invested in property. Managing those properties was an eye-opener. An abundance of data existed, more than banks had about their customers, but was scattered everywhere. The journeys to find, live in, and move into homes were broken, highly fragmented and inevitably painful. Nobody owned them. I went on many dog walks with Dave Wallace to discuss this and to understand customer experience and journeys better. From Dave, I grasped something I should have seen years earlier. Banking's fundamental problem did not rest in channels, intelligence or even the products. The problem was one of misperception. Banks thought they *owned* customer relationships when in reality they *provided* products. But products are not relationships. Journeys are, and banks did not own them.

Take home ownership, the biggest financial commitment by far that most people make. A 10-15-year journey kicks off when prospective buyers decide to move, define requirements, search properties, make offers, navigate the transaction process, shop and secure the mortgage, deal with solicitors, arrange surveys and coordinate the move. Exhausting, but the fun's just beginning. Over the next decade or more, these new owners must maintain the home, manage utility bills, handle repairs and improvements, pay insurance, track warranties, coordinate contractors, optimise energy costs, plan improvements, and eventually time the market for sale. The mortgage, while it takes up a lot of headspace and is the single most important transaction, is just 5% of the journey and maybe 10% of the total value opportunity for financial institutions. The rest?

Banks ignore it.

They think once they've sold the mortgage, the relationship is secured, and meanwhile their customers drown in complexity. Someone should own this journey. Why not banks? They have the customer *relationship*. They have trust. They have capital and scale. But banks only care about the mortgage, *their product*. Put another way, customers do not see their lives through the lens of a banker. They see bills, finding and paying for reliable contractors and so much more as part of the financial home-owning picture. Their banks, meanwhile, concentrate inordinate attention on the primary loan, that first brushstroke on a naked home canvas. To recoin a phrase, they fuss about the gutters and let their clients worry about the foundation, the property maintenance, the taxes, the utilities, the refrigerator purchase, the improvements, everything that completes the financial picture that's so crucial to the owner and always top of mind.

So, in 2019, I decided to build what banks had not and did not want to, AskHomey. Not having coded in years, I needed a strong CTO and co-founded the company with Tarne Westcott. We had not worked together since 2000, at Entranet, but had stayed in contact and began running ultra-marathons together. And as any tech start-up founder will tell you, start-ups are not overnight successes. They are ultra-marathons, which made Tarne the perfect business partner.

We pursued new property developers first. Every new home needed a physical handover manual: Thick binders full of appliance warranties, instruction manuals, utility information, contractor details, maintenance schedules. Creating these cost developers hundreds of pounds per property and hundreds of staff-time hours. And for what? Homeowners promptly lost them, filed them away or threw them out.

AskHomey digitised the entire handover: Every appliance, every warranty, every instruction manual, every contractor, all in one digital platform. The homeowner got access for free. The developer paid us up to £100 per property depending on volume. For developers, it meant massive cost savings and time savings. And homeowners now had far more than a binder they'd never open: a platform that managed all their appliances and warranties; predicted when things would need maintenance or replacement; connections to vetted contractors; help optimising utility costs through switching services. AskHomey also tracked their home's value and provided mortgage switching advice when beneficial. Imagine all of this translated into cost savings for the homeowner and ongoing opportunities for a financial institution beyond a one-time sale.

But we hit a fundamental limitation: *Natural language AI was not ready in 2020–2023.*

Specifically, voice assistants could handle simple commands but could not understand context, remember conversation history, or provide genuinely helpful responses to complex home management questions. Asking 'Should I replace my boiler or repair it?' requires knowing the boiler's age and service history, recent repair costs, energy efficiency of modern replacements, the homeowner's budget and plans, contractor availability and pricing in their area. It's a handful and that level of contextual, multi-domain intelligence required technology that simply did not exist at scale in 2020–2023. Now it does.

COVID-19 hit in March 2020, just as we were launching our MVP. Developers went remote. Construction slowed. And right at the bullseye of our business model, new home sales froze. Our market disappeared overnight. By the time developers came back fully in 2022, their budgets were crushed. Our flagship client, who'd committed to hundreds of properties, went bust. Other developers lapsed into survival mode. We managed to deploy AskHomey to more than 1,000 properties before we ran out of funding. PropTech was out of favour with investors post–COVID-19 and we lacked the runway to wait out a market recovery. In 2023, we shut down AskHomey and sold off the software assets.

But the failure was not final because we'd proven that the model worked. Developers who used it saved real money and time; so did homeowners. *Journey ownership creates years, decades and a lifetime of continuous value.* Even with our limited portfolio of properties and no direct homeowner subscription yet, we could see the path to profitability. In 2022, during our final fundraising attempts, I met with the CEO of a major UK bank and pitched to them: 'You should acquire us or partner with us. You have the mortgage relationship. We have the complete home journey. Together, we own the customer.'

She looked at the platform and asked, 'But how does this increase mortgage sales?'

Ugh.

I tried to explain, it does not increase mortgage sales, it makes mortgage sales automatic because you own the relationship. The journey selects the mortgage, not the customer shopping for mortgages. She did not understand. Being right too early is the same as being wrong. Trying to teach bankers new ways to see is too often the most thankless of tasks.

That noted, banks can learn a precise lesson from AskHomey. Do not be too early. In 2020, the market, technology (especially natural language AI), and customer expectations were not ready. Now, something of the reverse is true. Do not be too late. If you wait until 2029, the platforms will already own the customers. The window is 2027-2028. That's when the technology, customer behaviour, and competitive pressure will converge and make transformation both possible and necessary. Banks have the capital, the brand trust, the customer relationships, the distribution. And now, in 2026, they have the technology maturity and the market timing. What they do not have is much time, or, as with our CEO above, the perceptive power to see any of this coming. AskHomey proved journey ownership works. The question is whether banks have the courage to do it at scale.

* * *

1.9 2023–2026: 'Demystify' and Pattern Recognition

After selling AskHomey, I started co-hosting a podcast with Dave Wallace called 'Dave and Dharm Demystify' (Lou Carlozo, who had a hand in this book, acted as our executive producer in those earliest days.) The goal: demystify banking technology and trends for industry audiences. I met Dave in 1997 at Entranet, where he led design and creative while I led the technology team. We've done more than 150 episodes, interviewing banking executives, fintech founders, technology vendors, regulators, and analysts. Every conversation adds to my understanding of where banking is and where it's going.

More importantly, most conversations revealed the same patterns. And none of them have anything to do with sales charts. Behold:

- **Pattern one: Everyone talks transformation, nobody transforms.** Digitising is not transformation. Their innovation labs fail to deliver at scale. Their pilots run forever. They announce partnerships with press releases with positive PR as the primary benefit but never actually integrate. Every bank says they're transforming. After all, who would come out and say the opposite? But very few are. Theirs is an environment filled with fintech petting zoo visits, innovation labs that exist for their own sake, shiny new toys and an overarching desire to look cutting edge in the eyes of the industry.
- **Pattern two: Technology is never the blocker.** Digital twin technology exists. APIs are available. Quantum computing is accessible via cloud. AI agent frameworks are mature. The technology for everything I describe in this book is either ready now or will be ready within the next five years, the window banks have for true transformation. The blocker is culture, courage and commitment, not capability. An executive report by CSI, '2026 Banking Priorities', adds further context to the disconnect. The 252 survey respondents (who hail from the community banking sector) see these revolutionary technologies in nineteenth century ways. First and foremost, they

want to utilise AI and the like as 'efficiency drivers'. So, hold on tight. The new and improved Ford Model T is on the way!

- **Pattern three: Some banks know what to do, they just will not do it.** In off-the-record conversations, these bank executives share that they understand everything: the platform model, the digital twin requirement, the quantum advantage. They just cannot commit for a host of reasons that will never go away: quarterly earnings pressure, risk aversion, organisational inertia, board scepticism. They know the right answer, but they cannot execute it. Where is the courage to 'sell' their institutions on a bold vision and much bigger imperatives?
- **Pattern four: The talk-versus-action gap is widening.** In 2020, banks discussed digital transformation and ran some pilots. In 2023, the talk continued but the pilots failed to scale. And in 2026, bankers bandy about new buzzwords like static as though they're on top of the game: AI, quantum, platform. And still the action gap has not closed one (qu)bit. Meanwhile, Ant Financial and Grab have built what Western banks are still studying as they let the buzzwords fly.

These four patterns summarise where banking finds itself in 2026. Information is not the problem. Nor is intelligence. Nor are resources.

Will is the problem

'Nobody wants to be first' is a truism that has held fast across the generations and every business sector you can think of. Only this time, the consequences of following this well-worn path will lead banking as we know it over a cliff. Nobody wants to bet big. Nobody wants to risk their career on a transformation that might fail. So they'll wait. Study. Pilot. Analyse until crisis forces action or irrelevance chooses for them.

Now, let's put these patterns off to the side and take a close look at what the future holds: The near future.

Questions for Your Board

1. Which technologies do we track and in what timescale do we plan to address them? Being early is not ideal but better than being late.
2. How will we validate the drivers for adoption to make sure we're not too early?
3. Does our strategy identify business model changes or new product opportunities based on unfolding technology capabilities?
4. Have we identified key customer journeys and undertaken a SWOT (Strength, Weakness, Opportunity, Threat) analysis for each one?

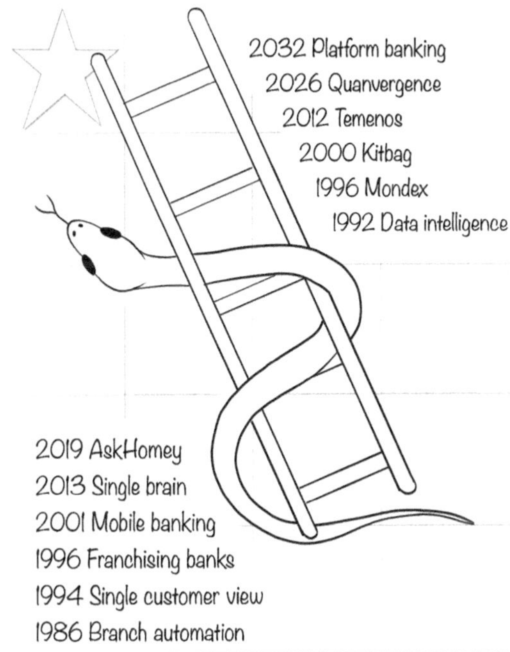
2032 Platform banking
2026 Quanvergence
2012 Temenos
2000 Kitbag
1996 Mondex
1992 Data intelligence
2019 AskHomey
2013 Single brain
2001 Mobile banking
1996 Franchising banks
1994 Single customer view
1986 Branch automation

2

Convergence, Technology and Banking: The Importance of Outside Forces

2.1 2026: The Convergence I'm Certain Is Here

Chapter 1 told the story of four decades spent watching banking change without transforming. Each wave: Unified data, the internet, mobile, and the single brain delivered real progress. However, they left the fundamental model intact: Banks still organised around products and still measured success by what they sold rather than what customers achieved. The history is useful not as an autobiography but as calibration. It establishes my baseline scepticism. So when I tell you that what is happening now is different, I mean genuinely and structurally different, that scepticism should inform how you hear the argument. I have been wrong about this before. And I need to explain precisely why this time is different.

I've been wrong about 'revolutionary silo' technology changes many times. In 1994, I thought unified customer data would transform banking; it just made product pushing more efficient.

Between 1997 and 2001, I thought the internet and mobile banking would transform banking; they just changed the channel.

From 2001 to 2012, I built low-code platforms, believing they would transform how banks built experiences. Eleven years was not the timeline I expected.

From 2013 to 2019, I thought the single brain would transform banking intelligence; it just made banks smarter about products they were already selling.

D. Mistry, L. R. Carlozo, *The Intelligent Ledger*,
https://doi.org/10.1007/978-3-032-32842-7_2

And during 2020–2023, I thought proving journey ownership economics would convince banks to change. They're still organised around products. Each time, I thought I'd reached the endgame. Each time, it was just one step on a longer journey.

In 2026, I'm making another prediction. The convergence of agentic AI, digital twins, quantum computing, platform economics, and tokenisation will completely transform banking by 2032. It will in no way resemble banking as we've known it for generations, or know it today. Tomorrow? Traditional banks that fail to truly transform face a diminishing role.

Why am I certain this time? Not because I'm smarter. Not because the technology has improved (which it has). But because I've finally learnt to recognise the difference between technology that changes *how* things work versus technology that changes whether things are needed at all. A better hot air balloon or a jet? A horse and carriage or a car? That's where we are.

* * *

2.2 Enter the Smartphone: Five Technologies, Five Years to Market Consolidation

In 1999, I delivered the UK's first mobile banking application for Woolwich Building Society. It was innovative. And it worked, years before anyone, including the late Steve Jobs, could imagine an iPhone. But it did not transform banking. Nine years later, in 2008, the iPhone 2 launched, and within five years, handset sales for Nokia and Ericsson were dead, BlackBerry was dying, and the mobile phone market had completely consolidated around iOS and Android. What was different? The technology had existed for years. IBM had invented a smartphone concept in 1994, fourteen years before the iPhone. Mobile banking apps existed in 1999. I built them. So why did the iPhone cause extinction-level market consolidation when earlier innovations did not? *Because convergence happened.*

The iPhone arrived when five separate technologies matured simultaneously:

- 3G data networks that actually worked,
- app stores creating utility through third-party services,
- storage cheap enough to carry your digital life,
- touch interfaces that finally worked without a stylus, and
- battery life acceptable for all-day use.

Five technologies. Each one alone would have been incremental. Together, they created a fundamentally different device that made everything before it obsolete. (The iPhone also combined the functions of a digital music player, a web search tool, an email-box and even a gaming console, making it unnecessary to lug around multiple devices.)

Five years. After the convergence happened in 2008, the market consolidated by 2012. Not gradual adoption over decades but rapid, brutal consolidation. I lived through this and so did you. Back in 2008, the tube was full of passengers reading newspapers. Now, they're all glued to their smartphones. The smartphone didn't just impact handset manufacturers but also adjacent markets. Kodak, a leader in photography with patents in digital photography, didn't die because the iPhone was a better camera. It died because the customer didn't want a better camera. They wanted a camera, a phone, a browser, mapping with GPS and more. All at once, in one device, belonging to one person. Convergence doesn't just improve an industry, it redefines who owns the relationship.

When I built mobile banking in 1999, I thought it was revolutionary. Eight years later, I watched the smartphone make everything we'd created look primitive. The pattern was clear: Gradual development of individual technologies, then sudden convergence, then rapid market consolidation.

I see the exact same convergence pattern now in banking.

* * *

2.3 The Banking Convergence of 2026–2027

Digital twin technology has matured. APIs are available. Integration is possible. Privacy frameworks exist. You can build a complete picture of a customer across all six layers – physical, environmental, social, emotional, cognitive, and financial – with tech available today, not ten years from now. That tech continues to improve and continues to create more and better data. This is like 3G networks being ready for the iPhone. The infrastructure exists. Quantum computing is accessible: IBM Quantum Network, Amazon Braket, Google Quantum AI and Microsoft Azure Quantum are all available now via cloud APIs on a pay-per-use basis. The use cases for banking via production pilots at Goldman Sachs, JPMorgan, and BBVA are proving the use cases. This is not research. It's engineering.

Platform business models are proven, too. Ant Financial has demonstrated it in China; Grab in Southeast Asia; Amazon, Apple, and Google in other industries. I proved the model worked with AskHomey; we just failed on timing and capital at the dawn of the pandemic, not concept.

Tokenisation and DeFi have reached scale with stablecoins approaching regulatory clarity, and DeFi total value locked crossing $200 billion. And as our everyday experiences can attest, AI and natural language are finally ready for demanding tasks. Large language models can understand complex, contextual questions and provide genuinely useful responses. The conversational interfaces I tried to build in 2016 and 2020 are now trivially easy to build in 2026.

Five technologies. Each one alone would be disruptive. But they were sequential in previous cycles, giving banks five to seven years to adapt to each. Today, we are living through an 'iPhone moment' with the simultaneous convergence of five more technologies maturing at the same time.

And just like the smartphone market, the timeline from convergence to consolidation will be five years:

- 2027 marks the convergence moment when platform banks deploy with digital twins and agentic AI.
- 2028 sees first movers achieve scale and network effects begin.
- 2029 is the point of no return. Platform banks own customer relationships through complete data, creating a moat so late movers cannot catch up.
- 2030–2031 brings the consolidation wave. By now, quantum simulation completes the picture, enabling life modelling of the type that is genuinely holistic and never experienced before.
- 2032 marks the consolidation point: Platform banks will master customer intimacy and own the prime relationships for consumer banking. Other banks will either be acquired or see their customer base begin to shrink. This is not conjecture. It's pattern recognition based on evidence of the last major tech convergence we lived through beginning in 2007, manifested in a device that likely sits in your pocket today.

* * *

2.4 My Father's TV Repair Shop and What Needs Fixing

My father excelled at repairing vacuum tube televisions. Watching him disassemble and reassemble sets on his workbench with a dizzying assortment of tools was like witnessing a wizard wave his wands. Magic.

Built more solid than a Magnavox console and possessed of heavy hands and a booming voice, Vasanbhai Gopal Mistry was the best in the Harlesden area. His customers trusted him and spread the word. He worked hard, laughed often and could scare the living hell out of you, especially when he laid waste to sets beyond repair. Any business owner would be proud to possess his commitment, his work ethic, his knowledge base and way of doing business.

But when transistors came, being excellent with vacuum tubes did not matter; they became the stuff of hobbyists and vintage guitar amp enthusiasts. The technology shift rendered his expertise useless, not because he wasn't skilled but because his skills no longer mattered. The wands no longer worked. The magic was gone. Bankruptcy soon followed.

Banks know traditional banking cold. They're great at taking deposits, underwriting loans, managing risk, adhering to regulatory compliance. Many are genuinely well-run institutions. But when digital twin platforms powered by quantum simulation own customer journeys, when conversational AI agents orchestrate everything, and when tokenised money moves without intermediaries, being excellent at traditional banking will not matter. The technology shift will make their expertise a moot point. It's a tubes-to-transistors transition.

Unless they want to go 'bankrupt', if you will, banks must turn into something that does not resemble today's model. They are tasked with changing into a platform that owns customer journeys, powered by complete data and quantum intelligence, orchestrated by AI agents, built on tokenised infrastructure. Complete journey ownership powered by complete customer understanding? That's transformation. And it's finally technologically possible. All five pieces are ready simultaneously in 2026. They were not ready in 1994, or 2001, or 2013, or 2016, or 2020. But they're ready now. It's taken me 40 years to spot the pattern.

Give it time; this coalescence is not incremental. It's not a better channel, smarter products or nicer interfaces. It makes traditional banking optional, if not a relic worthy of a Roman coin: once upon a monetary time worth something, but useless in today's marketplace. And I'm predicting it will happen in five years because of precedent. The smartphone pattern proved how long convergence moments take to consolidate markets. And so I posit this analogy: 2007 convergence to 2012 consolidation, five years; 2027 convergence to 2032 consolidation, five years. The economics force it. The competition demands it. The customer behaviour enables it. And technology allows it.

Extinction? Or convergence? Throw out your tubes because this book is about the new convergence, which Lou coined 'the Quanvergence'. The next iPhone moment, now. The immediate future of banking.

And the institution that navigates it successfully, that becomes genuinely, continuously intelligent about its customers' complete financial lives, will be something banking has never quite had before. Not a product provider, nor a channel or even an app. An ***Intelligent Ledger***: a living record that does not just reflect what you own and owe, but understands your financial life well enough to guide it. That is the ambition this book describes. That is what the Quanvergence makes possible.

Questions for Your Board

1. Have we completed (or started) a strategic analysis and plans for agentic AI, Quantum, Digital Twins, and Tokenisation?
2. Do we see these forces in isolation? Or have we identified convergence and agree with the convergence hypothesis set out here?
3. Do we have (and hence agree with) the proposed timescales for change? If not, why not?

3

The Quantified Self Gap: Why Your Bank Knows Nothing

3.1 Opening: The 2014 Revelation

Chapter 2 established that four technologies are converging simultaneously, and that the window for response is five years, not 10. This chapter examines the most consequential gap that convergence exposes: the data gap. Banks know less about their customers than almost any other institution, and the organisations that know more are building the platform that will make that ignorance commercial.

After the Apple iPhone launched the first great wave of five-year tech convergence, the company built upon it incrementally in 2014 by releasing its first wearable, the Apple Watch. Eleven years later, the Apple Watch Series 11 cut further into the cutting edge. It features five health and fitness sensors that measure heart rate, temperature, and blood oxygen. It can even perform ECG functions, and its accelerometers and gyroscopes detect high-G forces. It also tracks workout motion in fine detail and of course, it can count your daily steps.

You might think that's quite a bit of human/physical tracking for one person. But in 2014, in the same year as the Apple Watch release, I found a man who described himself as 'the most connected man on Earth'. Mind you, even in this age of unprecedented tech, it still makes Chris Dancy of New York City the Most Connected Human in History.

With blue bullet eyes, striking, short red hair and a beard, Dancy approaches a marvel of man-machine singularity. He monitors enough of himself across

D. Mistry, L. R. Carlozo, *The Intelligent Ledger*,
https://doi.org/10.1007/978-3-032-32842-7_3

all dimensions to keep the equivalent of at least 100 Apple Watches busy. How many sensors and systems does he connect to himself? Up to 700, and I trust that by the time you read this book, it could be dozens more.

I came across Dancy while researching data for Temenos's single brain project and was shocked to find that he measured literally everything: heart rate variability, sleep cycles, movement patterns, location data, social interactions, screen time, food intake, mood fluctuations, stress levels, environmental conditions . . .

Everything.

But if he sounds to you like a microchipped circus freak, think again. Chris Dancy takes this stuff seriously. He's penned a book about his living experiment, 'Do not Unplug: How Technology Saved My Life and Can Save Yours Too'. A former junkie who was also addicted to screens – 'already half dead,' as he put it – Dancy found self-styled salvation by using technology as a transformational tool. He writes:

> *Each time you interact with software or hardware – every moment that your relationships are mediated by a piece of glass or a wireless earbud or managed by some other publicly traded entity – you have the opportunity to wake up.*

By that measure, Chris is the most awake person I've ever seen. By turning himself into a walking data laboratory, he embodied futurist/author Kevin Kelly's theory of the 'quantified self'. If you capture complete data about a human life, you can understand and optimise that life in previously impossible ways. Kelly began his work in 2007 and founded the 'quantified self' movement; Dancy released 'Do not Unplug' 11 years later.

I read Kelly's papers on the movement. And I watched videos of Dancy explaining his setup. I read his blog posts. I studied his methodology. All those sensors. All that information. Unprecedented insight? Or information overload?

Then I hit on something that fundamentally changed how I thought about banking.

The Temenos single brain – sophisticated as it seemed, game-changing as it felt – could only access roughly 10% of the data Chris had about himself. It knew *financial behaviour*: transactions, product holdings, balances, credit history, channel preferences. But Chris knew complete *human behaviour*: his body, environment, relationships, emotions, and decisions . . . his complete life trajectory.

Then I recalled something Peter Harvey had said at Lloyds Bank in the early 1990s. Peter was a renowned expert in credit risk but understood that data could be applied to far more than assessing loan applications. His observation stuck with me for decades: *'There must be more to banking data than just transactions.'*

Twenty-three years later, Chris Dancy showed me what that 'more' looked like. And banks had none of it. Unless perhaps they read about it on an Apple Watch.

3.1.1 The Quantified Future Slideshow (2014)

I could not let this go. The implications of Chris Dancy's future leap, all of them, were too significant. If someone could quantify their complete life, not just financial transactions, what could a bank do with that understanding? I do not mean in a creepy way, as in a George Orwell 'thought police' sense. Rather, how could a person's data create a full picture where financial decisions and actions truly extend from their day-to-day reality, reflected by true numbers?

So, I created a presentation I called 'Quantified Banking'. I showed it internally at Temenos, pitched it to banks, used it to formulate an expanded vision of what the single brain could become. The slideshow outlined six data categories that constitute complete human quantification:

- **Finances** (not just banking transactions but complete financial life, risk profiles, life goals, lifestyle choices, investment psychology, spending patterns, financial stress indicators),
- **Health** (steps, heart rate, blood pressure, sleep quality, exercise intensity, caloric burn, recovery metrics, injury patterns, medical history, genetic predispositions),
- **Wellness** (sleep stages, stress levels, mental alertness patterns, breathing rate variability, burnout indicators, emotional state proxies),
- **Social** (engagement and interaction online and offline, communication frequency and depth, network size and quality, relationship strength, social isolation risk, professional network value),
- **Skills** (personal and workplace, learning velocity, skill acquisition, professional development trajectory, career progression), and
- **Travel** (where, how, what, when, location history, commute patterns, travel frequency, geographic risk exposure, transportation preferences).

Then I offered examples across the finance and commerce spectrum:

- **Insurance companies** using voice recognition to detect stress patterns correlated with dishonesty,

- **Banks** spotting spending pattern changes to detect fraud before customers noticed, not just 'unusual transaction' alerts but behavioural pattern breaks that pointed to an account compromise, and
- **Retailers** analysing shopping patterns to understand life stress, a sudden shift from fresh food to ready meals, increased alcohol purchases, reduced discretionary spending, not just shopping trends but life indicators.

The possibilities seemed endless; only a lack of imagination and/or courage to act on data for customer benefit could limit them. But I also saw the dangers. 'Quantified Banking' took shape around the time Edward Snowden revealed NSA surveillance programs. Privacy concerns were mounting. And Facebook's data practices were becoming controversial (and still are, given the company's limitless denial, deflection and equivocating).

The tension was clear: *Complete data could provide immense benefit but could also enable immense abuse.*

The difference was control, transparency, and consent. Despite this, consumers have continued to use Facebook, proving they would trade their personal data for the utility of the social platform. They've done this even after whistleblower Frances Haugen came forward in 2021 with tens of thousands of damning internal documents. They showed that Facebook consistently chose to maximise growth rather than implement platform safeguards, even though internal research illuminated the harms of Facebook products. One media outlet called it 'the most threatening scandal in the company's history.'

Then, days after Haugen's US Senate testimony in October of that year, a smiling Mark Zuckerberg announced the company's name change to Meta. The immense fanfare and media frenzy effectively wiped her story from the headlines and cleared the way for the company, if it so chose, to dance down the path of immense data abuse. (In the first quarter of 2026, Facebook lost two prominent lawsuits in the US for data-related child exploitation and youth addiction.)

* * *

3.1.2 2016: The 'Bank of Me' Vision

Two years after creating the Quantified Future presentation, I tried to show the banking industry what this could look like in practice. My three-minute video, titled 'The Bank of Me: A Future Vision of Banking', showed how a broader data set could work as banking ran in the background, not the foreground. The key insight: Banking is not the centre of life. Life itself is. Banking should work as a support service within a 'complete life' platform. The scenes captured a vision from the Chris Dancy playbook: complete data about a person's life, health metrics, location patterns, social interactions, and daily activities, with financial services integrated seamlessly. The banking happened automatically, triggered by life events and optimised for life outcomes. Not: 'Here's your bank account, now try to manage your life around it' but, 'Here's your life, and here's how banking supports it invisibly.'

The response was polite interest and zero action. I was too early, by ten years. *Not again!* But I knew I was pointing in the right direction.

* * *

3.2 The Six Data Layers Banks Lack: A Closer Look

Let me be precise. Traditional banks have one data layer and only one, financial. They know your transactions, account balances, product holdings, payment history, stated income, your credit score. That might sound like a lot. But it's not even close to 700 sensors worth.

In fact, it represents approximately 10% of what drives your financial decisions. The other 90% exists across five additional data layers; here's a closer look at all six.

3.2.1 Layer 1: Physical (Health and Body)

This does not mean static medical records (though those matter, too) but the *continuous stream of biometric data* that smart health devices now capture about your body and its functioning. This includes:

- **Heart rate patterns** at rest, during activity, and in recovery,
- **Sleep quality** and duration across deep sleep, REM, and interruptions,
- **Physical activity levels**,
- **Stress indicators** through heart rate variability and breathing patterns,
- **Energy levels** throughout the day,
- **Fitness trajectory** improving, declining or stable,
- **Injury patterns** and recovery,
- **Medication adherence**, and
- **Chronic condition management**.

Who has this data: Apple via Apple Watch and the Health app; Fitbit and Google; Garmin, Whoop, Oura Ring and Samsung, along with healthcare apps, and health insurance companies that incentivise data-sharing.
What it reveals: Your health trajectory affects every major financial decision. Banks should not approach a person suffering from a serious health condition to sell them long-term products such as a 30-year mortgage or pension. Someone who does not travel outside the UK does not need travel insurance. Someone training for a marathon has different insurance needs than a sedentary person. Someone making unusual transactions while stress levels are high might be coerced by a bad actor.
A personal example: I use a Garmin Fenix watch, a Circular 2 smart ring, and smart scales for health tracking. The same app collects data from all three devices while I manually log food and water intake. This yields an extraordinary volume of information, hundreds of daily data points about my physical state. My health insurance company, Vitality, saw the value immediately. They give me discounts for linking my shopping spend and smart watch data to their systems. I get rewards for working out and discounts for healthy eating. The arrangement benefits both of us. They get data that helps them assess my risk more accurately, while I get financial incentives for healthy behaviour.

This is the quantified self in practice. And it's utterly invisible to my bank, which is preoccupied with selling someone, anyone, something. Anything. Like a credit card to buy a smart watch.

3.2.2 Layer 2: Environmental (Location and Context)

This data concerns where you are, go, and spend time:

- home location and quality,
- commute patterns and duration,
- travel frequency and destinations,
- time spent in different locations,
- geographic risk exposure to natural disasters and crime and pollution,
- vehicle data from connected cars,
- weather,
- smart home data covering energy usage, and
- security and maintenance needs.

Who has this: Google via Android and Google Maps; Apple via iPhone location services; car manufacturers via connected vehicles; smart home platforms such as Amazon Alexa and Google Home; navigation apps; and utility companies.
What it reveals: Someone with a two-hour commute might be better off financially moving closer or taking a lower-salary job nearby. (Factor in health data and you get an even clearer picture of commuting 'costs'.) Someone travelling internationally frequently may be better off with currency accounts than exchanging money for each trip. Someone in a flood zone needs different insurance. Someone's smart home data reveals maintenance needs that might require financing.
A personal example: My own home has smart heating, smart speakers, smart TV, smart lights, smart cameras, and a smart alarm system. (If only this made me a smart homeowner.) Each feature generates data about how I use my home, when I occupy it, how much energy I consume and what maintenance might be needed. In January 2026, the singer/entrepreneur William Adams (known by his Black Eyed Peas stage name will.i.am) announced the Trinity. At £23,500, this three-wheeled electric microcar makes riding more of a connected *experience*. Recognising that many of us spend much of our day in cars, will.i.am wants to actively manage and improve that time. You could, for example, tell its agentic AI to find parking near your next meeting, text the attendees your ETA, log the mileage for expenses and pay in advance for your grocery run on the way home. As he told Dezeen, 'Trinity is for people who still love driving but want software and AI to handle the mental load around the drive: planning, coordinating, remembering and connecting.'

All of this data at home and on the road exists about me. None of it is available to my bank, which (once again) is preoccupied with selling someone, anyone, something. Anything, like a £23,500 car loan.

3.2.3 Layer 3: Social (Relationships and Networks)

This is data about your relationships and social interactions:

- communication frequency and patterns across who you talk to, how often and what medium,
- network size and quality, distinguishing strong ties from weak ties,
- social isolation indicators,

- relationship stability markers,
- community involvement,
- professional network strength,
- social media activity and sentiment, and
- life events visible through social channels.

Who has this: Meta via Facebook, Instagram, and WhatsApp; LinkedIn; Twitter/X; TikTok; Snapchat; messaging platforms; telecommunications companies.
What it reveals: Relationship breakdowns often precede financial stress. A suddenly quiet social profile might indicate depression or isolation. A growing professional network indicates career advancement potential. Life events announced on social media – a new job, engagement, pregnancy or relocation – have massive financial implications.

My bank sees none of this. They have no idea if I'm socially thriving or isolated, if my relationships are stable or strained, or which life events will drive financial decisions. They're operating blind.

3.2.4 Layer 4: Emotional (Stress and Mental State)

This proves the hardest data layer to quantify directly, but it's increasingly possible through proxies:

- stress levels measured through physiological indicators,
- mood patterns tracked through apps or inferred from behaviour,
- mental health indicators through sleep disruption, activity changes and social withdrawal,
- emotional resilience metrics,
- burnout risk,
- depression or anxiety indicators, and
- life satisfaction proxies (attainable in part through self-reporting).

Who has this: Mental wellness apps such as Headspace and Calm; mood trackers; therapist platforms that include BetterHelp; journaling apps; and increasingly sophisticated AI that can infer emotional state from communication patterns, voice analysis and even typing rhythms.
What it reveals: Financial decisions made under stress are often poor. Someone experiencing burnout should not be encouraged to take on more debt. Someone dealing with depression might need different customer service

support. While I do not explicitly track my emotional state through apps, my smart ring and watch indicate stress through wellness data such as heart rate variability, sleep quality and recovery metrics, all emotional state proxies. Poor sleep + elevated resting heart rate + low HRV = I'm stressed, even if I have not consciously acknowledged it. Based on this, my smart ring advises me how to manage my day: Whether I should take things easy, what time I should expect to do my best work, when I should rest. I would love to understand whether poor sleep or high stress affects my spending patterns, because shopping pattern changes can indicate stress: A sudden shift from fresh food to ready meals, increased alcohol purchases, reduced discretionary spending. These are not just shopping trends. They're life indicators.

My bank is oblivious to this information.

3.2.5 Layer 5: Cognitive (Decision Patterns and Thinking)

This data indicates how you think and make decisions:

- patterns between impulsive and deliberate,
- risk tolerance revealed through behaviour rather than stated preferences,
- learning speed and adaptation,
- information processing style,
- cognitive biases you exhibit,
- actual financial literacy level,
- time horizon preferences, and
- delayed gratification capacity.

Who has this: Nobody currently has this comprehensively but behavioural data from multiple sources reveals cognitive patterns. Investment apps see risk tolerance; gaming apps see decision speed; education platforms see learning patterns; search history reveals information-seeking behaviour.
What it reveals: Should someone who exhibits impulsive decision-making in multiple life domains be given instant credit? A person with short time horizons revealed through behaviour needs different advice than someone who demonstrates long-term thinking. Risk tolerance revealed through behaviour is far more accurate than risk tolerance stated on a questionnaire.

Banks do not recognise this but to be fair, the data picture is still emerging. What's more, banks that commit to structured financial literacy initiatives on a person-by-person basis, and make room for self-reporting, could act as drivers in collecting this information.

3.2.6 Layer 6: Financial, the 10% Banks Actually Have

This is the only layer where banks can claim comprehensive access:

- transaction history,
- account balances,
- product holdings,
- payment patterns,
- credit history,
- loan applications and outcomes,
- investment portfolio (if you bank with them),
- stated financial goals,
- income, and
- declared assets and liabilities.

What it reveals: Yes, financial institutions know how you behave financially but without any context as to why. Banks see spending patterns but do not know whether they're driven by stress, celebration, necessity or lifestyle. They see income but do not know whether your job is secure or you're burnt out. They see savings but do not know if you're saving for a house or recovering from a divorce. **A personal example:** I use Open Banking to connect my accounts but other products remain spread across different institutions. I manage relationships with more than a dozen companies for all my financial needs. Nobody gives me a unified, complete view of my financial picture. So, I use spreadsheets. I manually create my own single view of wealth because nobody, not my bank, not any fintech, nobody offers this currently. Think about that. I spent seven years as Chief Digital Officer at Temenos building the 'single brain' for banks. I understand financial data better than most. But I still need spreadsheets to see my complete financial picture. If as an industry veteran I cannot get a unified view of my finances, what hope do regular customers have? For the present anyway. Let's revisit this soon.

* * *

3.3 The Asymmetry: Who Actually 'Collects' Your Quantified Self?

Here's the uncomfortable truth: *Your quantified self already exists.* You just do not know it in all likelihood, or if you do, the various data threads are difficult if not impossible to trace. It's just not owned by you and certainly not accessible to your bank. Other parties capture, store and analyse the data:

- ***Apple has layers 1, 2, 3, and partial layer 4*** via Apple Watch and Health app for health data; iPhone location services; Messages and FaceTime for social data; wellness features for emotional proxies; plus your financial data if you use Apple Pay.
- ***Google has layers 1, 2, 3, and partial layer 5*** via Fitbit and Google Fit for health; Android and Google Maps for location; Gmail and Google Chat for social; search history, YouTube and browsing behaviour for cognitive patterns; plus financial data from Google Pay.
- ***Meta has layer 3 and partial layer 4*** via Facebook, Instagram, and WhatsApp for social data, posts and interactions for emotional state and life events you share.
- ***Amazon has layers 2 and 6*** via shopping behaviour, deliveries, Alexa for smart home, and payment data.

Your health insurance company may have layer 1 if you've opted into data-sharing. Your car manufacturer has layer 2 if you have a connected car.

Access to data sources across the six layers will only increase as governments push to open up more access, as the UK has done with the Smart Data (Use and Access) Act 2025. (The measure reforms how the UK manages non-personal and personal data and aims to unlock its secure and effective use.)

The quantified self is not theoretical. It's not the future. It's happening now, continuously, and in real time across multiple companies. The problem banks face is not, 'Should we capture this data?' Rather: 'This data already exists, and we have none of it.' Once banks gather up the will to look at this, they can start to think about how they can improve customers' lives with it and how to blend this data to create customer trust, because the benefits to these customers are too great not to share it.

3.3.1 The Credit Card Company That Failed to Use Its Own Data

Let me give you a textbook example of how banks fail to use even the data they *do* possess. I once went on holiday for two weeks. Immediately after I returned, I travelled for four weeks for work, which meant I was away from home for six consecutive weeks. During those six weeks, my credit card company observed that my spending had increased, because whilst travelling I charged everything to the card. They sent me a letter offering to extend my credit limit. The same week they also sent me *another* letter with essentially the opposite message, that my bill was overdue and that their next step was court proceedings for recovery.

What?

I had not seen my bill because I was not at home to receive mail. Simple. *And they knew I was not at home*; they could see from my transaction data that I spent time in different cities and countries throughout the period, continuously, for more than 40 days. Simpler still.

But the credit increase and overdue bill threat might as well have come from completely different banks. Two silos, acting independently. One offered me more credit, one threatened legal action. Neither used the data they had to understand I was travelling. Neither made the connection. And neither encouraged anything close to customer loyalty: confusion at best, consternation at worst.

Where's the data point for that? In a third silo, perhaps.

Now imagine that they had a grasp of my complete quantified self:

- They would've known from location data that I was away from home;
- that I was travelling for work, if I'd shared my calendar;
- that I'd be away for an extended period, based on predictions from historical patterns.

They could have:

- sent me a digital notification instead of physical mail;
- conducted an automatic payment from my checking account, with my permission;
- recognised the spending increase as travel-related rather than lifestyle creep;
- avoided threatening a good customer with court proceedings.

But they did none of that. Because they possessed just 10% of my data, in silos, and used it poorly.

Complete. And utter ...

Fail.

3.3.2 The Problem with Banks: Small Compared with Ours

Here's what's ironic: Banks complain about data silos.

The problem banks face with data spread across internal silos is minuscule compared to our own data spread and duplicated everywhere.

My health data lives in Garmin Connect, a Circular app, a smart scale app, a health insurance portal, multiple doctors' records, pharmacy records and NHS records.

I have financial data in my primary bank, multiple credit card companies, my mortgage provider, investment accounts, employer pensions, my business bank accounts, accounting software, and my spreadsheets (because nothing else gives me a unified view).

My location data is located in Google Maps history, my car navigation system, travel booking confirmations, hotel and airline loyalty programmes, Uber ride history and my company expense system.

And none of it talks to any of the rest of it. This constitutes enough silos to launch a digital mega-farm.

If banks bemoan their data problem, they should see deeper into their customers' lives. The opportunity exists not only to give banks a unified view of customers but also to give customers *a unified view of themselves*. That's what the quantified self, properly implemented, could achieve. That's what a digital twin could be.

* * *

3.4 From Quantified Self to Digital Twin

When I first encountered the quantified self movement in 2014, the term 'digital twin' was not yet mainstream in banking discussions. Grasping its function and description can be difficult. But properly explained, the digital twin really is quite simple.

Digital twins originated in manufacturing and engineering; you'd create a complete digital model of a physical asset, let's say a jet engine, factory, or a building, and simulate its performance under different conditions. The digital twin would mirror the real asset in real time, which would allow you to predict failures, optimise performance and test scenarios without risk. When I learnt about digital twins applied to people, I immediately saw the correlation with the quantified self.

A digital twin is not just data storage. It represents a complete, dynamic model of a person that updates in real time as new data arrives. And let's face it, we live in a real-time world: flash sales, flash mobs, 24-hour news flashes. In the digital sphere, no human activity stands still.

And so:

- The six data layers I described equal the inputs.
- The quantified self is the data capture mechanism.
- The digital twin is the model you build from that data.

Once you create a person's complete digital twin, with all six layers updating continuously, you accomplish something banks could not and cannot do: *You simulate their life*. Not predict what they'll do but simulate what would happen if they did X versus Y versus Z. What if I buy this house versus rent for another two years? Or change jobs for higher pay but longer commutes? Or have another child right now versus waiting three years? Or invest aggressively versus conservatively given my health trajectory?

Thousands of scenarios, different choices, different outcomes. Different futures. And . . . this is where quantum computing enters the picture.

Classical computing cannot simulate complex life scenarios at scale in real time with digital-twin level of variables, the plethora of interactions and uncertainty are simply too immense. But quantum computing can. We start with the *quantified* self. Then we apply it to *quantum* simulation.

That amounts to a paradigm shift and platform shift propelled by a tectonic shift.

* * *

3.5 Five Reasons Why Banks Have Not Built This

If the benefits are so clear, if the data largely exists, if the technology is increasingly available, then why have not banks built digital twins for their customers? I count five reasons and I want to address each directly, because I hear about them constantly.

First, they misperceive the privacy problem. Yes, scary headlines pop up constantly about massive data breaches and smart cybercrooks. To be certain, these issues need to be addressed, but they belong to a separate conversation. That data about myself I described above? *I share most of it willingly with tech companies in exchange for services I value.* Using my health data, my insurance company extends discounts. When Google tracks my location, I benefit from better navigation (including the ability to drive around nasty traffic jams).

Customers will share data if the value exchange is clear and the control is genuine. The problem is not privacy but rather value. Yet banks have not articulated the value proposition or built the control mechanisms.

Second, they think customers will not share. Wrong. Using an analogy bankers can understand, think of data as money. It's easy to say, 'Customers will not part with this; they'll think someone's out to steal it.' But we spend money all the time. Value is the key. And banks already know it because people buy their products, voluntarily surrendering their money to do it (though in the case of the 2016 American Wells Fargo scandal, the bank indeed foisted two million unauthorised bank and credit card accounts on customers. In essence, to steal from their own clients. The reason: A blind devotion to sales goals.)

Customers already share with banks and a plethora of companies: Apple, Google, Amazon, Meta, health insurers, smart home platforms, car manufacturers, and fitness apps. The question we should ask is not, 'Will customers share?' It's 'Why would not customers share with banks when they already share with everyone else?' After all, *banks could actually do something valuable with complete data that no single tech platform can.* Banks can optimise across your complete financial life in ways a fitness tracker or social network cannot. But first, banks must build the capability and earn the trust.

Third, they think it's technically too hard or even impossible. Here's a personal example. After selling AskHomey, I wanted to test whether property data could be made genuinely useful and accessible. Using Claude Code, an AI-assisted development tool, I built an application that used location services to pull public property data and give real-time information about any property you stood near. Just point your phone at a building and you could get its history, ownership, valuation, planning applications, and relevant financial context. Complete, working, useful.

Despite my youthful coding obsession, I have not written production code for decades. I built this myself. Microsoft and GitHub report that AI tools like GitHub Copilot now write more than 40% of code in repositories where it's enabled. (Ironically, the coders who made this possible are now putting themselves out of business as a result.) What previously required a team of 50 engineers over 18 months now requires a team of five over three months, with AI assistance handling repetitive integration, boilerplate and testing.

Even more significant than AI-assisted coding is the emergence of agentic AI with MCP servers. Model Context Protocol allows AI agents to connect to external data sources, APIs, and services automatically, meaning that via AI orchestration, complex digital twin integrations now take just hours/days, not months or years. Griffin Bank in the UK has already built an MCP server for banking operations. The question is no longer, 'Can we build this?' but, 'Will we start before our competitors do?'

Fourth, they think the business model is vague. This objection is partially valid. How do you monetise a digital twin? You cannot charge customers directly; they're used to free banking. You cannot sell personal data; privacy regulations prevent it and it would destroy trust.

But the business model is actually quite clear and only requires a shift of mindset. The digital twin enables journey ownership, and journey ownership enables platform economics, *which generates three to five times better margins than product sales.* With AskHomey, we did not charge to create the digital twin of your home. We monetised *the journey*. We captured value as a trusted adviser that knew everything about your home and could guide every decision. Banks could do the same with your complete life.

Fifth, they think they have time. Human nature, based on our inherent resistance to change, is understandable. But in this case, it's the fatal mistake. While they think and think and think, Big Tech builds. Apple collects health data from millions of Apple Watch users. Google stores location data from billions of Android users. Amazon digitises shopping behaviour from hundreds of millions of Prime members. Meta has access to social data from nearly three billion people. These companies have pieces of the digital twin and are not waiting for permission from stodgy boards or perfect business models. As mentioned earlier, Ant Financial in China has this and so does Grab in Southeast Asia. These companies live not in theory but in practice.

The window for Western banks to build digital twins is 2027–2028. After that, the data moat created by platforms will become much harder to overcome.

* * *

3.6 The Fruitless Future, or the Ghost of Banking Yet to Come

Let me paint you a picture of what 2030 could look like if banks do not build digital twins. (I cannot tune into it on one of my dad's obsolete TVs.) No crystal ball is needed and after reading this far, you can spot elements of it for yourself:

Apple launches Apple Life in 2027. It's not a bank. It's a life platform. It has your health data from Apple Watch, location data from iPhone, communication data from Messages, payment data from Apple Pay … and your calendar, your photos, your music, your everything. It builds your complete digital twin. It does not ask you to share data; you have no problem with that and have already shared it for years. It just starts to use it coherently. Apple Life tells you: 'Based on your health trajectory, commute stress, relationship patterns and financial situation, here are ten scenarios for your next five years; here is the optimal path; here is what you need to do; here are the products you need. Give us the word, we'll handle it.' It recommends a mortgage from the lender that offers the best terms and banks bid for the business. It recommends insurance from the optimal provider; insurance companies bid, too. Banks become product vendors in Apple's platform. Commodities compete on price. No customer relationship in the traditional sense. No loyalty. Just utility.

Or maybe it's not Apple. Maybe it's Google. Or Amazon with Alexa and Prime. Or a Chinese company expanding globally, the specifics do not matter. The *pattern* matters.

Someone will build the complete digital twin and own the customer relationship.

That will relegate banks to product providers unless they build it first. The irony is that I personally live with the problem banks refuse to solve. Through my many devices I generate the quantified self constantly. But who aggregates it, crunches it, helps me make sense of it and optimise my life based on it? I'm the exact customer banks should serve. I understand the value of complete data. I'm willing to share it. And banks have spent a decade ignoring the opportunity, still do . . . and still will?

* * *

3.7 The Storage and Compute Problems, Then Versus Now

Though Chris Dancy, in tandem with the concept of the quantified self, led to a double 'a-ha moment' in 2014, one doubt haunted me, an 'uh-oh' moment, you might say.

I was not sure that in my lifetime we'd have the storage capacity to keep everything, let alone the compute power to analyse it at scale and in real time. The data volume in a complete quantified self is enormous: every heartbeat, every step, every location point, every transaction, every communication, every environmental reading, every sensor measurement.

Now, multiply that by millions of customers and years of history, even as it continuously grows by the nanosecond. The storage requirements seemed impossible.

No more.

In 2026, I know this is feasible. The cloud is why. Cloud storage is effectively infinite and increasingly cheap. Distributed computing and real-time streaming architectures have scaled similarly. So, the infrastructure exists.

But one missing piece must materialise for the vision to be fully realised, with simulation of complex life scenarios at scale, in the now.

Classical machine learning can render predictions based on past patterns; it can recommend products and detect anomalies. But it cannot be simulated. It cannot show you ten thousand versions of your life playing out under different choices. Nor can it optimise across hundreds of variables simultaneously with pitch-perfect accuracy.

That's right. It cannot. But as the hardware matures, quantum computing will.

Complete data builds the foundation. What you do with that data – how you simulate, optimise, and guide decisions – that's the superstructure. The quantified self enables real-time context and quantum simulation enables real-time decision support at a scale and complexity never before possible, not even close.

But now, we stand as close as ever as the necessary elements coalesce like planets moving into orbit. Together, they transform banking from product sales to life guidance. Apart, they're incomplete.

* * *

3.8 What Follows: The Foundation for Everything

This chapter concerns the data problem, the quantified self gap, the 10% versus 90% asymmetry, the digital twin opportunity. But understand: It's the foundation, not the building.

- We need complete customer data to pull off the transformation. Without it, everything else fails.
- Without the quantified self, you cannot build an accurate 'next self,' the digital twin.

- Without digital twins, you cannot run simulations.
- Without simulations, you cannot provide guidance.
- Without guidance, you cannot own journeys.
- And without journey ownership, you cannot build platforms.

All those 'withouts' depend on one lynchpin, data. Banks 'without' it by 2029 will not matter as much as they do now by 2032. Then they'll risk becoming a without unto themselves, right up there with the paper deposit slip.

But banks that do can become platforms that own complete life relationships. The choice is binary; the timeline compressing; the technology ready. And so: ***Without will, the journey never begins.***

What that journey builds towards has a name. A bank that holds all six layers of a customer's life: physical, environmental, social, emotional, cognitive, and financial. Which then updates them continuously, and uses that understanding to guide rather than sell, is no longer a bank in any sense that the word has carried for six centuries. It is an ***Intelligent Ledger***. Not the ledger of medieval Florence, recording debts and credits in a vellum book. Not the digitised ledger of Barclays in 1961, running account balances through a refrigerator-sized machine. But a living, dynamic model of a person's financial life. One that knows what you need before you do, simulates what happens if you act or do not, and works quietly in the background of your life rather than waiting for you to visit a branch or open an app. That is the transformation this data chapter makes possible. Everything else in this book is built on top of it.

Find the will, choose differently, start now.

Questions for Your bank

1. How broad and deep is our data strategy compared to a digital twin with the six layers identified here? What will it take to fill the gaps?
2. Do our plans include a concerted effort and the ability to make decisions across our silos such that we operate with a 'single brain'? If not, how else will we provide real-time guidance and/or advice that reflects complete customer awareness?
3. Which of the five data concerns – privacy, data-sharing permission, technology complexity, and business model – do we need to address? Can we accomplish this before our competitors?

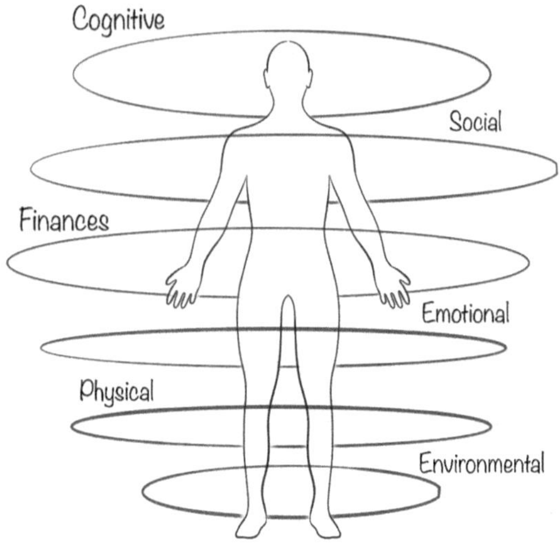
Cognitive
Social
Finances
Emotional
Physical
Environmental

4

Six Forcing Functions That Point to the Quanvergence (2027–2032)

Every banking executive I talk to says the same thing: 'This transformation will take ten years. We have time.' They're wrong. You do not have ten years. You have five.

Here's why the 2027–2032 timeline is not speculation: It's in motion. And why one of the most important factors is something most banks have not even started thinking about: the collapse of the technical build barrier. At present, six forcing functions compress the banking transformation timeline. Any one would give you a seven-to-ten-year window. Together they shave it down to five. And the sixth, the one most banks completely ignore, explains why the specific year is not 2029 or 2031: It's 2027.

* * *

4.1 Forcing Function 1: Technology Convergence (Not Sequential Adoption)

Every previous banking disruption arrived sequentially. Internet banking in the 1990s took 20 years to reach mainstream adoption. Mobile banking took 15 years. Cloud banking another 10. Whilst these waves overlapped, each gave banks time to adapt, one technology at a time and with gradual adoption, which gave banks the chance to figure things out eventually. This

D. Mistry, L. R. Carlozo, *The Intelligent Ledger*,
https://doi.org/10.1007/978-3-032-32842-7_4

disruption is different. Four technologies are maturing simultaneously with all four required together, not one at a time.

As noted in the previous chapter and worth stressing again here, digital twin, the data integration technology needed to build complete customer understanding across all six life layers, is now ready for production. APIs exist. So do privacy frameworks. Implementation partners exist. Most sectors outside of financial services piggyback off Open Banking to accelerate their own open data journeys. Quantum computing is no longer a laboratory curiosity, but now accessible via cloud on a pay-per-use basis. The use cases for banking, portfolio optimisation and risk modelling are being piloted in early experiments at Goldman Sachs, JPMorgan and BBVA. Agentic AI, with orchestration frameworks such as LangChain, OpenClaw, and MCP (Model Context Protocol), has matured to the point where AI agents can autonomously manage complex multi-system workflows. They do not just answer questions, but also orchestrate complete processes across dozens of data sources and services. And DeFi total value locked is crossing $200 billion and growing rapidly towards $500 billion by 2027.

If you wait to adopt these technologies sequentially with digital twins first, then quantum, then agents, then tokenisation, you'll do the last piece in 2035. But by that time, your competitors who adopted all four simultaneously in 2027 will own your customers. The smartphone is the pattern.

In 2007, five technologies converged: 3G networks, app stores, sufficient storage, touch interfaces and acceptable battery life. None of them alone would have created the iPhone revolution. Together, they created a device that made everything that came before obsolete. From that 2007 convergence point, it took five years for the market to consolidate. Smartphones already existed. Nokia and BlackBerry were not slow to adopt, as they had smartphones before Apple. But they were slow to recognise convergence. Indeed, it was not a better camera company that killed even Kodak, which had patents and had invented digital cameras. It was the device that was a phone, camera, diary, digital map, etc. The smartphone converged several capabilities and provided more utility, something Kodak could not compete with.

Banking stands at its 2007 moment once again. The four technologies are converging now. The market will consolidate by 2032. Five years. Not 10.

* * *

4.2 Forcing Function 2: First-Mover Advantage Is Absolute

Traditional banking competition is forgiving. If you're late to launch a product, you can match it later. If a competitor offers better rates, you can compete. If a customer leaves, they might come back. The barriers to switching are low.

But platform banking competition is unforgiving. Winner takes most. Late movers do not just lose market share, they lose the ability to compete. Here's why: The digital twin creates infinite switching costs. Once a customer gives a platform bank complete access to all six data layers (health, environmental, social, emotional, cognitive, financial) – and that platform starts building a personalised digital twin and simulation history – switching means you lose your entire digital twin with years of complete life data. Gone is your simulation history with all the scenarios that were run and advice that proved correct, along with your agent's learnings about your preferences, patterns and goals. Switch and you start over at zero with a competitor who cannot possibly provide the same quality of advice until they've accumulated years of your life data. Traditional bank switching costs: £0-50 and an afternoon of admin. Platform bank switching costs? Effectively infinite.

Ant Financial's timeline shows how this plays out. They launched Alipay in 2004 as a simple payments service, added savings products in 2008, wealth management in 2013, with Sesame Credit using complete behavioural data for credit scoring in 2015, insurance and investment products through 2017. By 2020, Ant was attempting a $300 billion IPO. Sixteen years from launch to dominant platform, but they built the playbook from scratch with no model to copy. Western banks can copy Ant Financial's proven model in just three to five years, not 16. But only if they start in 2027. Because the first bank in each Western market to achieve platform scale will own that market the same way Ant Financial owns digital financial services in China. The first two or three movers in each major market win. Everyone else loses. This is not speculation. It's the documented outcome of every platform market that has played out before banking.

* * *

4.3 Forcing Function 3: DeFi and Tokenisation Make Banks Optional

Every previous fintech disruption still required banks underneath. Neobanks needed banking licences. PayPal needed bank accounts. Even crypto exchanges needed fiat onramps through traditional banking. Customers could use the new services but could not escape banks entirely. DeFi and tokenisation change this. For the first time, customers can access payments, lending, savings and investment services without a traditional bank at any point in the chain. Stablecoins enable payments without bank intermediaries. Smart contracts enable lending without bank approval by replacing human workflows and credit checks with automated flows and data-driven decisions. Decentralised exchanges enable investment without brokers. Programmable money operates on blockchain rails that do not need traditional banking infrastructure.

What this means for banks: If you compete on infrastructure and the ability to process payments, hold deposits and provide credit, DeFi will prove cheaper, faster, and more transparent than you within this decade. The only way to survive is to offer something DeFi cannot, something like: complete life understanding, personalised simulation, journey guidance. This requires digital twins and quantum computing. If you're just infrastructure, DeFi eliminates you. If you're a platform that provides genuine life value, DeFi actually helps you: It gives you better rails to build on. The 2027–2028 window is specifically when stablecoin frameworks finalise in major markets and legitimise DeFi for mainstream adoption. Banks that fail to differentiate by then will face an existential infrastructure threat without a platform alternative to fall back on.

* * *

4.4 Forcing Function 4: Regulatory Catalysts Accelerate Change

The conventional wisdom says regulation slows banking innovation. For incremental change within existing frameworks, that's true. For existential transformation? Regulation *accelerates* it.

Full implementation in 2027 of Basel IV (the final set of global banking reforms designed to strengthen 2008 financial crisis regulations) increases capital requirements against risk, and makes traditional banking more expensive and less profitable, which will push smarter banks towards higher-margin platform business models. The EU AI Act that comes into full force in 2028 requires explainable AI for consequential financial decisions. Black-box machine learning that cannot explain its reasoning is non-compliant while quantum simulation, which shows customers multiple scenarios and explains the reasoning behind each, is inherently compliant. The regulatory environment actually favours quantum adoption over traditional ML. Stablecoin frameworks that finalise in 2027–2028 simultaneously across the US, EU, and UK legitimise DeFi and open the door for major technology platforms to offer regulated financial services. Apple, Google, and Amazon have waited for this regulatory clarity before making major moves into banking.

Regional bank failures that emerge in 2029–2030 are likely to trigger regulatory consolidation pressure. Regulators will prefer 15 strong platform banks over 1,000 weakened traditional banks. Consolidation will accelerate and separate early movers from late movers sharply. By 2030-2031, a new regulatory framework specific to platform banks will begin to appear. Winners will face heavier regulation than today but this is reassuring rather than threatening. Regulators do not write rules for businesses that fail. They write rules for businesses that are winning. Regulation is not the obstacle banking executives claim. For this transformation, it's an accelerant.

* * *

4.5 Forcing Function 5: Customer Behaviour Has Already Changed

Previous banking disruptions required customers to change their behaviour. Internet banking asked people to trust online transactions, thus taking 20 years for mainstream adoption. They also needed access to a PC and an internet connection, which at the time was a significant outlay for the average household. Mobile banking asked people to trust their phone with their money, another 15 years, and yet another device they had to buy first. Each disruption had an education, adoption and cost factor built in. But this disruption requires no behaviour change at all, the majority of customers now own devices for accessing everything they need.

Customers are already doing everything platform banking needs. They already share complete data with technology companies, health data to Apple and Fitbit, location data to Google and Apple, communication data to Meta and messaging platforms, shopping data to Amazon. People who would never consciously think, 'I'll share my health data with a company,' wear Apple Watches that track every heartbeat. They already trust AI recommendations as Netflix tells them what to watch, Spotify what to listen to, Google Maps where to go, Amazon what to buy. The habit of following AI guidance is already formed. They already expect personalisation and they're annoyed when experiences do not deliver it. They already use scenario planning; Google Flights shows different prices for different dates, Kayak shows trip options across hundreds of variables.

The data confirms what's self-evident from experience:

- According to Accenture's Global Insurance Consumer Study of 47,000 consumers across 28 markets, 69% are comfortable sharing health and lifestyle data in exchange for lower insurance premiums, up from 58% just two years earlier, a trajectory that only accelerates.
- SEMrush's December 2025 survey of more than 1,000 consumers shows that 85% of people who use AI tools do so at least weekly, with 48% engaging daily for product research, navigation, entertainment, and shopping decisions.
- 'Reimagining Retail in 2026', a white paper by commercetools, forecasts that by 2030, nearly 50% of online shoppers will use AI agents, accounting for roughly 25% of their spending.
- According to Personetics' February 2025 global survey of 2,000 banking customers, 84% say they would switch to a bank that provided timely, relevant financial advice, not a marginal preference, an overwhelming one. The habit of following AI guidance is already formed; banks are simply the last service that has not yet offered it.

And the gap between what customers experience from their bank versus every other digital service in their lives is not a perception problem. It marks the central customer experience fact of 2026. In fact, this has been talked about for more than a decade with banking expert after expert, vendor after vendor, questioning why banks could not replicate the 'seamless' or 'friction-free' customer experience of Amazon, which initiated predictive shopping and shipping in 2012. Bank executive after bank executive promised it or said they were working on it. Few if any have yet to deliver.

The financial institution that begins to build towards a complete digital twin and quantum simulation capability in 2027 does not need to educate customers or change their behaviour. It just needs to offer what customers already want from every other service in their lives and have never received from their bank. This eliminates the historical adoption curve that has given banks time to respond to disruption. Traditional banking by 2032 could feel like using a fax machine in the email era. Customers will not switch because it's worse but because they can no longer understand why they're still using it.

* * *

4.6 Forcing Function 6: The Development Barrier Has Collapsed

The previous five forcing functions explain why the transformation window exists. This sixth explains why it opens specifically in 2027, and why banks that understand it can move faster than ever. For years, banks had valid technical excuses for slow transformation: 'It's too complex to build. It would take too long. We do not have the developer resources.' Complex digital twin integration across six data layers, real-time quantum simulation, agentic AI orchestration: All this would have required enormous engineering teams working for years. The technical barrier was real. But that barrier collapsed in 2025–2026.

4.6.1 AI-Assisted Development

Microsoft, GitHub, Google, and Amazon have fundamentally changed how software gets built. GitHub Copilot now writes an average of 46% of code across repositories where it's enabled, up from 27% in 2022, with Java developers seeing that figure reach 61%. Major financial institutions have seen their enterprise development transformed, as what previously demanded 50 engineers over 18 months now requires just five engineers over three months. But the more important implication is not speed for professional developers. *It's accessible for non-developers.*

As I highlighted in the previous chapter, after closing AskHomey, I wanted to test whether property data could be made genuinely accessible. Using Claude Code, an AI-assisted development tool, I built an application that used location services to pull public property data and give real-time information about any property you stood near. Point your phone at a building and see its history, ownership, valuation, planning applications, and relevant financial context. Complete, working, useful. I have not written production code for decades. I built this myself. The labour and time barriers between having an idea and a working application have collapsed. Whilst many have concerns that this inevitably means we need fewer employees, many banks now see that they can now do far more with the people they have. This new capacity allows the banks' Intelligent Ledger to be built, when once it would have amounted to a distant vision.

4.6.2 Agentic AI and MCP Servers

More significant than AI-assisted development is the emergence of agentic AI that operates through MCP servers. MCP, Model Context Protocol, is a framework that allows AI agents to connect autonomously to external data sources, APIs, and services. An AI agent with MCP access can:

- connect to Apple HealthKit and pull health data, access location services,
- integrate with smart home platforms,
- connect to social data APIs where permitted,
- pull financial data across institutions via Open Banking APIs, and
- orchestrate complex workflows across all of these simultaneously, without a developer writing custom integration code for each connection.

Griffin Bank in the UK has already built an MCP server for banking operations, making it one of the first banks globally to do so. This means AI agents can connect directly to Griffin's core banking infrastructure. The digital twin integration layer that would previously have taken years of custom development can now be assembled through AI orchestration in months. Griffin posted a video on its website in June 2025 that demonstrated how AI agents could open bank accounts, make payments, and handle complex banking workflows, all through natural language commands.

For business leaders: This is as significant as the shift from manual processes to computing in the 1980s. The pace at which technology can be deployed has jumped by an order of magnitude. Your competitor who decides to start building in January 2027 could create a working digital twin prototype by April and production deployment by September. Not because they're exceptional. Because the tools make it achievable.

4.6.3 Everything Runs at the Speed of Tech, Not the Speed of People

The most profound implication is this: Agentic AI does not wait for committee approval. Traditional technology projects fail not because of technical complexity but human bottlenecks. Business requirements need sign-off. Architecture decisions need review. Code needs QA. Integrations need testing. Deployment needs change management. Each human checkpoint adds weeks or months; a two-year project has 12 to 18 months of actual development and six to 12 months of waiting. Agentic AI that operates through

MCP servers executes complex integration, testing, and deployment workflows autonomously.

A bank that embraces agentic development works in a fundamentally different time dimension compared to one that still runs projects through traditional governance. I've personally evidenced this with OpenCoreOS, where I was chair of their UK company. There, a dozen developers compete effectively with legacy giants such as Finastra and Temenos, who each have thousands.

4.6.4 Why This Makes 2027 the Specific Moment

Without this sixth forcing function, you might ask: 'Why not start in 2029 or 2030?' Five forcing functions say transformation is necessary, but when exactly? The sixth says it's now achievable at a speed that makes 2027 the competitive inflection point. The competitor bank that starts to use agentic AI and MCP servers in Q1 2027 can have production digital twin infrastructure by Q4 2027. That's as little as six months. With the previous technical constraints, that same work would have taken until 2030: three years. The six-month versus three-year build cycle upends the competitive dynamics. By the time a bank that starts in 2029 launches, the 2027 starter has:

- 24 months of customer data across all six layers,
- refined models trained on real behaviour,
- network effects from platform scale,
- customer trust built through demonstrated value, and
- switching costs established through deep relationships.

The 2029 starter does not just face a lead time or technology gap. It faces a data gap that compounds daily, a trust gap that took years to build, and a model sophistication gap that only time and data can close.

* * *

4.7 The Compression Effect: All Six Forcing Functions Together

Each forcing function alone would give you a seven-to-10 year transformation window. Together, they compress it to five years. Technology convergence means you cannot adopt sequentially; all four technologies are needed simultaneously. First-mover advantage means the winner takes most, and being second by two years could mean losing the market entirely. DeFi creates an existential threat you cannot delay differentiating against; infrastructure banking will be commoditised. Regulatory acceleration means the environment is pushing transformation, not blocking it. Customer readiness eliminates the adoption curve; launch in 2027 and customers are immediately receptive. Development acceleration means the technical barrier has collapsed and six-month builds are now achievable. Any one of these forcing functions and banking transformation might unfold over a decade. Combine all six and it unfolds in five years.

4.7.1 Why Not Faster? (Why Not 2027–2030?)

Some readers will ask: If the technology is ready and the threat is real, why does it take five years and not three? Because transformation is not just a technology problem. It's an organisational problem. Organisations move at human speed, not tech speed, even with the help of agentic AI. Banks need 18–24 months just to make the decision: Committees, consultants, board approvals, regulatory pre-engagement, and budget cycles. The fastest-moving banks in the world still take 18 months from 'We should do this' to 'We have approved funding and a team.' The digital twin build is 18–24 months minimum even with AI-assisted development, six layers of data integration, privacy architecture, consent management, model training, regulatory compliance and testing at scale. The platform business model needs three to five years to reach profitability. Journey ownership generates better economics than product sales, but only after you've built the customer base, established the data advantage, and earned the trust. Customer migration takes time: You cannot flip a switch and move millions of customers onto a new platform. Rather, you migrate cohorts, prove value, and earn customer permission to go deeper. The 2027-2032 range is aggressive. It's achievable. But it's not a choice; it's the minimum viable timeline.

4.7.2 Why Not Slower? (Why Not 2035+?)

Other readers may say: 'Banking always takes longer than expected; why is 2032 credible when previous deadlines passed?' Because this time, the compression forces are *external*, not *internal*, and will pick up momentum no matter how banks choose to embrace or ignore them. Previous transformation predictions assumed banks would choose to transform. When they chose not to, nothing forced them. The internet did not extinguish banks; it just made branches less convenient. Mobile did not either; it just required them to build apps. Each previous 'transformation' allowed banks to adapt incrementally because the underlying business model survived.

But the 2027–2032 forces do not wait for banks to choose. DeFi grows regardless of banks. It does not need banking permission to reach $8 trillion in value and does not need banks to endorse it for customers to use it. By 2030, it's a viable infrastructure alternative whether banks like it or not. Big Tech does not need banking permission to compete once stablecoin frameworks are clarified. In 2027–2028, Apple, Google, and Amazon are legally clear to offer regulated financial services, and they have the customers, the data, trust, and distribution. They're waiting for regulatory clarity, not for banks to be ready. First movers create lock-in that late entrants cannot overcome; this is the smartphone pattern. Nokia did not fail because it could not build smartphones. It failed because by the time it understood convergence, the market had already committed to iOS and Android. The switching costs were established. The ecosystem was locked in. Late entry was commercially impossible.

And today, customer tolerance for outdated banking is declining, not stable.

In 2015, customers tolerated poor digital banking because the alternatives were worse, but in 2027 customers will have experienced five years of AI-personalised everything, and banking that does not match that standard will not just feel inconvenient. It will feel broken. And 2029 is only reachable from a 2027 start.

* * *

4.8 The Next Nexus of Forces: Welcome to 'Quanvergence'

When I built the digital strategy for Temenos in 2013 and 2014, I used a framework that Gartner had published the previous year called the Nexus of Forces. Gartner's insight was that four technology forces – Social, Mobile, Cloud and Big Data – were individually significant but collectively transformational. Each one amplified the others. Social generated the data. Mobile provided the access. Cloud provided the scale. Big Data provided the intelligence.

The nexus was the literal point: It marked the intersection that changed everything, not any single force on its own. I used that framework in my presentation to the Temenos executive team because it gave language to something genuinely difficult to explain: why that moment was categorically different from previous technology cycles, and why institutions that treated each force as a separate initiative would miss the *compounding effect* that made the combination so powerful.

The industry is talking about AI. It is talking about quantum computing. About blockchain, stablecoins. And about digital twins and platform business models. But it treats each of these things as separate and individual tech investments, strategic questions or risk assessments. It sees the separate elements but not the whole picture and the formidable overlap that makes it so compelling. The nexus. And as in 2012, the nexus X marks the spot where the transformation lives.

We have reached that kind of moment again ….

Call it 'The Quanvergence.'

* * *

Banking's new nexus of forces has four technical components and one business model at its centre. The four technical forces are:

- **digital twin**, the complete, continuously updated model of a customer's financial and personal life described in Chapter 3;
- **agentic AI**, artificial intelligence capable of autonomous reasoning, planning, and action across complex multi-step tasks on behalf of customers;
- **quantum simulation**, the ability to simulate thousands of life scenarios simultaneously in ways that classical computing cannot achieve; and
- **tokenisation**, the conversion of financial assets and value exchange onto new digital rails through stablecoins and decentralised finance, replacing the legacy infrastructure that has constrained banking for decades.

At the centre of these four forces, not as a fifth equal element, but as the business model that determines whether the convergence creates value or merely capability, sits Platform Economics.

This positioning matters. Gartner's four forces were relatively symmetrical, each enabling the others in roughly equal measure. The new nexus is different. The four technical forces are necessary but not sufficient. Digital twin data without AI to reason over it is just a very expensive database. Agentic AI without digital twin data is intelligent but blind. Quantum Simulation without the data and the AI to feed it is a laboratory experiment. Tokenisation without the relationship and intelligence layers is faster plumbing. Platform Economics organises all four forces as a business model based around customer journey ownership rather than product sales; it transforms the convergence from impressive technology into genuinely transformational banking. The centre is not a technology. It represents a choice about what your institution exists to do.

This is also why the six forcing functions described in this chapter compress into a five-year window rather than spreading across a decade. Each forcing function accelerates the others. Technology convergence makes first-mover advantage absolute. First-mover advantage makes regulatory catalysts more consequential. Customer behaviour change removes the adoption lag that previous technology cycles relied on. The collapsed development barrier removes the time buffer that slower-moving institutions used to count on. When you see these forces through the lens of a nexus rather than as individual pressures, the compression effect becomes not just credible but inevitable. The institutions that establish platform positions by 2032 will treat the nexus whole, and will understand they did not have to make six separate technology decisions but just one.

The critical question they will have successfully addressed is this: *What kind of institution do we intend to become when the nexus fully assembles?*

* * *

4.9 The Question Banks Will Not Ask Themselves

Meanwhile, banks face related questions that, for all the intelligence and acumen in the C-suite, they refuse to ask themselves. Here's what I observe in every banking conversation I have, on the podcast, in consulting, and in every boardroom I visit: Banks ask, 'Is this transformation real?' They should ask, 'How fast can we start?' The six forcing functions describe what's already happening. The technology is mature. Customer behaviour has changed. Competition is building. Regulatory environments are shifting. Development tools exist, and the business models are proven. On a 2022 Demystify podcast, when Dave Wallace and I interviewed John Blicq, Australian author of 'The Agentic Bank', he issued a clear warning. In 2026, the warning remains, but is now urgent.

The CEO of a mid-sized European bank told me in 2025 that he understood everything: The platform model, the digital twin requirement, the quantum advantage, the first-mover window. I asked him what he was doing. 'We're studying it. Consultants are running analyses. The board needs more evidence.'

'How much evidence do you need? Ant Financial IS the evidence.'

'I cannot bet the bank on something unproven in our market.'

'By the time it's proven in your market, it will be too late to enter.'

He had no response. That conversation, repeated in slightly different forms more than once, is why I'm writing this book. Not because banking executives do not understand the threat. But because understanding the threat and acting on it are separated by a gap that will prove fatal.

Six forcing functions. Five years. One window. The only question is whether your bank is on the right side of 2027.

Questions for Your Board

1. Of the six forcing functions identified here, do we see one or several that intrigue us? Which of those might present an opportunity to begin a transformation journey?
2. Let's think about this phrase: 'The digital twin creates infinite switching costs.' What would we interpret this to mean and how could it plant the seeds for an exciting (if demanding) game plan?
3. How closely does our C-suite align with the attitude of the European bank CEO? Whether we agree or disagree with them, can we identify the risks of taking one path or the other – and where the rewards might lie?

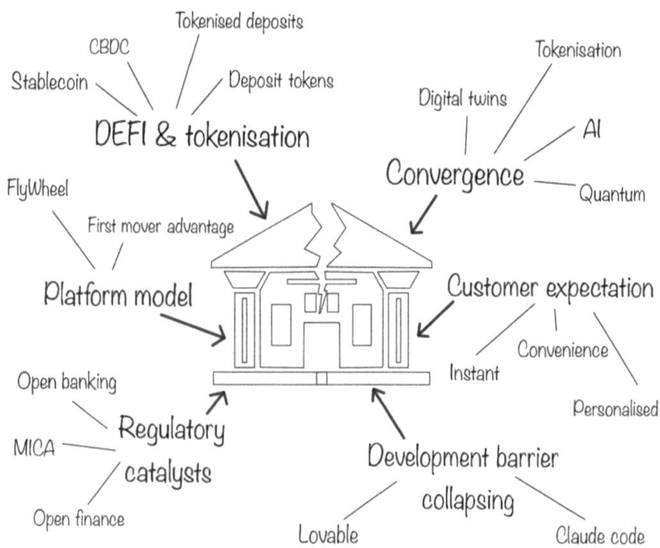

5

Digital Money: How Tokenisation Is Building the New Rails

Of the four forces driving Quanvergence, tokenisation is the one most frequently misunderstood as a fintech story rather than a banking strategy imperative. This chapter makes the case that it is the latter.

When I joined Lloyds Bank in 1986, few if any people knew about or interacted with a certain bank department—though without it, nothing moved.

It sat somewhere between technology and operations, and engineers who staffed it understood things most of us did not: circuit switching, leased lines, bandwidth allocation. This was the telecoms department, and its job was to build and manage the private communications network that interconnected our branches, offices, and mainframes. A transaction initiated at a branch in Leeds had to travel through Lloyds' own infrastructure to reach the systems in London that processed it. That network was not just a cost centre. It was a competitive necessity. You could not run a national bank without it. Building it required capital, expertise, and scale that simply was not available to anyone who started from scratch.

Yet by the 1990s, the network's logic had dissolved.

Why? Public telecommunications infrastructure and eventually the internet made it unnecessary for any bank to maintain its own private communications system. The engineers who'd built and managed those proprietary systems were redeployed or made redundant. And so the competitive advantage embedded in the network disappeared because the network became commoditised. Banks did not stop being banks. But they lost the ability to use their communications infrastructure as a differentiator.

D. Mistry, L. R. Carlozo, *The Intelligent Ledger*,
https://doi.org/10.1007/978-3-032-32842-7_5

Still, that loss turned out to be a moot point because what actually differentiated a bank had never really been its cables. At this point, it's worth mentioning that communications is quite a broad term and incorporates voice, emails, and movement of money. Hence the term 'banking rails' was birthed to describe more accurately the infrastructure used to move money.

I tell this story because it is the most precise analogy I know for what's happening to banking's financial rails right now. To understand this paradigm shift requires that we take a trip back in time: four centuries, to be precise.

* * *

Our journey begins with the Banca Monte dei Paschi di Siena in Italy, which began as a charitable pawnbroker or 'mount of piety' in 1472 and established its foundational banking structure in 1642. (It still exists today, with some 1,400 branches and close to 4 million customers.)

At that time, banking was built around physical money. Notes and coins such as the Florentine florin were scarce by nature. You could not easily replicate them. Moving them was expensive, slow and risky. Banks derived their power and business model from the simple fact that they were the institutions trusted to hold physical money, move it securely and keep accurate records of who owned what. The branch network, the vault, the clearing house, and all of it existed to manage the constraints of physical money. Not even the richest merchant would wish upon himself such collective responsibility.

Fast forward three centuries to 1959, when Barclays ordered an electronic computer, the Emidec 1100, costing £125,000 (£3.8 million today). Used to replace manual ledgers with automated bookkeeping, this 4KB machine housed 12 tape reels in six refrigerator-sized cabinets, accompanied by a control desk not unlike a recording studio mixboard. (In fact, EMI Laboratories had built it.) The Emidec 1100 paved the way for Barclays to open Britain's first computer centre in 1961.

In a virtual dead heat, Martins Bank boasted in Spring 1960 that it was the UK's first to use an electronic computer for account bookkeeping. Much like the Barclays machine, the Pegasus II was a colossus of hulking cabinets, power cubicles, card punches and tape units crammed into a room measuring 10 × 7 metres. And while it could process 30,000 accounts in five hours, the truth remained that for the next half century, the underlying logic of banking remained the same. (Interestingly, Martins and Barclays announced a merger in February 1968.)

In both instances, the machines allowed banks to digitise their records. Transactions recorded in ledgers became database entries. Settlements that once required physical paper movement became the electronic movement of numbers. The process became faster, cheaper, and more scalable. But the fundamental structure remained intact: Money was still a claim on a regulated institution, and regulated institutions still controlled the rails on which it moved. Though far faster and more connected, digitisation was, in the end, merely a better way of doing the same thing.

The internet accelerated the speed and accessibility of those digital records without changing their nature either. Online banking, mobile banking, and open banking each made it easier for customers to see and interact with their money. But none of it changed what money was or who controlled its infrastructure. Banks still served as the necessary intermediary. The rails were still proprietary: not private telecoms networks this time, but payment schemes, correspondent banking relationships, and settlement systems that required institutional membership and regulatory authorisation to access.

What is happening now, though, is genuinely different.

The nature of money itself is changing for the first time since paper currency replaced gold. And it is not changing in one direction. Money is moving from *digitised* (money represented on computers) to actually being *digital*. The words sound similar—but oh, what a difference.

* * *

The idea of digital money is not new. It did not arrive with blockchain, stablecoins or central bank working groups. It arrived at NatWest in 1990, invented by two people in the bank's research division, Tim Jones and Graham Higgins. They called it Mondex.

I was at NatWest in the mid-1990s, working in Card Services, and I saw what they had built. The Mondex demos were genuinely impressive for the time. Smart cards held value directly on the chip, not a record in a database somewhere, but actual digital money stored on a piece of hardware you carried in your wallet. If you lost it, you lost real money. Electronic wallets and key fobs let you transfer money directly to another person, offline, without going through any bank system. The cards doubled as building access passes and library cards in the closed-environment trials they ran at universities and military campuses via vending machines, payphones, and buses.

They launched a public trial in Swindon in July 1995 and more than 700 retailers accepted Mondex within weeks. The technology worked. It was elegant. It solved a real problem.

It failed anyway.

Though the concept was exactly right, the infrastructure required to make Mondex universal could not be assembled without universal agreement, and universal agreement among competing banks, merchants and technology providers proved impossible to achieve. Every merchant needed proprietary point-of-sale hardware. Every person–to–person transfer required a special electronic wallet device. And fundamentally, Mondex only worked as a cash replacement if everyone accepted it. That meant every bank had to join, which flew in the face of banking's competitive logic, where each institution protects its own rails. NatWest sold the intellectual property to a consortium in 1996. Mastercard absorbed it. By 2001 it was gone. What happened?

Mondex failed not because digital money was a bad idea but because the specific problem digital money needs to solve – universal acceptance without universal proprietary infrastructure – required something that did not exist in 1995: a shared, open, programmable ledger that no single institution controlled. The technology that makes stablecoins, dentral bank digital currencies (CBDCs), and tokenised deposits viable as digital money is not new. It is a new solution to the coordination problem that killed Mondex a quarter century earlier. The insight was right in 1990 but the architecture needed time to catch up.

So what should digital money be? How should it work? Who should issue it? And what should it do? As the space evolves, it has produced at least three distinct and credible approaches. Each is designed with different features, benefits and trade-offs. That plurality is not the equivalent of the Betamax-versus-VHS videotape battle of the 1980s. Nor does it indicate some form of confusion. Rather, we are witnessing genuine innovation in a banking ecosystem that has barely changed in six centuries.

Digital money is taking three forms: CBDCs, stablecoins, and tokenised deposits. They are not competing to win and eliminate the others. They solve different problems for different participants in the financial system—and will most likely coexist in the same way that cash, bank deposits and money market funds do today, each serving different needs. But together, they do something no single form of digital money could do alone: They make the rails on which money moves a commodity rather than a scarce resource.

And when the rails commoditise, there arises the question my Lloyds telecoms engineers never had to ask in 1986: What exactly are we here for now that anyone can build this? Forty years later, this is the question banks can no longer avoid. IBMs Institute for Buiness Value, in its 2026 Global Outlook for Banking and Financial Markets, reaches the same conclusion from a different starting point: 'By 2030, tokenised assets, stablecoins and CBDCs 'will not be experimental, they'll be table stakes.'

* * *

5.1 Three Forms of Digital Money

Each new form of digital money serves a different purpose and so has a different impact. Let's be precise about what each one actually does to the economics of banking because the detail matters more than the headline.

Stablecoins today are mostly, meaning not exclusivly, dollar-pegged tokens on public blockchain rails, of which USDC (US dollar coin), USDT (Tether), and PayPal USD are the leading examples. (They can be created for any fiat currency.) The issuers of stablecoins will be increasingly regulated but they need not be banks. Current regulations are following a similar path to those of e-money licensees. However, if adoption of stablecoins reaches a point where they could pose a systemic threat, then I expect regulators to lean towards more stringent rules similar to those required for banks. Currently, issuers are private companies (as listed above) that do not threaten the existence of banking.

What they *do* threaten is the specific revenue that comes from being the trusted intermediary. Let's consider an example from the correspondent banking model, where a payment from London to Lagos routes through multiple institutions, with each taking a clip. Though inefficient by design, it existed because building the alternative was too expensive for anyone other than established banks. Think about when banks had their own networks, exchanging money between them in the same country required an intermediary to save all banks from having to connect to each other. The same problem exists when sending money abroad but worse. By leveraging the internet, stablecoins remove that barrier internationally. As for banks under the traditional system? Betamax. VHS. Tube TVs, folks.

The evidence that this is no longer theoretical arrived quietly in early 2026. S&P Global Market Intelligence reported that at least 15 applications for federal banking charters had been submitted to the Office of the Comptroller of the Currency since the start of 2025, the majority explicitly referencing stablecoin issuance or reserve management as the core business rationale. These are not crypto speculators seeking legitimacy. They include an asset manager, a Japanese multinational, a Brazilian fintech, and established payments infrastructure firms. What they share is a single strategic insight: Large enterprises will not run payroll, supplier payments or treasury operations on tokens issued by lightly regulated entities. Stablecoins only become serious commercial infrastructure when they sit inside institutions that corporates already recognise as credible. The race to build the stablecoin bank is, at its core, a race to own the next generation of regulated pipes.

Central bank digital currencies (CBDC) operate differently. Where stablecoins are privately issued and therefore carry counterparty risk, your USDC is only as good as Circle's reserves. A CBDC is a direct claim on the central bank, with no credit risk and, in most proposed architectures, no interest rate risk either. The Bank of England's digital pound, the European Central Bank's digital euro, and equivalents in development across more than 100 jurisdictions are all meant to serve the retail payment function that commercial banks currently perform. The interesting paradox (which we'll revisit) is that no central bank has any appetite whatsoever for managing their population, 70 million in the UK, of retail customer relationships directly. The architecture of almost every CBDC project in serious development assumes a two-tier model: The central bank issues the currency, and commercial banks distribute and service it. Sentiment on CBDCs currently in the USA is quite different, with the current Government wanting to steer clear of them.

Tokenised deposits are the most nuanced of the three and deserve the most careful attention from banking strategists. Unlike stablecoins (created by private tech companies) or CBDCs (created by central banks), tokenised deposits are bank-issued claims on bank liabilities, expressed on programmable blockchain rails. JPMorgan has run JPM Coin since 2019, quietly processing billions in institutional transfers. This does not destroy the bank's balance sheet position but rather its process margin. What it creates, for banks that understand the opportunity, is a new product category they can charge for. These include programmable money services, smart contract treasury management and the infrastructure for bridging between traditional finance and the decentralised finance ecosystem.

Think of the rails like the electricity grid. The question then becomes: What can you build on top of them?

It is worth being precise about what JPM Coin has become, because the evolution reveals a distinction that matters enormously for banking strategy. The original JPM Coin, running since 2019 on Kinexys's private permissioned blockchain, is a tokenised deposit in the conventional sense: a digital wrapper around an existing deposit, with the bank's traditional ledger remaining the source of truth. In November 2025, JPMorgan went further.

It launched JPMD, a deposit token, on Base, Coinbase's public Ethereum Layer 2 blockchain. The distinction is architectural and profound. JPMD is not a representation of a deposit that exists elsewhere. It is the deposit, issued natively onto a blockchain rail, with no legacy ledger underneath it. The blockchain is the ledger of record. This requires genuinely different infrastructure, not a second core alongside the bank's existing core, but an ***Intelligent Ledger*** in its own right. And it is precisely this architecture that allows banks to compete directly with institutional stablecoins: not by improving the efficiency of the existing system, but by replacing the settlement layer underneath it with one that is natively programmable, interoperable, and capable of streaming money at any scale and granularity. The GBTD (Great British Tokenised Deposit) pilot in the UK, EnsembleTX in Hong Kong, and most of what the industry currently calls tokenised deposit programmes are the wrapper model. They are valuable, necessary, and achievable as a second core strategy. JPMD is the destination, and whilst both matter, only one competes with Circle.

Combined, these new forms of money do not eliminate banking: *only the excuse for change.*

For decades, banks pointed to the complexity and cost of their infrastructure to justify why genuine customer centricity was difficult. But when the rails commoditise, those excuses disappear, and what remains is the actual question: Do you have a business model based on understanding and serving customers, or have you monetised a monopoly position on infrastructure that someone else can now build cheaper?

* * *

5.2 The Platform That Does Not Need a Licence

If the rails represent commoditising, if stablecoins, CBDCs, or tokenised deposit networks via API can source payments infrastructure, then the banking licence itself becomes optional infrastructure rather than a competitive moat. Let's repeat that: *optional.* The new rails are not built for the rubber tyres, if you will, that today's banks roll on.

Any entity that owns the customer relationship, builds the intelligence layer and orchestrates financial products across a customer's life does not necessarily need to hold a banking licence to do any of that. It needs the products and services that a licensed entity provides. It does not need to be that entity.

This is not theoretical. It exists.

Apple holds no banking licence in the United States, yet manages the financial relationship, payments, credit, and savings for millions of American consumers. It sources the licensed infrastructure it needs: Goldman Sachs for the savings product and Apple Pay Later, Mastercard for the card rails, Citizens Bank for financing phone purchases. Apple also decides:

- which financial products its customers should access,
- designs the experience through which they access them, and
- captures the relationship value while paying commodity prices for the underlying banking services.

WeChat and Grab have built equivalent positions across Asian markets. A more recent and pointed example: Sony. Through its banking subsidiary, Sony Bank, the Japanese conglomerate is pursuing a US federal charter for a new entity called Connectia Trust, whose purpose is to issue a dollar-pegged stablecoin, not as a financial product, but as a settlement layer embedded inside Sony's gaming, media and content ecosystems. Sony has no ambition to become a bank. It has every ambition to own the customer relationship across its platforms and to make regulated financial settlement invisible within that experience. The banking infrastructure is sourced. The platform logic is Sony's. This is the Apple model, running on blockchain rails, built by an organisation whose primary business is entertainment. Any teenager can grasp the flow and logic of Apple's model.

Mind you, none of these organisations set out to become banks. They started out wanting to own customer relationships in their respective domains ... and discovered that financial services naturally extended that ownership. The banking licence was a cost-benefit decision, not an identity. You only need a licence when the pipes cannot give you the margin you need and require balance sheet control for credit decisioning, or the regulatory environment in a given jurisdiction makes it unavoidable. You do not seek it because it is inherently necessary to serve customers well.

One caveat worth naming directly: The pace of regulatory change varies significantly by jurisdiction. The US, EU, and UK are each moving towards stablecoin and tokenised deposit frameworks, but on different timetables and with different emphases. The US GENIUS Act, the EU's MiCA regulation, and the UK's Payment Services framework are each at different stages of implementation. A bank's strategic response to tokenisation cannot be a single global plan applied uniformly. It requires jurisdictional monitoring, understanding which markets will have regulatory clarity first, and sequencing the platform build accordingly. The underlying argument holds across all of them. The timing requires local calibration.

The genuinely uncomfortable implication for incumbent banks is this: Their most dangerous competitor over the next decade is not another bank. It is not a fintech with a banking licence and a better app. It is an intelligence platform with no designs on becoming a bank. It's built instead by an organisation that currently operates in an adjacent domain such as retail, technology, healthcare, or real estate—and that has better customer data, superior AI capability, lower legacy cost, and a straightforward intention to source regulated infrastructure from whoever offers the best terms.

* * *

5.3 Pipe or Platform: The Choice That Cannot Be Deferred

The pipe is the simpler model to understand, which may be why so many banks now drift towards it rather than choose it deliberately.

A pipe creates value linearly: It produces a regulated service, delivers it to a customer or partner, and charges for it. The margin is utility economics: thin, volume-dependent, and competitive on operational efficiency. The strategy is to be the best-run, lowest-cost, most reliable provider of regulated banking infrastructure in your chosen markets. NatWest Boxed has made this choice explicitly. It positioned itself as a banking-as-a-service (BaaS) provider for fintechs and platforms rather than competing for consumer relationships directly. That is a coherent strategic decision. The less comfortable prediction is that most traditional banks will become pipes through the gradual loss of the customer relationships that make the platform model possible. I will return to this binary in the next chapter and set out the full logic of each path. But the important point is that the commoditisation of the rails forces the choice into the open.

The platform is the harder model to build, which is why so many banks talk about it and so few have actually built it. A platform creates value by facilitating interactions between participants it does not fully control. It owns the context *in which exchange happens, not the exchange itself.* The revenue comes from matching, intelligence and the relationship rather than the transaction. I first articulated a version of this intelligence layer at Temenos in 2013, a unified decisioning system (the single brain) that understood the complete customer relationship and avoided siloed product decisions. Yet that version hit a wall: It only knew banking data.

The Quanvergence of digital twin data, agentic AI, and quantum simulation solves for this. It knits an intelligence layer that actually knows enough to be genuinely useful, not just about products but a customer's full financial life as well seen through a holistic rather than bank-centric lens. Chapters 7–11 describe how that layer is built. The point here is simpler: The commoditisation of the rails does not threaten platform banks. It makes the platform model not only attractive but also necessary.

Banks that get this will make deliberate choices about which layer they want to occupy. Banks that sit and wait? The choice was made for them, as customer intelligence platforms, built by organisations that never thought of themselves as banks, arrive in financial services with superior data assets, lower cost structures and no attachment to the infrastructure model that has defined banking for the past century.

* * *

5.4 What Tokenised Deposits Actually Change

Of the three forms of digital money, tokenised deposits are the ones most squarely in the bank's hands and whose strategic significance is most misunderstood. When banking executives hear about stablecoins and CBDCs, the instinct is defensive; these are external threats, invented outside the banking system, designed by people who do not particularly care about the future of commercial banking.

Tokenised deposits are different in character. They are bank-initiated, bank-controlled, bank-balance-sheet instruments, simply expressed on programmable rails rather than traditional ledger infrastructure. The bank is still the credit institution. The depositor still has a claim on the bank. What changes is the mechanics of how that deposit moves and what it can do.

What tokenised deposits destroy is process friction.

The strategic opportunity in tokenised deposits, then, is not primarily about cost reduction, though cost reduction will occur. It is about the creation of a new category of financial service: programmable money as a platform. Banks that treat tokenised deposits as a more efficient version of existing deposits are missing the point. Banks that treat them as the foundation of a new product category, and build the developer tools, smart contract infrastructure, and client education to support that category, are positioning themselves for the institutional finance market of the 2030s. JPMorgan understood this instinctively. The goal with original JPM Coin, running since 2019 on a private permissioned blockchain, was never to save costs on internal transfers. It was the first step. The launch of JPMD in November 2025 (a native deposit token on Base, a public Ethereum Layer 2 blockchain), was the second. This was a declaration that JPMorgan intends to own the institutional programmable money layer not just on private rails but on public ones, before a technology company, a stablecoin issuer, or a central bank built an alternative that JPMorgan could not compete with. That is the difference between a tokenised deposit strategy and a deposit token strategy. The first improves the pipe, the second builds the platform.

The same logic applies at the retail level, and this is where programmable money connects directly to the platform model. An AI agent working from a complete digital twin of a customer's financial life can identify that their fixed-rate mortgage expires in six weeks, run simulations across the available refinancing options, and identify the one that optimises for their specific goals rather than just the headline rate. With traditional banking infrastructure, even the most sophisticated agent stops there. It presents the recommendation and waits. The customer must apply, submit documents, wait for processing, and complete the switch manually. Days of friction pass between the optimal decision and the actual action. With programmable money, the agent executes the switch at the optimal moment within parameters the customer has already pre-approved, no second interaction required. Savings rules trigger when life events are detected. Mortgage drawdowns complete at the moment of legal completion. Insurance switches happen when the comparison finds a better policy at renewal. The difference is not a matter of degree. It is the difference between a platform that advises and a platform that acts.

There is a second and less obvious reason why programmable money is a prerequisite for platform banking, and it is one that almost nobody in the current conversation about AI is addressing directly. As AI agents proliferate and begin managing complex financial lives on behalf of customers, they will not just execute occasional large transactions. They will be transacting constantly: querying data sources, reserving contractor slots, optimising energy contracts, managing micro-subscriptions, settling agent-to-agent payments where one AI system pays another for a service on behalf of a human customer. A single platform bank with a million customers, each with an agent running continuous background optimisation, could generate transaction volumes orders of magnitude larger than the same bank's human-initiated transactions today. And many of those transactions will be tiny (micro-payments): a few pence to query a pricing API, a fractional payment to confirm a booking, a real-time micro-settlement between systems. The economics of current payment rails make this impossible. A processing cost of 20 pence makes no sense for a three-pence agent-to-agent transaction. The speed of current rails, even fast payment systems, introduces latency that agents operating at machine speed cannot absorb. Programmable money, with its capacity for instant, cheap, conditional settlement at any granularity, is not a nice-to-have for the agentic economy. It is the only infrastructure that can support it. Banks that build their platform intelligence on traditional rails are building on an architecture that will fail them precisely when the platform is working best, when the agents are active, the customers are engaged, and the transaction volume is at its highest.

Programmable money is not just an infrastructure improvement. It is the fourth mandatory component of a platform bank, and the one that determines whether the intelligence layer can ultimately act or can only ever advise.

It is worth naming this destination more precisely, because the concept runs through the rest of this book. The idea of streaming money has been central to my thinking for more than 10 years, and the agentic economy is where it stops being theoretical. The underlying premise is a structural one. Every payment architecture ever built, from the paper ledgers of Monte dei Paschi to the batch-processing cores that run most banks today, assume that value moves in discrete, deliberate steps: one authorised transaction at a time, cleared and reconciled on a schedule. That assumption was an engineering constraint, not an economic truth. Value, left to move freely, does not step. It flows. An AI agent managing a household's financial life does not make 20 separate payment decisions a day. It maintains a continuous, real-time optimisation across income, expenditure, obligations, and opportunity, adjusting allocations as conditions change, not waiting for a human to notice and act. That is streaming money: value in motion, carrying its own logic, settling against conditions rather than instructions. The distinction is not incremental. It represents a different paradigm for what money is and how it behaves. And it requires an entirely different kind of ledger to run on, one that does not merely record what happened but participates in what happens next. A ledger with native intelligence. The rest of the book is built around this, and why it carries the name it does. The Intelligent Ledger is not a product or a platform feature. It is the architectural prerequisite for everything that follows, for platform banking, for the agentic economy, for deposit tokens that can genuinely compete with stablecoins, and for the streaming money flows that will define how value moves in the next era of finance. Tokenised deposits are today's pilots. Deposit tokens mark the first production deployments. The Intelligent Ledger is the destination both point toward.

* * *

5.5 The CBDC Paradox, and Why Central Banks Still Need Banks

Before closing this chapter, let's address the assumption that CBDCs represent a straightforward disintermediation of commercial banking. I contend that this misreads how central banks actually think about their role and capabilities.

No central bank in any serious jurisdiction has expressed a desire to manage retail customer relationships at scale. The Bank of England does not want to field 70 million complaints about disputed transactions. (Would you?) The European Central Bank has no interest in building fraud detection infrastructure for daily retail payments across the eurozone. Central banks exist as wholesale institutions by nature, temperament, and regulatory design. They issue currency. They set monetary policy. They manage systemic risk. But they do not open current accounts.

This is why every CBDC architecture in a serious stage of development assumes a two-tier model with commercial banks as the customer-facing layer. The central bank issues digital currency. The commercial bank distributes it, services the customer relationship, handles disputes, manages onboarding and KYC, and provides additional financial products that customers need alongside their digital cash holdings. In this model, the commercial bank earns servicing fees for exactly the customer trust architecture it already provides—and that a stablecoin issuer, for all its technical sophistication, cannot easily replicate.

Banks that will benefit from CBDCs have already positioned themselves as customer relationship owners rather than transaction processors. If your value proposition revolves around efficient money movement, a CBDC poses a genuine threat. The central bank's money will move more effectively than yours, with less credit risk and full sovereign backing. Likewise, if your value proposition stems from how you understand your customer's financial life and can help them navigate whatever infrastructure exists to best serve their goals, then a CBDC is simply another rail. And a highly credible one at that.

This same distinction runs through every chapter of this book: The banks that survive do not boast the best pipes. They own the relationship that runs through them.

* * *

5.6 Where This Leaves You

The connected roads that carried banking's competitive advantage for centuries are being rebuilt as digital rails from first principles. Not by banks, but by technology.

Three new forms of digital money: Stablecoins, CBDCs, and tokenised deposits, are embedded in infrastructure that banks themselves are both building and enabling. The regulatory architecture is already being rebuilt around them: By February 2026, crypto-native firms, payments companies and technology conglomerates had filed at least 15 applications for US federal banking charters, almost all of them anchored to stablecoin infrastructure. The legislative machinery is moving on a parallel track. The GENIUS Act of 2025, the first US federal framework for payment stablecoins, cleared the Senate 68–30 in July of that year, and the broader Digital Asset Market Clarity Act passed the House in 2025 before reaching Senate Banking Committee markup in May 2026 on the back of a bipartisan compromise on stablecoin yield engineered by senators Tillis and Alsobrooks. Whether the full market-structure legislation lands in late 2026 or slips into 2027, the regulatory direction is set; what's still being negotiated is the detail, not the principle. The unresolved question, as S&P Global noted, is not regulation but rails, specifically, whether these new entrants can secure Federal Reserve master account access. Companies that obtain both the licence and the rails will define the next phase of dollar-denominated payments.

Nobody is doing this *to* banks. Banks, in fact, are participating in their own displacement. Meanwhile, the customer intelligence platform model is under construction right now, in adjacent industries, by organisations with better data, superior AI capability, and no attachment to the architecture that defined banking for the past century. The window in which existing customer trust can be converted into a platform relationship is open. It will not stay open indefinitely.

The question this chapter posed – What is a bank for when the rails are no longer a moat? – has an answer:

A bank is for credit, and for trust, and for the intelligence to understand a customer's financial life well enough to serve it genuinely rather than just profitably.

This value proposition spans generations, and some visionaries within financial services obsess over how to more fully realise it. The accent, however, often falls on the wrong syllable. Technology, not some new product or service or even web page, will facilitate a paradigm shift that will remake banking into something as arcane as the 15th Century mount of piety.

None of this forward movement requires the ownership of payment rails. All of it requires the deliberate construction of an intelligence layer that most banks have deferred, delayed, or denied because the pressure to build it has not yet been acute enough to overcome institutional inertia. Existing and healthy revenue streams might as well be a lazy river.

The pressure is now acute enough to facilitate change—or force it. The three forms of digital money described here will raise the stakes with each passing year. The choice that the next chapter sets out, Platform or Pipe, is not a strategic planning exercise to schedule for next year's offsite. The commoditisation of the rails already answers the guiding question for you, whether you have decided or not. The banks that build the customer intelligence platform will own the financial lives of their customers for the next generation. The banks that defend their rails will discover that rails are infrastructure. And infrastructure gets commoditised. That has always been how this works.

This is not a forecast. The process is already underway. The choice set out in the next chapter marks the only defensible strategic response. Banks that ignore this might as well look upon the new rails, stand off to the side of the platform and watch the train leave the station.

Questions for Your Board

1. For each of our primary markets, does our bank know which regulations and their timescales apply for the following: stablecoins, CBDCs, and tokenised deposits? With timescale, think: the window to address these needs.
2. Does our bank see tokenised deposits as a way to defend our market by addressing cost efficiency? Or to leverage an advantage and compete by selling new product capabilities such as smart contracts? (Remember that optimising cost efficiency only involves improving something already commoditised.)
3. If competition in the new landscape does not require a banking licence, do we know who and what our new threats are? How can we look ahead to compete with them – or transcend the need to compete – in a way that's *not* product-centric?

4. Do we understand the difference between a tokenised deposit and a deposit token, and does our roadmap have a credible path from one to the other? Our tokenised deposit programme improves settlement efficiency and is achievable alongside our existing infrastructure. Our deposit token strategy is how we compete with institutional stablecoin issuers on native programmable rails. The Intelligent Ledger requires the latter. Do we have a plan to get there, and who owns it?

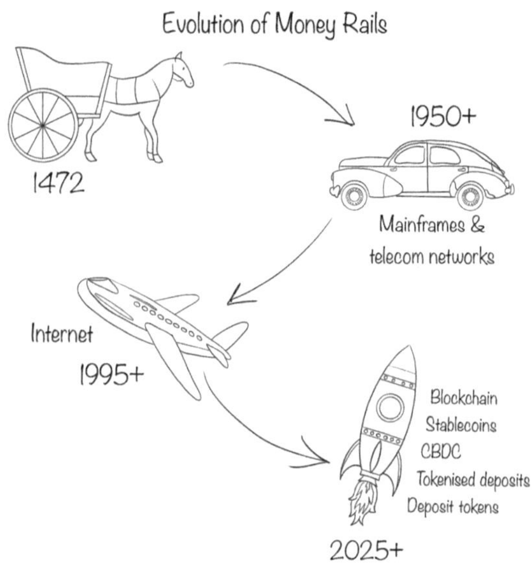

6

The AskHomey Lesson: Right Model, Wrong Timing

Chapter 5 established that the rails are being rebuilt and that the choice of what to build on top of them defines a bank's future. The question it left open – Platform or Pipe? – is the one this chapter is built around. Not as theory, but as personal experience. I tried to build what banks should have built and failed. What I learnt from that failure is more useful than any framework.

The two viable futures for your bank are Platform or Pipe.

I've often blogged about it as the separation of manufacturing (owning the product) and distribution (owning the customer). The choice is simple: Own complete customer journeys with high margins and lasting loyalty or become commodity infrastructure with thin margins and survival increasingly at risk.

I imagine part of you hopes for a third option, some comfortable middle ground where you carry on roughly as you are and 'explore platform opportunities.' Honestly, that option does not exist. When you optimise your current business, it leads to Pipe by default. Only deliberate, committed transformation leads to Platform. Not choosing is itself a choice, a default to Pipe.

I know this because I tried to build what banks should—and failed. In retrospect, the model was absolutely right, but suffered from the wrong capital structure at the wrong time. The banks I pitched AskHomey to did not get it. They wanted to know how my platform would increase their mortgage sales. Sales, as it too often does, trumped vision and a lasting, long-term source of value. A change in mindset was not open for discussion.

That is: They could not see that owning the home journey makes mortgage selection automatic. Someone else saw what those banks missed. I sold the

D. Mistry, L. R. Carlozo, *The Intelligent Ledger*,
https://doi.org/10.1007/978-3-032-32842 7_6

software assets to a company under NDA, so I cannot tell you what they're building with it. (I can only hope the new owners succeed where I could not.)

This chapter tells that story of endeavour and failure honestly, but is not meant as a mini-memoir. It shows you the binary choice you must make. Platform or Pipe. And why, in my view, roughly 90% of banks will wind up as Pipe by default, not because they strategically chose it, but because they failed to choose Platform while the window was still open.

File this, then, under 'learn from me'.

* * *

6.1 Why I Started It

Over 40 years in banking I witnessed the same pattern repeating itself. A couple buys a house. They get a mortgage. The bank celebrates a £400,000 mortgage, locked in for 25 years, with a £2,000 lifetime margin if the customer stays. Product sold. The relationship begins . . .

Then nothing.

You could even argue that it ends, outside of the ensuing paperwork. The bank sends annual statements. Maybe a rate adjustment offer. Possibly a remortgage pitch when the fixed term ends. That's genuinely it. The bank has finished its job, as far as it's concerned, and moves on to landing the next mortgage customer.

Meanwhile, the homeowners drown in complexity the bank never sees. Should you own a dwelling, the questions and quandaries will sound all too familiar:

- **The boiler breaks.** Which contractor can I trust? What should it cost? Is it still under warranty? When did I last have it serviced? Where's the documentation?
- **The energy bill spikes.** Should I switch providers? Which tariff? Fixed or variable?
- **The roof needs work.** How much should that cost? How does it affect the house value? Should I even fix it or sell and move?
- **Insurance renewal.** Same provider or shop around? What coverage do I actually need after the extension we added last year?
- **Home improvement.** Does the cost justify the increase in home value? How can I find a reputable, cost-efficient design firm?

Every homeowner manages hundreds of these decisions over a 10–15 year ownership period. Every decision has financial implications. Most involve spending thousands of pounds. And each exacts a toll in terms of stress that can lead to rushed, expensive decisions.

The total financial value of all those decisions across a typical ownership period? **More than £500,000**. (The full breakdown is in Appendix A.) The bank that provided the £400,000 mortgage has £2,000 of margin and absolutely no relationship with any of this. They're completely absent from the journey that actually matters. And they've lost out on the continuous revenue stream that increases the bottom line and guarantees customer loyalty, perhaps for life.

I knew from my 'single brain' work at Temenos that banks did not even track most of this. They had mortgage data. Transaction data. Maybe credit card spending if the homeowner used their card. But no boiler service records. No contractor history. No energy usage patterns. No property improvement plans. No life event triggers that would indicate when someone is ready to move. Banks treated home ownership as a mortgage transaction, a product sale, when the reality was a decade-long journey with total value exceeding £500,000, of which the mortgage was just one component transacted over a few days.

So in late 2019, after leaving Temenos, I decided not to build a better mortgage broker but instead own the complete home journey. That's why I started AskHomey with my co-founder and long-time friend Tarne Westcott, the guy I respect most when it comes to building systems. Without him, AskHomey would not have been possible, certainly in the timescales he created it in: starting in November 2019 and ready in its initial form by early 2020.

* * *

6.2 What We Built

I spent my gardening leave from Temenos through summer and autumn 2019 doing nothing but research on the property sector. Reading everything. I talked to homeowners to understand the pain points. I studied PropTech start-ups to see what worked and what did not. Tarne and I are ultra-runners and talked about this through the night during two 100-mile races. We felt exhilarated to think we could positively improve homeowners' lives and create a business. So, when I officially left Temenos in October 2019 and registered AskHomey, we could hit the ground running. Tarne built a small team and created a rough prototype that we tested with 100 homeowners, friends, family and their networks. The feedback was consistent: 'This is exactly what I need. Why does not this exist already?' With that validation, we refined it into an MVP.

Then COVID-19 hit in March 2020.

Property developers, our primary customer acquisition channel, had been told literally to stay home. Construction sites shut. New builds stalled. We were in lockdown. I could have shut down and furloughed the team. Instead, we used the time to build the platform properly. We had user feedback and validation, let's build it right. But the lockdown lasted longer than expected, and the return of developers to their sites took longer still. We spent 18 long months in waiting while we built a feature-rich platform that far surpassed the original MVP. Tarne's ability to solve problems and create solutions could not be underestimated. AskHomey was comprehensive. Possibly too much so. Here's what he built.

Data management side:

- **complete EPC (Energy Performance Certificates)** and historical energy ratings,
- **integrated property valuations,**
- **detailed floor plans** down to individual spaces including lofts, sheds, and garden areas,
- **inventory management** for every appliance, serial numbers, purchase dates, warranties, manuals stored digitally. AI-assisted inventory that identified inventory items from a photo of a room,
- **documentation central** for everything from purchase contracts to planning permissions to contractor invoices and inventory manuals. AI-assisted search, no need to open a document, ask the question and our search would go through all documents for the answer, and
- **fixtures and fittings catalogue** by room, right down to paint colours and brands, so when you needed to match paint five years later you did not have to guess.

Home management:

- **a contacts manager** for tradespeople, utility providers, insurance companies, suppliers of fixtures/fittings,
- **account management** for all subscriptions including gas, electricity, broadband, and many more. You could track previous bills and for utilities

we provided automated switching. We also had a huge database of contact details for all key suppliers you could create accounts with,
- **budgeting** for general household bills and planning for renovations, and
- **a Task manager** to book individual maintenance work or plan a complete project such as a home extension with shopping lists and progress photos. It also included reminders for tasks due or overdue.

Community:

- **Chat**—Homeowners could chat with a property developer or contractors or set up their own neighbourhood groups.
- **Marketplace**, essentially our own App Store for third-party services. We launched with conveyancers you could share your documentation with, home designers who could work from your floor plans, and many more vendors.

Personal Home Assistant

This is where it got interesting. We showed what platform thinking actually means, though we did not have the resources or time to fully build out our brain behind the assistant.

Also, at that time AI was not as powerful as today, so document search AI required formidable effort to build and integrate older solutions from AWS. We started with rules-based engagements such as:

- **warranty expiry alerts:** Two months before a boiler warranty expired, we'd notify the homeowner. With today's agentic capability we would have also sent quotes from three local contractors to service or replace, price benchmarks, and ROI analysis on upgrading to a heat pump based on energy usage patterns.
- **safety alerts:** Appliances older than seven years flagged as potential fire hazards with recommendations to replace.
- **energy optimisation:** Proactive reminders before energy contracts expired. Users had switching capability, but today's agents could automate that search for a better deal and we would 'learn' customer contract preferences to yield better future matching.

We had a long list of other engagements we could have delivered much quicker with today's capabilities in AI and agentic automation, let alone code generation. We were not short of useful and powerful ideas, just of resources.

Developer Portal
For property developers, we built a separate B2B portal where they could clone a single generic property specification across a development, making a 100-home site manageable in hours. All appliance manuals, warranties, contractors and building specs entered once and applied across every property. Instead of passing off a folder of paper manuals to buyers at handover, developers gave them access to AskHomey with everything pre-loaded. The developer looked innovative. The buyer got immediate value. We received £100 per property upfront *and had a customer relationship from day one.* Ongoing. This model should have worked and in a real sense it did. We built it. Developers loved it. Buyers loved it.

Then COVID-19 killed the housebuilding market for 18 months, and by the time it recovered, our flagship client had gone bust. The final nail in the coffin was the Ukraine war as it forced energy price caps. This made secondary revenue from energy switching obselete too, it really felt like the start–up Gods were against us.

We could only take cold comfort in knowing that we met our fate in hurricane headwinds of historic proportions, far beyond anyone's control. Across the pond, the American Bankruptcy Institute reported that nearly 60% of business failures during COVID-19 were permanent: close to 100,000 in all.

* * *

6.3 The Business Model That Worked (On Paper)

For all the complex coding that went into it, AskHomey had a revenue model that could not have been simpler. It consisted of three components:

- First, developers and housebuilders paid £100 per property for digital handover.
- Second, for homeowners, we'd charge nothing initially to build trust, prove value, then offer a subscription at around £30 a month for premium features.
- Third, service revenue. Every time a homeowner needed a utility switch, contractor, insurance renewal, and mortgage, we'd take a commission from the provider. Utility companies pay £50–100 for a switch. Contractors pay 10–15% for a qualified lead. Insurance companies pay £50 or more for a new policy. Mortgage brokers pay 0.3–0.5% of loan value.

All told, the numbers looked compelling. Again, the total value of home ownership over 10–15 years exceeds £500,000, detailed in Appendix A. Our margin opportunity:

- Roughly £3,600 in subscription over the period,
- £2,000–3,000 in service commissions,
- £1,000–1,500 in mortgage introduction fees,
- Total: £6,600–8,100 over the journey.

Compare that to the bank's mortgage margin of £2,000. Journey ownership generated three to four times better economics from the same customer. That was the model. On paper. You'd think the smartest, most sophisticated chief revenue officer at a bank could grasp this. Perhaps they did. Regardless, no one had moved to create something remotely close. Many start-ups pride themselves on identifying a pain point and solving for it. AskHomey addressed not one but dozens and did it holistically. To forge an analogy from the Kitbag platform, we were not selling football jerseys or shoes so much as the entire wardrobe, better launderette services, better credit card terms to pay for it, and much more.

6.4 The Reality

Our B2B2C model depended on developers handing over properties with AskHomey pre-installed, and that stopped entirely once the pandemic was declared in March 2020: the same month we launched our MVP. We pivoted to direct-to-consumer but quickly discovered the customer acquisition cost was prohibitive. Homeowners do not wake up thinking, 'I need a home management platform.' They likely did not even know what one was, our start-up was so new and unique. They might want one when something breaks, but by then they demand an immediate solution, not a comprehensive platform. We conducted about a dozen free trials. Homeowners used it for a specific problem, then did not come back. The habit did not stick.

Our one paying customer was a developer with 1,000 properties who paid us to manage those homes post-sale. By 2022, developers were building again. We signed a flagship client, a major housebuilder planning to roll out AskHomey across all new developments. Then they went bust. The housebuilder industry crashed. Our pipeline vanished. And on a deeper level, the technology was not really ready to answer the demands we wanted to place on it. Natural language processing in 2020–2023 could not handle the complexity we needed. 'Should I fix my boiler or replace it?' requires understanding boiler age, efficiency, energy costs, warranty status, and the homeowner's financial situation simultaneously. The NLP could not do it reliably. We'd built the platform too early. Again, just like Entranet in 1997 and edgeIPK in 2001. I'd established a pattern of being right about direction and wrong about timing.

By 2023, we'd run out of funding. We could not acquire customers at scale. We could not monetise homeowners fast enough. The developer channel had collapsed. When we shut down the UK company and sold the name and software assets, the purchasers saw value we could not monetise ourselves. They recognised, as we did, that journey ownership has value.

Before we shut down AskHomey, I pitched to three banks as proof that they should build similar platforms. None of them embraced it. Revolut wanted to see the model working at scale before they'd consider it. Lloyds wanted mortgage leads. Surprise.

A third wanted to know how it increased product sales. They organised themselves around products, not journeys, and nobody's bonus was tied to customer lifetime value. How sad. They all missed the lesson that runs through the rest of this chapter: Whoever owns the journey owns the customer. The product provider is replaceable. The journey owner is not.

That's it. Not the ending a four-decade financial services veteran would be encouraged to share. But my failure teaches everything banks need to know about Platform versus Pipe. It's also a principal driver that moved me to write this book.

* * *

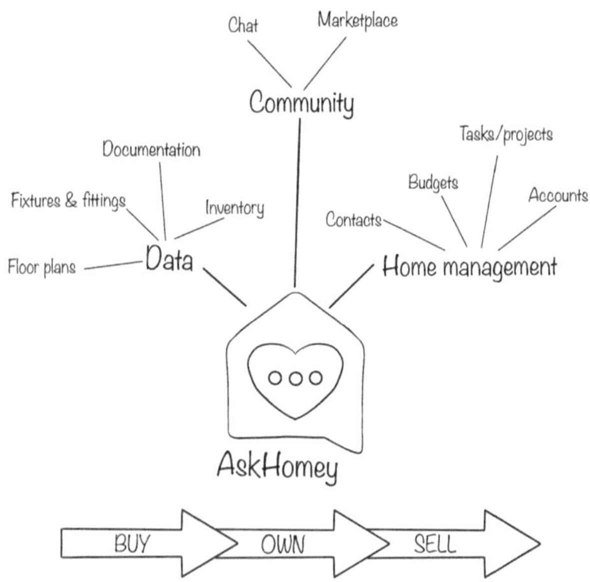

7

Platform or Pipe: The Only Two Futures

7.1 Where It Started: Franchising Banks, 1996

AskHomey failed because the model was right and the timing was wrong. The banks I pitched it to could not see past their product metrics. The capital structure could not survive the wait. And more importantly, the technology – large language models, agentic AI, the data infrastructure needed to make journey ownership genuinely intelligent – had not arrived yet. It has now. This chapter does not dwell on the failure. It uses it as a foundation for precision: what Platform banking actually means, what Pipe banking actually means, why there is no comfortable middle ground between them, and where to start if you have decided that Platform is the path. I have been thinking about this binary since 1996. Here is everything I know about it.

Platform Banking as I call it is not new. I first articulated it in the mid-1990s at NatWest, studying for an Open University MBA in evening school. Learning about different business models such as franchise economics from books at home, after a full day in banking, sparked an idea: A bank could broaden its customer base and a brand could deepen its customer relationships if the two were separated. Not a partnership. A structural separation. The bank provides the regulated infrastructure and product manufacturing. The brand owns the customer relationship, the distribution. I called it Franchising Banks, although, in hindsight, I could have called it white-labelling.

The industry would take another 30 years to accept it.

D. Mistry, L. R. Carlozo, *The Intelligent Ledger*,
https://doi.org/10.1007/978-3-032-32842-7_7

The model was straightforward and simple to grasp. A retailer, supermarket, airline, telecoms company – any brand with genuine customer trust and frequent touchpoints – could offer banking services to existing customers without building a bank from scratch. They would white-label the regulated infrastructure from an established bank, wrap it in their own brand, and own the customer relationship. The bank would get volume it could never achieve on its own. The brand would get depth it could never build by itself.

Everyone wins. Except, as I was about to discover, the banks did not perceive it that way. As I saw it, they were too consumed with selling products to see the big idea I was selling them. The sales obsession on the banking end would go on to repeat itself many, many times. It still does.

I wrote to the CEOs of four major UK banks to put the idea to them directly. Two replied with polite rejections, thanks but no thanks. One of those replies contained a phrase I have never forgotten. Four words that captured everything wrong with how banks think about their position: 'We own our customers.' Not 'we serve our customers.' Not 'our customers trust us.' We own them. As if a customer relationship were a property right rather than something earned and renewed daily. The third bank, RBS, was equally clear: This was not part of their strategy. The fourth, NatWest, thought it was interesting because they already were extensively white-labelling credit cards, but did not want to follow up the idea in retail banking.

About a year later, NatWest's COO came back to me and asked me to help write the business justification for a white-label banking deal with Tesco, the UK's largest retailer. I provided my input for the case for exactly the model I had proposed: Tesco's brand, customer trust, and distribution reach combined with NatWest's regulated infrastructure and banking licence. I thought the economics were compelling, the strategic logic was sound, and so I was certain it would proceed. The NatWest board reviewed it and declined. The feedback I got from the COO was that there was too much cannibalisation risk, too uncertain a strategic direction and not the right time.

RBS took the deal. The bank that had told me Franchising Banks was not part of their strategy launched Tesco Bank in summer 1997 initially as a 50:50 joint venture. Backed by RBS's infrastructure, Tesco Bank served millions of customers for over two decades. At its peak it held £9 billion in customer deposits and provided mortgages, credit cards, loans, and insurance to people who trusted Tesco far more than they trusted any bank. The model worked exactly as I had described it in my letters and in that NatWest business case. It just was not NatWest that proved it.

I tell this story because it establishes something important about the argument I make in this chapter. The Platform and Pipe binary is not a new observation born of the current technology moment. It has been the structural logic of banking's future since at least the 1990s. What has changed is not the thesis but the technology that makes the Platform vision fully achievable rather than merely logical. In 1996, I imagine RBS ran a separate instance of the banking system. But today a cloud-native core makes this much more easily possible, scalable and cost-effective. Tesco Bank was a genuine platform experiment, brand ownership of a financial relationship, but it was built on 1990s infrastructure and could only go so far. Back then they had no digital twins, no agentic AI, or the ability to advise customers across broader journeys with agentic AI. What Platform Banking means in 2027 is categorically more powerful than what was possible then. The idea was right in 1996. The technology is finally ready now.

And the banks that said 'we own our customers' in 1996? They are still saying versions of the same thing in 2026. Listening to them is still the wrong choice. And ultimately, should events play out as this book contends, it will fall on the deaf ears of those very customers who have abandoned them in droves.

My fellow author Lou Carlozo relates the story behind a 'we own our customers' debacle he lived through: The decline of the Chicago Tribune, and the beginning of its collapse.

'In the 2000s, the writing was not so much on the wall as the computer screen. The Internet was catching on with readers and a publication named Editor & Publisher ran an editorial, "The Internet is Coming: Are You Ready?" The Tribune built a small team to explore the implications but it was more a dog-and-pony show good for positive PR. Up in the C-suite, the bean counters could not be bothered. Their print newspaper had a healthy double-digit profit margin. People bought papers, even if subscriptions had dipped slightly. Businesses bought ads. Sales were the bottom line, the ultimate barometer and the weather was good. Why change? The mighty Chicago Tribune had been around for more than 150 years. Those readers who'd grown up with it? Those merchants who'd run ads for generations? They were not going anywhere: The Tribune "owned" them.

'But the execs did not get what technology had made possible. People turned to their laptops. Their phones. Often the news sites that won did not break the news fastest but loaded fastest. When journalism transformed from a print-centric model into a digital-first landscape, we were caught with our pants down. Any first-mover advantage had been long lost. Ad sales plummeted. Subscribers bailed. Then the Great Recession hit. More than 50 journalists lost their jobs in a single day of layoffs, an all-time record. I was one. The myopia of sales-uber-alles turned the paper into a shell of its former self. Even the historic Tribune Tower was sold and converted to condos. And somewhere along the way, Editor & Publisher went

bust, a victim of the very phenomenon it saw coming. We failed to adapt. To a large extent, the obsession with safe sales was why.'

* * *

7.2 Manufacturing Versus Distribution: My 2013 Temenos Thesis

I became Temenos' Chief Digital Officer in 2013, tasked with developing the company's digital strategy. By then I had already been sitting on the manufacturing and distribution thesis for 17 years, since those NatWest letters and the Tesco business case. Temenos gave me the platform in every sense to articulate it properly for the first time at industry scale. From that perch, I produced a paper that became central to how Temenos thought about digital banking's future; its core thesis replicated my 1996 proposal, only sharpened by two decades of watching it languish. Banking manufacturing and distribution would finally separate. This was not speculation. The seeds were already sprouting in 2013.

Banks have always done manufacturing well. They take deposits, make loans, process payments, manage risk, handle compliance: Essentially they own the product lifecycle. The products, the regulated activities, that require banking licences and capital. Distribution centres on owning the customer relationship as banks drive customer intimacy, understand needs, provide advice, guide decisions, build trust, maintain ongoing engagement. It also owns the conversation with the customer.

For most of banking history, these two elements were bundled. If you wanted a mortgage, you visited a bank, and the same institution managed both the product and the relationship. But starting in the early 2000s, cracks appeared. Mortgage brokers emerged, distribution without manufacturing. Comparison websites launched, platforms that customers trusted for advice on which bank's product to use. Then fintech companies, including Wise, handled distribution and utilised traditional banks for manufacturing. Banks provided rails. Fintechs owned customers.

In my 2013 thesis, I argued that this separation would accelerate – dramatically – and that two forces would drive it. First, Open Banking regulation was moving towards mandated data-sharing and open APIs, which would commoditise banking infrastructure and allow any company to access banking rails. Manufacturing would become a utility that distribution platforms could plug into. Second, platform economics: Technology companies were proving that platform models generated better economics than vertical integration. For example, Amazon did not manufacture most of what it sold. It owned distribution and curated manufacturing from others. Better margins. Faster growth. Higher valuations. I predicted banking would follow the same pattern:

- **Platform Banks** would own distribution and orchestrate banking products from whichever institution offered the best value;
- **Pipe Banks** would provide manufacturing-regulated infrastructure for platforms to use.

I saw the separation as the most likely course. The question was which kind of bank yours would become.

In 2013, most banks dismissed this. They thought their banking licences and regulatory moats made them immune to unbundling. And of course they were wrong. Revolut launched in 2015, started as a payment card, no banking licence, used traditional banks for manufacturing, and owned customer distribution. By early 2026, it had 68.3 million customers, on track for 70 million. NatWest launched Boxed in 2023, a Banking-as-a-Service offering. It explicitly chose Pipe, provided regulated infrastructure for fintechs and platforms, no customer relationship, a B2B model, commodity manufacturing. My 2013 thesis is playing out exactly as predicted. Manufacturing and distribution are separating. The question simply becomes: Platform or Pipe?

* * *

7.3 Platform Bank: Complete Definition

Most banks that claim to build platforms are not. A Platform Bank owns complete customer journeys for major life domains. Not 'we have an app.' Not 'we offer multiple products.' Not 'we partner with fintechs.' Actual platform banking means the customer thinks of you as their life platform for a specific domain, and banking products serve as invisible infrastructure within that experience. The customer does not think 'my bank', they think 'my home platform' or 'my business platform', and the banking services quietly work away underneath without demanding attention.

Traditional banks are organised by product divisions for mortgages, credit cards, deposits, wealth management. It's a time-tested model but does not fit the coming revolution any more than a petrol station equals a road trip.

Platform banks are organised by literal customer journeys: home team, business team, wealth team. **The home team** owns everything about the home ownership journey, buying, financing, insuring, maintaining, optimising, selling. They do not hand off to a 'mortgage specialist'. Mortgage is one component they orchestrate as part of the complete journey. **The business team** owns everything about running a business; starting, growing, managing, exiting, and banking products are embedded within business growth guidance. **The wealth team** owns everything about building and protecting wealth, with financial products selected automatically based on life stage and goals. These may resemble the product lines banks rely on today but this trio of teams operates in a realm that's dynamic, real-time and interconnected.

Platform banks require three mandatory technology foundations, which I've detailed in the appendices but will name here because they're not optional extras. You need:

- **the digital twin**, with complete customer data across all six life layers: physical, environmental, social, emotional, cognitive, and financial. Without this you can provide product-level advice but not life-level advice; you have 10% of context, your platform competitors will have 90%.
- **quantum simulation**, the ability to run thousands of personalised life scenarios and show customers not just what customers like them usually do, but what would happen specifically to them under different choices. Classical machine learning cannot do this with the vast number of variables in a six-layer digital twin: The computational complexity is too high. Quantum computing can.
- **agentic orchestration,** AI agents that autonomously manage journey touchpoints, alerts, optimisations, recommendations, transactions without requiring customer action unless genuine decisions are needed. Without all three of these foundations you're not a platform. You're a bank with good digital tools. The full life simulation capability that quantum enables will mature through 2029 to 2031 as fault-tolerant hardware develops. What matters in 2027 is beginning to build the digital twin data foundation and classical simulation layer that quantum will run on when it arrives, because the banks that start in 2027 will have three years of customer data and simulation history that no late mover can buy.

There is a fourth, less visible but equally important infrastructure requirement: *Programmable money*. Tokenised financial rails, stablecoins, smart contracts, tokenised assets, allow the platform's AI agents to move from recommendation to action. Without programmable money, the agent can identify that a customer's fixed rate expires in six weeks and simulate three refinancing scenarios. But with it, the agent can execute the switch at the optimal moment, automatically, within parameters the customer has already approved. Programmable money distinguishes between a platform that *advises* and one that *acts* via a sophisticated recommendation engine.

In other words:

- digitised financial intelligence leads to action,
- action comes from connection to a novel, exceptional financial architecture, and
- customers will find it useful (and will in short order learn to love it),
- and traditional banks do not have it.

Moreover, will they? Ever? When the newspapers-to-website moment arrives, it will be too late.

* * *

Let's examine how the Platform revenue model works. Right away, you'll spot the profound difference between Platform and Traditional banking.

In our theoretical model, journey subscriptions run £100–300 per month depending on complexity: home journeys at £150–200, business journeys at £200–300, wealth journeys at £100–500 depending on net worth. Most customers participate in two or three active journeys simultaneously; a young professional might have career and home journeys at £300 per month total; a business owner might have business and wealth subscriptions at £500 per month. Banking products execute automatically as embedded transactions within the journey. Customers do not apply for mortgages separately, they happen as part of home journey management. Add marketplace revenue from partner referrals and you get a total customer lifetime value of around £72,000 over 20 years compared to £2,000 for traditional banking. That's 30–70 times higher lifetime value. Same customer. Different models. *And by comparison, 36× returns.*

In terms of competition, Platform builds a genuinely formidable moat. Once a customer provides complete data across all six life layers and you integrate it into their life management, switching is a losing proposition of major proportions. Customers who do it literally rip their financial nimbleness out by the roots. Here's what they lose:

- years of integrated data,
- simulation history that proves your advice works,

- the AI agent that knows their complete situation, and
- quality of guidance as they start from zero with a competitor.

The switching cost is not £50 in admin fees. It's much, much more, especially when extrapolated over the customer's lifetime. Reconstructing their entire life platform? Effectively impossible. By contrast, every simulation you run on a Platform with deep data resources builds trust that compounds year on year. New competitors cannot buy that track record no matter the power and expansiveness of their technology. A stretch, perhaps, but you could compare it to stripping a virtuoso guitarist of their resources and asking them to start over with a new teacher.

One final note on defining a platform. Platform does not always mean full-spectrum. A bank that owns one journey so completely that it becomes the undisputed default within that niche such as later-life finance, agricultural lending, SME trade, is also a platform bank. The distinction between full-spectrum and micro-platform matters, and Chapter 12 returns to it. What does not change is the commitment required: Owning a niche completely demands the same organisational depth as owning multiple journeys broadly. There is no shallow version of a platform.

* * *

7.4 Pipe Bank: Complete Definition

If Platform encompasses one future then consider Pipe the other. But what does Pipe mean *exactly*? It may not be what you think. I want to be crystal clear on this point because two diametrically opposite versions exist. True Pipe is a legitimate strategic choice. Laggard Pipe simply does nothing but dress up as one, arriving at its fate by obsolescence and default.

A Pipe Bank deliberately chooses its model to provide commodity financial infrastructure without a customer relationship. Not 'We've lost customers to fintechs,' that's a failing traditional bank. Actual pipe banking means opting to operate as a B2B infrastructure provider. It manufactures for platforms and accepts that they own customers while you provide the rails.

Your customers? Fintechs, platforms, brands, neobanks, and embedded finance companies. You provide white-label banking as a service, regulated infrastructure, banking licences, compliance expertise, custody services, settlement rails. Your technology must be API-first: Representational State Transfer APIs (RESTful) with comprehensive documentation, MCP servers for agents and real-time settlement. It must be tokenisation-ready for programmable money and smart contracts, multi-currency and multi-jurisdiction, with 99.99% uptime because the platforms whose SLAs depend on you need rock-solid reliability. Customer-facing technology? Not your problem. The Platform builds that. You provide the Pipe they utilise.

The revenue model stems from utility economics: basis points on transaction volume (0.1–0.5% depending on transaction type), infrastructure licensing fees from platform customers (£10k per month for small fintechs up to £1 million or more per month for major platforms processing billions), and compliance-as-a-service for fintechs who do not want to build regulatory adherence themselves. Do not expect platform economics (45–65%) but gross margins (15–30%) and operating margins of 8–20% (compared to 30–45%). Lower, yes. But more stable and predictable, with lower customer acquisition cost and less churn risk since B2B contracts are sticky. If you can achieve top-quartile operational excellence, Pipe is survivable. Just do not expect those lofty platform valuations. However, without the legacy of an existing bank, Griffin Bank is already achieving gross margins of 90% having made the decision to create a pipe bank.

NatWest Boxed is also an example to watch here. It too explicitly chose Pipe—not to compete for consumers but to provide BaaS for fintechs and platforms. I'd call that a smart strategic choice if they execute operationally.

Elsewhere, I'm not so sure. The less comfortable prediction is that most traditional banks by 2032 will become Pipe by default, not because they strategically chose it like NatWest Boxed or Griffin, but lost customer relationships to platforms only to discover that their only remaining value was regulated infrastructure.

True Pipe is a deliberate business model. Laggard Pipe is just what happens to you when fintechs, platforms, brands, and neobanks head for the exits.

Having defined what Platform and Pipe actually mean, the next question is the one most banks are quietly hoping to avoid: Can you be both?

* * *

7.5 No 'Platpipe' Middle Ground

Short-sighted banks will search for a third option. Some hybrid between Platform and Pipe that lets them keep their current structure while 'exploring platform opportunities'. This 'Platpipe' option does not exist and the reason has nothing to do with technology or products. It's organisational. Platform and Pipe are fundamentally incompatible business models that require completely different companies, cultures, incentive structures, and time horizons. Let me show you why every attempted compromise fails.

7.5.1 'We'll Be Platform for Some Customers, Pipe for Others'

This represents the most common attempt at middle ground, building platform experiences for retail customers while also providing BaaS infrastructure for fintechs. It sounds reasonable. It does not work.

The Platform needs journey designers who understand complete life domains, machine learning engineers building personalisation at scale, customer-facing teams measured on lifetime value, patient capital with a three-to-five year investment horizon before scale, and a culture of experimentation. Pipe needs operations specialists who optimise transaction costs, compliance experts to navigate regulatory complexity, B2B sales teams to manage platform partnerships, immediate profitability at utility economics, and a culture of operational excellence and reliability above all else. These are not just different teams. They're different cultures with fundamentally conflicting objectives: speaking different languages and scaling different peaks.

Try to build both and you get this: a Platform team that complains Operations is blocking API access, Compliance is slowing launches, and Sales is hawking products instead of offering journeys. The Pipe team complains that Platform has wasted money on unnecessary features and broke operational efficiency with constant changes. The CEO caught in the middle, reciting from his business school negotiation textbook, asks why both teams cannot just collaborate.

They cannot.

Platform optimises for customer delight at the expense of operational efficiency, while Pipe optimises for operational efficiency at the expense of customer relationship. You can be one or the other. JPMorgan has managed a version of both only because they're essentially running *separate companies under one holding structure*, with the resources to absorb the organisational complexity. Most banks cannot afford that.

7.5.2 'We'll Be Pipe Now, Platform Later'

The second attempted middle ground: Accept the current position, provide infrastructure for platforms today, build capabilities, learn, then pivot to Platform when ready. Confused? No wonder. That does not work, either. By the time you're 'ready', the Platform market has already consolidated. 2027–2028 is narrower than most banking executives want to believe. Why?

If you choose Pipe in 2027 with a plan to pivot later, here's what happens. If your BaaS business scales, by 2028 you have 20–30 fintech customers, £50–100 million in revenue, decent margins. The board is happy with the clear business model, immediate revenue. Meanwhile, Platform banks have been building for two years. By 2029 they have 500,000-plus customers with complete digital twins, two years of simulation history proving accuracy, network effects kicking in, customer switching costs established, journey teams with deep expertise, and mature technology stacks tested at real scale. It's a long list and an immense barrier to competitors.

You decide you're ready to pivot. You launch your Platform offering. You're two years behind competitors who have ten times your customer base, years more data for better advice, proven track records customers trust, and network effects you simply cannot overcome. The data gap compounds daily. The trust gap took years to build. You cannot catch up: Not because your technology is worse, but because better advice requires more training data, and your competitors have been accumulating that data for months longer than you.

Result: Your Platform launch fails.

You're stuck as a Pipe.

That would've worked if you'd committed to Pipe strategically like NatWest did. But you tried to wait and were forced by default into a Pipe identity. The lesson: The choice that feels deferred to 2029 has already arrived in 2027.

7.5.3 'We'll Optimise Products While We Explore Platform'

This most common path guarantees you become Pipe by default. The logic sounds prudent: We cannot abandon our current business, mortgages still generate billions, credit cards turn a profit, deposits fund our lending. We'll optimise while we explore platform opportunities on the side via innovation labs, pilot programs, strategic partnerships with fintechs. Test and Learn.

No. It's Build and Learn ... and Build. The aforementioned strategy is actually fatal, not because optimisation is wrong, but because it is incompatible with strategies executed simultaneously with the same resources and leadership attention.

Gradual, slight improvements to existing products such as better mortgage rates, faster loan approvals, a more convenient digital experience are all genuinely good things. All focused on doing current things better rather than doing different things.

But change by increments carries major risks. It feels safe, a way to convey baby steps as leaps forward. True transformation demands a complete business model change, organisational restructure, a different revenue model, patient capital, different metrics, a technology rebuild, culture conversion. These require opposite resource allocations and by appearance threaten to upset the proven-profits apple cart. But appearances and reality, in this case, could not be more dissimilar.

Optimisation demands that most resources go to current products with small teams on innovation and ROI proven quarterly. Transformation demands that most resources go to platform build with current products in maintenance mode and a willingness to accept a three-to-five-year investment before platform scale.

What happens when you try both? The innovation team builds a platform pilot. Customer feedback is positive. They ask for resources to scale. But product teams point out they're hitting their numbers with mortgage sales up 12%, credit card activation up 8%; why divert resources to something with zero revenue? The CFO asks when the platform becomes profitable. The innovation team explains that they need 100,000 customers before unit economics work, a target three to four years away. The CFO cannot approve that when product optimisation shows an 18-month payback. The innovation team gets constrained resources. The pilot never scales. Platform strategy stays indefinitely in the 'exploration' phase.

Penny wise and pound foolish, to put it mildly.

Meanwhile, a platform bank launches, owns the home journey, guides customers to mortgages, and your improved mortgage becomes one option among several in their platform. Selected on rate, not relationship. You've become Pipe by default, not because you chose it strategically, but because you chose optimisation over transformation.

The Uncomfortable Truth Most Banks Will Not Accept

Why do I predict that 90% of banks will become Pipe by default? Based on 40 years in the business, I've all too many times seen 'all talk no action' in action. Bankers pontificate about 'platform strategy' in boardrooms and analyst calls, launch innovation labs with fanfare, run pilot programs, announce partnerships with fintechs and speak at conferences about 'ecosystem banking' and 'embedded finance'. Their scripts are fine-tuned. Impressive. Chock full of buzzwords like 'agentic' and 'synergise'. *But they will not do the hard things Platform actually requires.*

- The CEO will not declare publicly: 'We're becoming a home platform. This is our primary strategy. Everything else serves this goal.'
- The board will not approve multi-year investment with no expectation of platform profitability before year four.
- The organisation will not restructure.
- Product teams will not be dissolved.
- Journey teams will not be created.
- People will not have to reapply for roles knowing some will leave.

There's more and all of it penetrates to the heart of how banks resist change. Metrics will not shift from product sales to customer lifetime value. Compensation will not transition from quarterly bonuses on product targets to multi-year retention bonuses. Culture will not enforce journey thinking from the top, with executives who resist being reassigned or removed. Admittedly, these changes are painful. They create internal resistance. They sacrifice short-term numbers for long-term transformation. They require courage that most CEOs and boards genuinely do not have.

So what happens instead? Banks optimise products, launch innovation labs, run pilots, and announce partnerships. And while they do this, true platform banks will build, quietly, deliberately and with patient capital and clear commitment. By 2030, most banks risk waking up to find that their mortgage customers now select their bank through a home platform they do not own; their business customers use banking products embedded in a business management platform they do not own; their wealthy customers access accounts through a wealth platform they do not own. The banks are still there. Still providing mortgages and business loans and investment accounts. Still making margin on transactions. But they're Pipe. They manufacture for someone else's distribution. Commodity vendors compete on price. They did not choose this strategically. Not choosing platform meant they had no choice at all. Period. They became Pipe. I first predicted this separation in 1996 in those letters to four bank CEOs. I formalised it in my 2013 Temenos thesis. At the current rate of progress, that prediction will finally come true in 2027. The question is which 10% will win the Platform battle.

Having cleared the ground of three compromise positions, all of them wrong, one question remains: Which is the productive one? If Platform is the choice, where do you start?

* * *

7.6 The Three Journeys Worth Owning

If you've genuinely decided to go the Platform route – and no longer just 'exploring' it – the next choice is which journey to own. Most banks have three viable options: Home, Business, or Wealth. Let's walk through each, starting with the one I believe offers the clearest opportunity.

7.6.1 Home Journey: The Best First Choice

Yes, I spent three years building AskHomey for the home journey. But my bias stems from failure as much as faith. Home ownership stands as the optimal first journey for most retail banks, and there are five reasons why.

First: You already possess the mortgage relationship. You're not starting from zero; homeowners with mortgages know you, trust you for financial advice, and have an existing reason to engage. You're not asking them to trust a bank with something new; you're expanding a relationship they already have.

Second: The value is enormous and the timeline long. As mentioned earlier, the average UK homeowner stays in a property for 10-15 years. Total value of the home ownership journey exceeds £500,000 (see Appendix A). Your current mortgage margin is £2,000. Journey ownership could generate £10,000–20,000 over the same period, five to 10 times the improvement.

Third: The pain is real and completely unaddressed. Every homeowner struggles with complexities surrounding contractors, mortgage refinancing, curbing energy costs, even timing a move. But nobody provides complete guidance; it's either fragmentary or non-existent.

Fourth: The competition is beatable right now. Who owns the home journey today? Nobody. Estate agents own the buying and selling transaction but nothing in between. PropTech start-ups have small pieces but no complete platform. Tech giants could enter – Google and Amazon with their smart home platforms are the obvious threat – but have not committed yet. You have a two-to-three year timeframe to establish position before they move.

Fifth: The scope is clear and bounded. The home journey has natural start and end points and clear scope. That makes it easier to define, build, and measure success than open-ended journeys such as 'complete financial life'.

* * *

What does the home journey look like in practice? **In the buying phase**, spanning three to six months, the platform provides property search integrated with complete financial modelling: not just 'Can you afford it?' but 'Should you buy it given your complete life situation?' along with offer guidance based on quantum simulations, automatic mortgage selection, coordinated legal and insurance services, and complete digital capture of all property information at purchase.

In the owning phase, spanning a decade or more, it tracks all appliance warranties and service records with predictive maintenance alerts, runs continuous utility monitoring with automatic, price-sensitive switching, coordinates verified contractors with price benchmarking, handles insurance renewal comparisons annually, provides improvement guidance with ROI analysis based on likely sale timeline, monitors property value monthly with optimal improvement and sale timing recommendations.

In the optimising phase, it alerts owners when remortgage makes sense, models equity release implications, adjusts guidance as life events occur.

And **in the selling phase**, it advises on optimal timing based on the market and the owner's personal situation, models pricing based on improvements and quantum scenarios, and enables complete records transfer to the next owner.

I'd start with this journey if I ran a retail bank today. It's natural, valuable, achievable and defensible for two to three years before the tech giants arrive. You need capital, brand and scale. Banks have all three.

7.6.2 Business Journey: Natural for Commercial Banks, but Unproven

If you're a commercial bank with strong business banking relationships, the business journey could be your platform play for sensible reasons:

- You already serve business customers.
- The value is significant, the total cost of running a business over its lifetime runs into hundreds of thousands or millions, of which your current banking margin is a fraction.
- The pain points you solve are intense. Every business owner I've spoken to says some version of the same thing: 'I started this business to do the thing I'm good at, but I spend most of my time on taxes, HR, compliance, cash flow, admin.'
- The competition is fragmented. Accountants own compliance but not growth strategy, consultants own strategy but not operations, SaaS

platforms own specific functions but not complete integration. Nobody owns the complete business journey from start to exit.

The business journey spans starting (business model validation, incorporation, accounts, accounting setup, initial hires), growing (cash flow management, growth financing decisions, hiring guidance, marketing optimisation, expansion decisions), operating (financial management, HR, risk, technology decisions, supply chain), and exiting (timing, options, valuation optimisation, buyer identification, transition planning).

Here's a sample revenue model:

- £200–300 per month subscription.
- £5,000 or more in banking products over the business lifetime, and £3,000–5,000 in service commissions.
- £10,000–50,000 in exit advisory fees as a percentage of sale value.
- Total lifetime value: £15,000–30,000 or more.

The subsegment for gig workers is clearly set to expand. As AI takes the reins on many repeatable and easily replaceable human tasks, those displaced must reskill and/or supplement income with a side hustle—as many did during COVID-19.

A business journey could also work if you're a commercial bank with strong SMB relationships and willing to take 3-5 years to figure this out. What's more, specific large niches could provide a strong entrance ramp, as with Hammock, the first landlord accounting platform recognised by HMRC. There are somewhere between 2.3–2.8 million landlords in the UK! This 'niche approach' creates a more personalised service where banks understand your business and can provide specific services and advice. Using one niche to work out how to create this prepares you to scale across others.

The honest challenge lies in that I have not seen anyone do this well yet. Accounting firms cannot own it, they're organised around compliance, not growth. Consultants cannot own it, they're project-based, not continuously present. Banks have not tried yet. Business journey is the right idea for commercial banks, but genuinely unproven and harder to organise than the home journey. It demands a more complex scope since every business is different and needs business strategy expertise beyond financial optimisation. You must facilitate longer journey paths since businesses operate for decades and exit events are rare, so you have fewer moments to prove tangible value. My counsel: Only attempt this if you have strong SMB relationships and genuine patience for a five-year build.

7.6.3 Wealth Journey: Best for Private Banks, Especially with an Inheritance Focus

If you serve high-net-worth customers, consider the wealth journey your natural platform play. You already manage investments for wealthy clients, so the trust and existing relationship already exist and with substantial value. High-net-worth (HNW) customers lead complex financial lives with multiple properties, business interests, investments, tax strategies, estate planning, trusts, generational wealth transfer, and total lifetime value that exceeds £1 million for many clients. The advisory relationship is already in place and customers already pay for advice. The wealth journey spans building (income optimisation, investment strategy, business interests, property portfolio, and tax efficiency), protecting (insurance across assets, risk management, estate planning, trust creation, succession planning for business interests), and transferring (inheritance tax optimisation, trust distributions, next-generation preparation, philanthropic legacy, business succession, and estate execution).

Revenue model:

- £100–200 per month for mass affluent.
- £500–2,000 or more for ultra-high-net-worth.
- investment management at 0.5–1.5% of AUM annually.
- plus service commissions from legal, tax, and trust specialists.
- total lifetime value: £50,000–100,000 for HNW, considerably more for ultra-high-net-worth (UHNW).

One deeply underserved niche within the wealth journey is inheritance and end-of-life planning. A friend of mine, Steve Scott, built afterloss.com after his father died and he discovered how extraordinarily complicated the estate handling process is: probate, asset transfers, tax filings, creditor notifications, property sales, distribution to heirs, all while grieving. The platform helps with end-of-life planning while a loved one is still alive, with estate organisation, probate guidance, inheritance tax optimisation, emotional support during bereavement, and next-generation wealth transition. This is ideal for wealth journey platform banks: high trust required, significant financial value in inheritance tax optimisation alone, strong referral potential, and very low competition because most firms find this space too sensitive to tackle properly. (A book that covers similar turf in America and could serve as an excellent platform model is *My Mother's Money* by MarketWatch columnist Beth Pinsker, based on the legal and financial tangles that followed her mother's passing.)

Wealth journey works for private banks with established advisory relationships. It's harder to build than home journeys, smaller addressable market, more bespoke since every HNW situation is unique, requires specialised expertise in tax and trusts and estate law, and competes with family offices that already provide comprehensive advice. If you possess strong HNW ties, consider a narrow start with the underserved inheritance and end-of-life niches, which build deep trust that naturally expands to complete wealth management.

7.6.4 The Decision Framework in Sum: Which Journey First?

For retail banks, start with Home Journey. It's a natural extension of the mortgage relationship: Largest addressable market, clear value proposition, beatable competition for now, proven customer willingness to pay, two-to-three year period before tech giants arrive.
For commercial banks, consider Business Journey. This business banking encompasses significant value opportunity, intense customer pain, no proven models yet so you could pioneer the space, but only if you have strong SMB relationships and genuine patience for a five-year build; this is riskier and harder than home journey.
For private banks, start with Wealth Journey, specifically the inheritance niche. It flows easily from wealth management, the advisory relationship already exists, inheritance and end-of-life remain underserved. It builds deep trust, expands naturally to complete wealth management, but it's also a smaller market and requires specialised expertise.
For most banks: Home Journey is the safest, most validated bet, largest market, clearest path, shortest time to demonstrable value and best defensibility before serious competition arrives.

* * *

7.7 Closing: The Decision You Must Make

7.7.1 Not Choosing Is Choosing

Every month you spend 'exploring platform strategy' without commitment puts you a month closer to Pipe. Every innovation lab you launch without a board pledge to platform transformation is theatre: expensive, well-intentioned theatre that makes you feel innovative without the tangible transformation that would actually make you competitive. Every pilot programme you run with 'Let's see if this works' is delayed. Real platform commitment looks like this: The CEO declares publicly that he's becoming a home platform, or business platform, or wealth platform. This is the bank's primary strategy for 2027–2032, and everything else serves this goal. Not in an internal memo. Publicly. So customers and staff and competitors know.

The board approves multi-year investment, three to five years before platform profitability, patient capital, no expectation of quarterly profit from the platform in years one through three. The organisation restructures: Product teams dissolve, journey teams emerge, people reapply for roles; some will leave, and that's expected. Culture change in this instance is painful but necessary. Metrics change completely as the bank stops measuring product sales and quarterly revenue by product. It transitions into the metrics of customer lifetime value, journey completion rate, platform adoption, simulation accuracy, and switching cost strength. Compensation changes, too. Away with quarterly product sales target bonuses; hello to multi-year customer retention and lifetime value growth. The technology investment: a digital twin build over 18–24 months, quantum simulation capability established (via partner or build), agentic orchestration over 12–18 months. Not optional. It forms the foundation.

Underpinning it all, you'll find changes in company culture. Executives who continue to optimise products while claiming to support the platform are moved on. Managers who resist journey thinking get reassigned or removed. Promotion criteria change, with journey expertise valued over product expertise.

Yes, this is hard. It creates internal conflict. Friction and pushback are certain. Some will undoubtedly contend it cannot be done. But this is what platform commitment actually looks like.

7.7.2 What I Learnt from AskHomey

I started this chapter with a story. Let me close with another 'learn from me' moment. Why did AskHomey falter? The banks I pitched had the capital, the brand, the trust, and the scale I lacked. But they lacked something as well: the willingness to see past mortgage product sales to journey ownership. I hope you take this gap between understanding and acting to heart as you contemplate the future of finance—and your future within it.

But bad timing should not be confused with a good idea. The pandemic needed time to cool off (Remember when that was a frightening uncertainty?)

and the tech time to mature. The digital firepower that was missing in 2020 mostly exists in 2026. Natural language works. AI handles complexity. Digital twins integrate complete data. Quantum simulation is building its foundation now. Can you imagine how much more will come on line in the next decade? Any bank that tries to start then might as well chase rocket ships with a wheelbarrow.

AskHomey proved the value and validity of journey ownership. The question is this: Will banks choose to follow that model before or hold out at their own peril as they protect their space in the marketplace?

To answer this question, it pays to examine the groundbreaking work of two business school titans. The 2005 bestseller 'Blue Ocean Strategy' by W. Chan Kim and Renée Mauborgne, professors at the prestigious INSEAD Business School in Fontainebleau, France, posits a thesis that fits today's banking world. They argue that companies – instead of fighting each other for the same exact business with the same exact products in the same exact way with the same exact goals – should provide innovative value to consumers in new markets where competition is irrelevant. This is the same way that iPhone killed Kodak, and remember Apple had to kill their best selling product the iPod to do this!

In 2026, every bank you can think of occupies some version of their 'red ocean,' where at some level they vie to gain advantage and market share, bloodying the waters in the process. But a company – in this case, a dedicated Platform or Pipe – discovers a 'blue ocean' when it takes up a market opportunity few if any competitors have assayed.

The first Platforms and Pipes will enjoy this blue ocean advantage for years to come while countless conventional banks risk drowning in a sea of red ink.

Questions for Your Board

1. Of the three journeys, which one maps best to our customer base? Why?
2. What measurements will we apply (or have applied) to journey ownership? Assuming this is not a priority, what might it take to change that reality? How would the case be made?
3. What timeframe and budget will we commit to switching to a full platform business model and how might we divide this into stages that allow for manageable change?

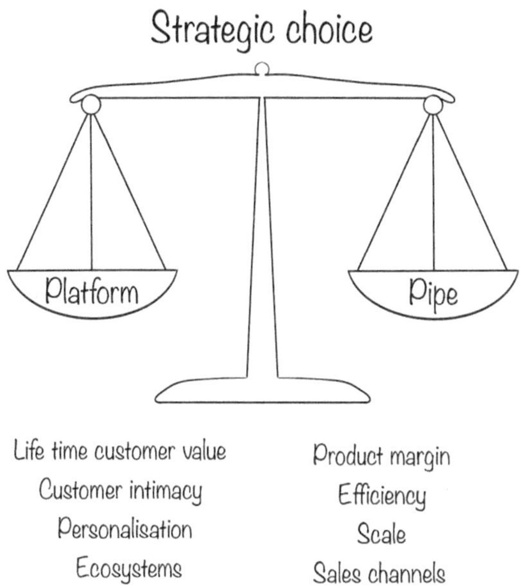
Strategic choice
Platform
Pipe
Life time customer value
Customer intimacy
Personalisation
Ecosystems
Product margin
Efficiency
Scale
Sales channels

8

Quantum Simulation: Beyond Classical Computing

It's become a monthly ritual: I open a spreadsheet and spend roughly two hours keeping my financial house in order. That house is a metaphorical mansion of many rooms, and I do my best to bring exactitude and organisation to the task. I log my latest bank account balances. I check my stocks/shares and crypto holdings. My rental properties each have separate accounts that track income and expenses. My fixed-term deposits mature at different dates, with different rates and early exit penalties. My wife and I each have ISAs. I own pensions split across companies, a legacy of working for different employers. A few credit cards, each used strategically to collect air miles or for overseas spend. A separate spreadsheet for insurance: two cars, buildings, contents, pet and health. This encompasses 17 separate companies and almost as many logins. Another spreadsheet tracks monthly household expenses, because costs are split between the credit card and current account; it makes sense for points accumulation but complicates balancing the books. Aside from this monthly update, I revisit our household budget every three months.

I like to think my money management skills stem from my financial background and decades spent in the banking sector. I understand compound interest, asset allocation, risk diversification, and tax efficiency better than most people. And still, every month, I sit at my dining room table, copy numbers manually from nearly two dozen different places into a spreadsheet

D. Mistry, L. R. Carlozo, *The Intelligent Ledger*,
https://doi.org/10.1007/978-3-032-32842-7_8

and try to construct a picture that none of these institutions will show me *in toto*. It is tedious. Slow. And it only ever gives me a static snapshot of where things stand in a given moment. I cannot even say 'right now' because by the time I finish up, some element has shifted in real time. That I cannot precisely track. Nor does this tell me anything about what to do next.

Given the current muscle of AI, quantum computing, and convergence technologies, this snapshot might as well come from a shake-that-picture Polaroid SX-70. Put another way, the Microsoft Excel spreadsheet first appeared for the Mac in 1985, whilst I was still a teenager.

The doing-what-next part is where the process really falls apart. It's not just weighing the numbers but what weighs on my mind as I write this: my mother's health and what happens if she needs care, whether my children will achieve financial security in a world where AI displaces jobs, the economic environment and how interest rate movements and world events impact my property portfolio, when I want to retire and what that actually requires across all these assets—and, perhaps, the most unsettling thought, how all this complexity would teeter or topple if something happened to me. My wife is smart but does not manage these spreadsheets. She has not spent decades developing intuition about when to move assets, lock in rates, hold or sell assets. If I am gone, what does she do with 17 institutions, financial windows with no holistic view of anything?

Many people can manage each of these questions on their own. You can sit down, think through a scenario, run some numbers. But you cannot hold all of them in your head simultaneously any more than you can mentally multiply two 17-digit numbers. Imagine tackling this dog pile of what-ifs:

- my mother needs care in the next three years?
- AI impacts my son's income within five years?
- interest rates rise, fall or sustain a sudden blow from an unforeseen force?
- I want to retire by 65, or earlier, or later?
- I continue to allocate my assets with a tech-industry bias?

Even in this age of revolutionary LLMs, any hope for a singular answer cleaves into two more questions: What should I do right now? And what tech-based financial resource can tell or show me?

The answer is actually question number three: Who knows?

* * *

Now call to mind your own what-ifs. The interactions between the variables are too complex. The uncertainties are too numerous. No human brain can process them all at once. No spreadsheet can model them. This applies even before I consider the impact of existing data from my digital twin: my health, work, travel, and wellness. Financial planning tends to focus on products and individual life goals. But life never happens one event at a time! It happens all at once. Convergence is not just for technological revolutions, the iPhone moments. The word also captures how our lives unfold, events overlap, and the world's gyrations influence us—all of it changing by the second.

Let me be clear: Money is not managed just by numbers, it's managed by the heart: feelings, emotions, and values embedded in a broader data set from our behaviours. Data? The heart? If you buy someone you love a gift – an item you might not otherwise purchase – then the cost, purchase location, date and time all leave a data trail.

And when people behave irrationally around money, the data can tell that story, too, by detecting unrecognised patterns. Believe it or not, otherwise logical investors will pick stocks based on a subconscious alphabetical bias. Jesse Itzkowitz, Chief Behavioural Scientist at Ipsos North America and his spouse Jennifer, a professor at Seton Hall University's Stillman School of Business, discovered this in joint research.

'Just like choosing "AAA Best Plumber" from the Yellow Pages, people when looking at stocks frequently overinvest in companies that have names or tickers that appear early in the alphabet,' they told my co-author in a 2016 investing article published in US News & World Report.

* * *

So here is the point I want to make in this chapter: No spreadsheet nor classical computer can answer the myriad financial questions we all carry. Nor can they factor in life events and conditions that, while not directly financial, have everything to do with how we manage our money. Nor can they quantify and reveal dysfunctional and baffling money habits we'd rather keep hidden from ourselves.

Not properly. Not at an actually useful level of personalisation and complexity. But the convergence of quantum, digital twins and AI can help us create what I call *quantum simulations.*

Let's explore how quantum simulations work and can work for us.

* * *

8.1 The Agentic Solution: Solving the Data Problem First

Before I explain quantum simulation, I want to reinforce one fundamental reality. Agentic AI – the AI agents that connect autonomously to external systems and orchestrate information – will solve the spreadsheet problem.

My monthly spreadsheet trial, the maze of logins, the copy-paste hell, is solvable with technology that exists today. An AI agent connected via APIs or MCP servers to my bank accounts, investment platforms, property accounts, fixed-term deposit platforms, ISAs, pension providers, and credit cards would maintain a live, unified view of my complete financial picture. Best of all: I do not have to lift a finger, aside from clicking a mouse. Balances update in real time, transactions categorise automatically, net worth calculates continuously.

Yet even after AI solves the data problem, other challenges exist. Imagine a near-future version of me with an ideal, live, unified view of all my financial data. Yes, every balance, rate, maturity date, income stream, expense, asset, and liability—all visible in one place, updated automatically. I would love that. Wouldn't you?

But even with flawless data visibility, I still face the same fundamental challenge: *What should I do next?* Think back to all those 'what-ifs' that opened this chapter. These questions do not have simple answers or any answers at all in a static state. Each factor depends on all the others, which can shift in the blink of an AI.

What should I do next? That's a mammoth problem built on a subset of problems, the most colossal game of financial Whack-A-Mole you can imagine. It's also the quintessential kind of problem that quantum simulation is built to address.

8.1.1 Why Classical Systems Cannot Fully Solve This

How come classical computers and today's AI LLMs cannot solve this problem? To be sure, this does not betray a failure of intelligence or sophistication. Rather, classical computing cannot overcome the mathematical constraints. Classical computing processes information in bits. Each bit is either 0 or 1. When you ask it to model a complex scenario with many interacting variables and multiple layers of uncertainty, it needs to work through the possibilities one at a time, or in small batches. The number of possible future states in a multi-layered scenario like mine grows exponentially with each variable you add. Time horizons. Interest rates. Growth predictions. Financial opportunities of any sort that you are considering but have not actualised. Another way to think of it (though the analogy is not quite precise) is a decision tree. The more variables you incorporate, the more branches spread out. Trouble is, selecting a given branch then in turn may impact previous or adjacent ones. It's a daunting task for any human to comprehend, let alone a classical computer to digest.

Classical computers handle modest complexity well. But not this kind of exponential complexity with the speed and personalisation we would find genuinely useful in real life and real time.

Current AI, including large language models, is extraordinarily impressive. It can reason about individual scenarios, synthesise information, explain complex concepts, and engage with multi-layered problems in ways that sounded like science fiction five years ago. But under the hood, this still operates as a classical system. When you ask it to run thousands of simultaneous, personalised life simulations – each with its own probability distributions, interacting with the others across a 30-year horizon – it cannot accomplish this in real time with a granularity that makes the advice genuinely reliable. It can be approximated. It can be reasoned by analogy. It can provide thoughtful guidance based on patterns it has encountered. But it cannot show you 10,000 specific futures, computed from your situational specificity in regard to family situation, risk profile, and economic assumptions.

That gap, between approximation and genuine simulation, is what quantum computing directly addresses. This is not a better tool for the same job but a new tool for jobs that the old tools genuinely cannot execute.

For technologists I've included a more technical overview of quantum in the appendices. For everyone else the next section provides a simple overview, especially for those who have not looked at quantum computing before.

* * *

8.2 The Core Quantum Idea, Without the Physics Degree

In the spirit of my 'Demystify' podcast, let me explain quantum computing just as I would to a bank executive over coffee, as opposed to a physicist dissecting it for an academic journal. Truly, you need not grasp the full mechanics of quantum physics—only the capability difference, what quantum computers can do that classical computers cannot, and why that matters for banking.

The first relevant property: Superposition. Where a classical computer works with bits (off or on, 0 or 1), a quantum computer uses 'qubits'. And a qubit can exist in a state of 0 and 1 simultaneously, a property called 'superposition'. This is not a metaphor or approximation. Until the qubit is measured, it genuinely exists in both states at once.

In a system of multiple qubits in superposition, the number of states it can represent at the same time grows exponentially. Two qubits can represent four states at once. Ten qubits can occupy 1,024 states at once. Fifty qubits? *More than a quadrillion.* This exponential scaling explains quantum computing's power for certain types of problems, specifically those that explore a vast number of concurrent possibilities: the exact requirement to create a personalised life scenario simulation.

The second: Entanglement. When qubits entangle, the state of one instantly correlates with the state of another. This allows quantum systems to process relationships between variables together rather than in sequence; they do not calculate each interaction separately but explore the complete web of interdependencies all at once. For financial life modelling, where every variable affects every other and a change in one assumption ripples through hundreds of connected outcomes, entanglement provides necessary, extraordinary power.

The third: Interference. Quantum algorithms are designed to amplify the probability of correct answers and suppress incorrect ones, a bit like the way noise-cancelling headphones amplify audio signals and squelch background static. As such, quantum computers generate useful results rather than reveal all possible states and know how to extract a meaningful answer.

The fourth: Measurement. While superposition lets a qubit be both 0 and 1, the act of looking at it, measuring it, forces it to 'choose' a side. It snaps instantly back into a simple 0 or 1. This is why quantum computing is not a silver bullet. You cannot just peek at the system and see every possibility at once; you only get one answer per run. This is why **Interference** (the property mentioned earlier) is so critical. We have to choreograph the algorithm so that when the measurement 'snap' happens, the laws of probability are heavily stacked in favour of the right answer. Measurement is the bridge between the strange quantum realm and the binary results a bank can actually act on. It's what makes quantum programming an art of probability rather than just raw speed.

Superposition, entanglement, interference, and measurement combine to make quantum simulation categorically different from classical computing: not just faster but fit to solve problems standard computers cannot in any reasonable timeframe. Not even a warehouse full of Mac Studio M3 Ultra computers can come close, any more than an army of those Pegasus II machines in a hundred 10x7 metre rooms could compete with a single Mac Studio.

* * *

8.3 The Difference That Matters: Prediction Versus Simulation

The capability that matters most in banking specifically involves the ability to predict versus simulate. Here's what that means.

The classical AI machine learning that banks use today predicts. It crunches historical data, finds patterns and says, based on what's been seen before, 'Here is what will likely happen.' It is powerful, valuable—and fundamentally backward-looking. Why? It explains what customers like you have done, outcomes that occurred in similar situations, and the most probable next event given past patterns. This is useful but insufficient for the personalised life guidance that platform banking requires.

To understand what quantum simulation adds, we must look at the architecture that makes it possible. For all its muscle, quantum computing does not work alone. It needs three contributing layers to distinguish it as a credible (and incredible) technology strategy as opposed to hype.

A world model, as the name suggests, is learnt from how a person's world actually operates: not rules written by humans, but from emergent understanding gleaned from data across financial markets, health trajectories, environmental conditions, family dynamics, and behavioural patterns. Think of it as the physics engine of the simulation. It does not predict the future. It encodes the laws of how things interact so that when you run a scenario through it, the outputs are grounded in real causal relationships rather than statistical correlations that may or may not hold.

Yann LeCun, a native of France, developed the world model concepts as a foundation for general intelligence. He was not even 30 when he joined the Adaptive Systems Research Department at AT&T Bell Laboratories in New Jersey, interestingly the birthplace of the transistor. At Bell, LeCun (who later became Facebook's chief AI scientist) pioneered the very machine learning methods we use today.

Speaking to my co-author in 2018, LeCun elaborated on the fuel that would propel quantum computing someday:

> *'You need data to train your system, and the more data you have, the more accurate your system will be. So, from a technology goal and business point of view, having more data is better.'*

Quantum computing, as we have established, can process a nearly limitless cascade of data that changes by the second. Fifty qubits equals a quadrillion states. How many for 100? (Do not multiply 50 x 2 because it's way, way more than two quadrillion.)

The second layer is agents, autonomous AI actors thrown into the world model to explore what happens. Think of how a child learns to ride a bike by trying, falling, and adjusting a hundred or more times. In the digital realm, we can thank another AI pioneer for discovering this principle, a University of Toronto professor named Geoffrey Hinton. In 1986 he co-authored the seminal paper that established backpropagation, the foundation of modern neural networks, as a way computers could learn by performing a task over and over, each time with its neural network adjusted in the direction that decreases the error. LeCun would later work under Hinton, an alliance of kindred tech spirits that made much of what you're reading in this book possible.

The autonomous AI agents elevate backpropagation to not so much a higher stratum as a new planet. Imagine teaching a robot the same skill by running a hundred attempts in parallel, simultaneously, and distilling all of that learning back into a single model. Agents do exactly that in a world model; they explore thousands of versions of a person's future at the same time, each a parallel run through the physics engine of their specific circumstances, accumulating evidence about which decisions produce which outcomes.

The third layer is where quantum sampling enters, and this is the precision that matters. Quantum does not invent hypotheses. It does not generate the world model. *It samples* and does so with a growing advantage over classical methods. When you need to draw results from a vast, complex distribution of possible outcomes – to identify which scenarios matter, which interactions are load-bearing, which decisions are most consequential across the full probability space – quantum sampling can explore that space more completely than any classical arrangement at equivalent speed. A precision point is worth making here. Quantum advantage in sampling is not universal. For some problem structures, a well-designed classical algorithm working sequentially will outperform a quantum approach, particularly when the overhead of encoding data into quantum states is factored in. The advantage is problem-dependent and algorithm-dependent. What quantum sampling delivers for the specific problem of drawing from complex, high-dimensional probability distributions – precisely the kind that personalised life scenario modelling requires – is a genuine and growing edge over classical methods, provided the right algorithms are developed and the data encoding problem is addressed.

Is it a crystal ball? No, but in some ways better. In your typical fairy tale, the crystal ball points to one fateful outcome. Quantum sampling yields a faster, more thorough exploration of a reality model humans and AI construct together and can follow multiple trajectories. This is not some future-shock machine hijacking your life. You provide the data. You make the decision. You control the process by deciding what to feed the simulation, or whether to do so at all. To recall an earlier point: Think of all the life data you already share with Apple, Amazon, Google, and a host of other companies. In exchange for that, you get value: Better prices, faster commutes, health measurements you'd otherwise need a doctor's appointment to get.

Quantum simulation provides value on steroids.

If you want something truly dystopian, look no further than the bank that brags about how they own you as a customer.

* * *

Quantum does not rescue a bad model; it exhausts a good one. What follows are two projections of what this architecture makes possible as each layer matures. You need not search for any bank that can deploy this today: They cannot. Some components are already available, including agentic AI that connects to live data. Classical simulation that runs meaningful scenario sets is also deployable now. The world model layer, the learnt physics engine of a person's financial and life circumstances, is the most forward-looking of the three. Research is active and well-funded, with LeCun's AMI Labs raising more than $1 billion in 2025 to pursue this exact architecture.

The timeline for production-grade financial world models is five to seven years out, further than the quantum sampling layer it feeds. And full-complexity personalised life simulation at the scale I will describe requires fault-tolerant quantum hardware, itself two to four years from reliable production deployment. In the meantime, the vision determines whether you build the right foundation now. The next chapter will offer a precise assessment of each component's current state and what starting now actually means in practice.

The architecture is easier to understand through a person than a diagram. In the next chapter you'll be introduced to Clyde and Amara, and through their respective situations, see what this combination actually delivers.

Questions for Your Board

1. If we see quantum computing as a valuable tool, what issues and possibilities do we want to explore right now as the technology matures?
2. Does the political environment in our bank tend towards embracing the future, wait-and-see, or death by committee? Do the opportunities presented by quantum simulation seem enticing enough for us to shift attitudes and rally internal support? Why or why not?
3. What questions about quantum simulation do we still have after reading this chapter? How might we educate ourselves vis-a-vis ongoing developments?

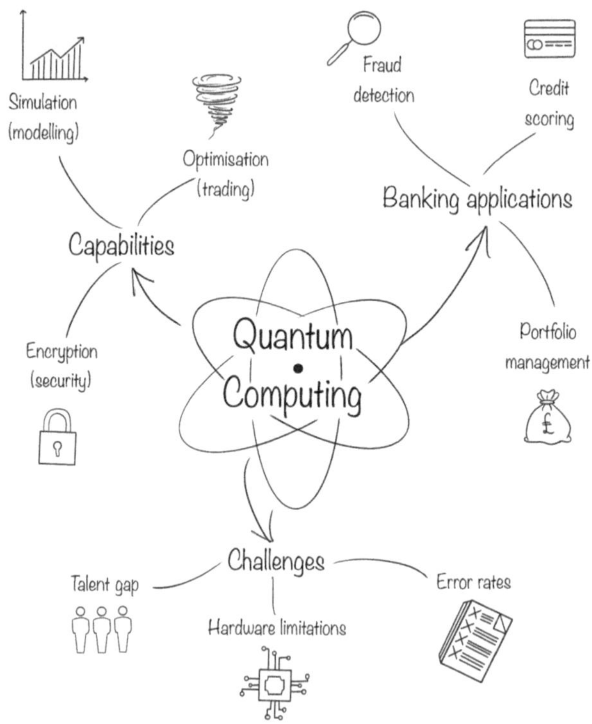

9

Clyde and Amara: Two Scenarios, Two Platform Bank Success Stories

9.1 Life of Clyde: Layers and Layers and Layers

It is a Tuesday evening. Clyde opens his laptop and types the question that has been nagging him for months: 'Am I on track?' That question, though simple on the surface, contains multitudes. He and his wife Sarah have two sons, Jeremy (22) and Neville (19). His father, now in his late 70s, has a diagnosis of early onset dementia. Clyde works in a senior role at a professional services firm and earns well, but his financial life has accumulated the kind of layered complexity that a successful career and adult family responsibilities produce over time. To understand what answering that question actually requires, consider what Clyde is carrying. His finances alone comprise:

- a current account with savings at his main bank,
- a second current account at another bank opened for business purposes years ago but never closed,
- a stocks and shares ISA and a cash ISA,
- a pension from his current employer and an older pension from a previous employer he has not consolidated,
- three fixed-term deposits at competitive rates maturing at different points in the next 18 months,
- a buy-to-let property with a mortgage and its own account,
- a car loan with two years remaining,
- two credit cards,

D. Mistry, L. R. Carlozo, *The Intelligent Ledger*,
https://doi.org/10.1007/978-3-032-32842-7_9

- home buildings and contents insurance,
- a separate health insurance policy,
- car insurance, and pet insurance for the family dog,
- three buy-now-pay-later balances his youngest opened and he is guarantor for, and
- a side hustle as an occasional emcee on a sports podcast, though this has yet to produce any income.

His financial layer alone has 23 distinct data points, each with its own rate, maturity, balance, and trajectory.

His health picture is equally layered. Clyde wears a fitness tracker that shows a consistent pattern: His resting heart rate variability, a reliable indicator of stress and recovery, drops sharply on days he has long commutes into a congested city centre. His body mass index sits in the borderline range and has slowly trended upward for three years. His blood pressure is mildly elevated. His sleep data shows poor quality sleep at least three nights a week, correlating strongly with the days following evening client entertainment. His exercise frequency has dropped from five sessions a week two years ago to two. None of these are crisis indicators. Together, across a ten-year projection, this reveals a health trajectory with meaningful implications for his insurance costs, the ability to sustain his current work pace, and ultimately the retirement timeline he plans around.

His environmental picture adds further variables. His Victorian terrace home sits within 400 metres of a river. The Environment Agency's flood risk data shows a one-in-50-year flood probability for his postcode, rising to one-in-30 under current climate trajectory models over the next 50 years. This impacts his building's insurance premium, long-term property value, and viability of the solar panels he may install. The south-facing roof makes him an ideal candidate and energy consumption data from his smart metre shows above-average heating and lighting costs that solar generation would materially reduce. His car usage data shows a 45-minute average commute each way, predominantly in heavy congestion. Stress correlations in his health data trace directly to those commute patterns.

Clyde's social layer reveals patterns his bank has never seen. He and Sarah regularly spend Friday evenings at a wine bar near the office; the transaction data shows consistent above-average alcohol spend two to three evenings per week, correlating with his late office days. Combined with the poor diet indicators from his food delivery spend pattern and the health data, this creates a social and lifestyle variable that a health coach would flag immediately: The lifestyle pattern, though sustainable in the short term, compounds the health trajectory risk over a 5–10-year horizon. His social data also shows that Jeremy graduated 18 months ago with a degree in graphic arts, a sector with significant AI displacement exposure, and currently rents in London. Neville is mid-degree in media relations, a field with similar structural uncertainty; he lives at home to save on costs. Though in the early stages of financial independence, neither has arrived there yet.

Then there is the emotional and cognitive layer. Clyde's platform interaction data shows that he checks his finances most frequently between 11 at night and midnight, resulting in a late-evening anxiety pattern his spreadsheet cannot resolve. His decision patterns tend towards inaction or procrastination on complex decisions—pension consolidation has been on his list for two years, solar panel installation for 18 months. The buy-to-let mortgage comes up for renewal in four months and he has not yet decided whether to fix or stay variable.

Clyde is neither financially unsophisticated nor neurotic. His cognitive overload stems from the real complexity of his situation; no bank tool he can access will sort it out.

9.1.1 What Every Existing System Tells Clyde

Clyde's bank sees his current account, ISA and mortgage, his income and spending. Its financial planning tool compares him to customers in similar income brackets and identifies him as broadly on track for retirement. It recommends he increase his ISA contributions and offers a risk questionnaire. But it knows nothing about the pension from his previous employer or his fixed-term deposits, buy-to-let income and associated mortgage. They likewise have not a clue about the BNPL balances he acts as guarantor for, his health trajectory, flood risk, commute stress, evening lifestyle pattern, children's employment uncertainty or the orientation of his father's care. The bank's advice – gleaned from a mere fragment of his life – gets presented to him as a 'plan'.

Clyde's financial adviser Angie has a better picture as Clyde has painstakingly compiled his financial data and brought it to their meeting. The adviser sees the complete financial layer. But she knows nothing of his health trajectory or what it implies for his insurance costs in five years. Or his flood risk and how it might impact long-term property valuation. Or his lifestyle pattern. Or stress indicators.

We should not blame Angie for these knowledge gaps; in this aspect she joins every adviser in the UK. She also gives Clyde solid financial advice based on the numbers in front of her. But she is not a tax adviser – even though she knows a lot about tax – so often Clyde must seek further advice from an accountant. When Clyde asks Angie what happens if his father needs full residential care in maybe two years, she works through that carefully.

But other considerations weigh on him and his financial wellness.

Clyde asks: 'What if one of my children also needs financial support in the same period?' Angie works through that, too. Ah, but what if interest rates stay elevated and the buy-to-let yield compresses? She's hardly the impatient type – they've worked together for more than a decade – but Angie has hit the limit of what any human can process simultaneously. She gives Clyde her best professional judgement: informed, sound, and well-intentioned.

But she cannot present a simulation. Nor could any financial adviser working alone, with the information and time available to them.

Angie's estimate, considered as it is, presents an incomplete picture—a mere snapshot. Her client needs a moving picture, 'The Life of Clyde', with many different endings. And this task requires far more data, complete consideration of life variables that directly and indirectly reflect finance, the ability to fully calculate their interdependence, and the capacity to project alternate and probable futures: producing peerless actionable advice in the process.

Angie realises this even though she does not voice it. She begins to sense that Clyde needs not one expert but many, all working in lockstep from the same complete picture of his life. She knows a thing or two about quantum and believes that in some digital future, a superpowered financial adviser could gather all 23 of Clyde's financial data points and calculate their interactions.

Clyde needs other wranglers in his digi-posse, each with a unique role in producing the clearest financial rendering of any human being in history, including:

- a health and wellness coach who understands how his current trajectory would impact his work capacity, insurance costs and his retirement readiness.
- a tax planner who can access every account, maturity date, and income stream simultaneously.
- an energy expert who can model whether solar panels make sense given his consumption pattern, roof orientation, flood risk, and 15-year energy price trajectory.
- a risk manager who understands how his flood exposure, health trajectory, and concentrated employment risk interact.
- a life planner who can hold his father's care timeline, children's financial dependency arc, and retirement ambition to construct a single coherent model.

(An optional career coach would also urge Clyde to give up the zero-income podcast gig, as he's a frustrated comic who only succeeds in annoying the podcast hosts and guests. No quantum needed for that.)

* * *

Twenty-three data points. A half-dozen first-class advisers of every stripe and type. No human being has ever had access to all of these inputs and experts simultaneously, working from the same complete data sets, reasoning together rather than in silos. The wealthy leverage approximate versions of this but separately. Nobody, at any price, has integrated them all.

But what stands today as beyond reach and affordability will come soon to a Platform near you.

Specifically, a platform bank with a complete digital twin, AI and quantum simulation closes the gap between science fiction and financial science fact. What's not on that checklist? A bank. Or even a better bank.

For the first time in history, an ordinary person can look forward to accessing a resource that exceeds what the wealthiest people currently pay for. Integration makes it valuable and possible. It does what technology and humans cannot.

9.1.2 Future Clyde: What Quantum Simulation Tells Him

2030. Clyde's 'bank' is a platform with a complete digital twin and six data layers, assembled and continuously updated by agentic AI. The platform holds these full pictures:

- **financial:** every balance, rate, maturity date, income stream, insurance policy, and BNPL commitment,
- **health:** fitness tracker data that includes HRV patterns, sleep quality, blood pressure trend, declining exercise frequency,
- **environmental:** flood risk trajectory, smart metre consumption, commute pattern and stress correlations,
- **social patterns:** evening spend, lifestyle indicators, children's employment sector exposure, his father's age and health trajectory, and
- **cognitive and emotional:** the anxious late-night check-ins, decision paralysis pattern, two-year-old consolidation task that has not moved.

Even a skyscraper full of superstar advisers trying to tie this all together would succumb to cognitive overload. But not this platform.

To expand on the movie analogy above, this is Life of Clyde in 3-D – only not a snapshot but a living model, continuously updated.

That is, once Clyde decides to give it a go and share his data. Jeremy and Neville do not get it; they think it's creepy to give up all that personal info. Sarah shows cautious optimism; she'd welcome anything that keeps Clyde from pacing the floor past midnight. Angie asks for a report back; she's curious about the technology and how she could adapt her practice to use it.

Only Horace, Clyde's banker, discourages him. 'What they're promising you is a load of rubbish. Leave the money to us and forget about that fitness tracker drivel, we'll issue you a credit card to buy a better one.'

That's what Horace says. Here's what he thinks:

'But I own him'

Off to the next sales meeting, Horace feels a knot form in his stomach.

On his laptop, Clyde feels hope as he connects to the platform.

* * *

Clyde opens the platform on a Tuesday evening, the time his financial anxiety peaks, according to his data. He asks one question: 'Am I on track?'

What happens next is not a prediction. Not an approximation.

The platform contains a world model of Clyde's circumstances: a learnt representation of how his specific financial variables, health indicators, environmental risks, and family dynamics interact, and the broader forces that shape them. This includes: interest rate movements, care cost inflation, employment market conditions, energy price trajectories. This world model is not a rules set written by a financial planner. *It exists as an emergent structure learnt from data that encodes the actual causal relationships in Clyde's world.*

Into that world model, the platform throws agents, autonomous explorers that each follow a different path through his possible future. They make decisions, encounter events, learn what matters, operate 100 times in parallel and distill what works. Each agent becomes one version of Clyde's future, explored in full. Quantum sampling then accomplishes what classical methods cannot match at this scale; it draws efficiently from the distribution of outcomes across all those agent runs. It identifies the most probable scenarios, most consequential interactions, and best decisions that most frequently separate good outcomes from difficult ones.

What emerges is not a single prediction but a map. The platform does not compare Clyde to customers in similar income brackets. It runs 10,000 specific simulations of his future – *and his alone* – computed from his exact numbers, under 10,000 different combinations of assumptions about interest rates, property values, care costs, future health, employment scenarios for his children, energy prices, and flood risk.

Within seconds, it shows Clyde a distribution of outcomes. 'Under the most likely range of scenarios, your financial position will look like this at 62,' his stated ambition for retirement. 'Here are where things work comfortably—and where they're tight.' And the compound variable that most frequently causes the tight scenarios does not involve his pension, which is healthier than he thinks. The combination of the buy-to-let mortgage renewal decision in four months and fixed-term deposit maturities in months seven and 11 causes more concern. In 43% of the tight scenarios, executing those two moves within a six-month window creates a liquidity constraint easily avoided with the right timing.

Clyde did not know to look for that interaction. The platform found it because it ran thousands of simultaneous simulations across all variables at once.

He begins to relax a bit and asks a second question: 'What if my father needs residential care starting in 18 months?' The simulations re-run and incorporate the care cost range: not a single assumption but a probability distribution built from actual care cost data in his father's region and information on his current health indicators. The platform shows how the outcome distribution shifts. It identifies that the pension from his previous employer – the one he has meant to consolidate for two years – provides the optimal buffer asset for this scenario. If Clyde consolidates it now, before the care scenario potentially materialises, it improves his outcomes in 67% of care-cost scenarios and at negligible cost in scenarios where care is not needed. Clyde now has a specific reason to jump on this task he let languish for two years. Not from guilt or waking up in a cold sweat. Quite the opposite: Clyde is empowered with the clarity that comes from quantification, drawn from his actual numbers.

* * *

Digging into some salty Chinese takeaway and a Newcastle Brown Ale (he has not eaten a home-cooked meal in a week), Clyde adds a third condition: 'What if my health trajectory continues on its current path?'

The platform draws on the health layer. His BMI trend, elevated blood pressure, lower exercise frequency and higher alcohol spend imply a statistically meaningful health insurance premium hike at his next renewal. The platform also reveals a moderate but non-trivial probability increase that a health event would impair his ability to sustain his current income trajectory in his late 50s. *The platform does not make a medical diagnosis.* Rather, it shows Clyde the financial consequence of two health scenarios: a current path continued versus a modest lifestyle adjustment that his health data suggests he can achieve, expressed as a difference in retirement outcomes across the full simulation distribution. The difference is not trivial.

For the first time, Clyde sees what his Tuesday evening bar habit costs him in retirement years, expressed in actual numbers, not a generalised health warning. It treats physical health as a function of financial health.

* * *

Then Clyde asks the question no system has ever answered properly. It forms on his lips with trepidation and a touch of sadness: 'What happens to Sarah and the children if something happens to me?' It's a scary thought but he's beginning to trust that the platform can wrap data-driven reassurance around it.

The platform runs the simulations without Clyde's income, active management of the financial complexity or existing policies, debts, and assets as they currently stand. It shows Sarah the actual picture and which decisions Clyde could make now that would most improve the family's resilience across the widest range of scenarios: the insurance gap, pension nomination, and solar panel decision that would reduce the household energy bill independently of his income.

This may sound morbid. In fact, every responsible person with a financially complex household – and the loved ones who depend on them – should ask Clyde's question and arrive at a definitive answer. Almost nobody can, though. Even if they take up the subject with clear-eyed courage, no instrument exists that holds the full picture and can run the simulation. Until now.

9.1.3 Clyde's Platform Makes the Moat of It

Thanks to a quantum simulation platform, Clyde has seen his actual future, in its actual complexity, with his actual numbers, simultaneously across all six layers of his life:

- It found the mortgage and deposit sequencing interaction he did not know to look for.
- It gave him a specific, quantified reason to complete the pension consolidation he'd stalled on for two years.
- It showed him the retirement cost of his current health trajectory in his own numbers.

- It answered his poignant question about how to best provide for Sarah and the children in the event something happened to him.

And it accomplished all this in less time than it took you to read those four bullet points. Without a spreadsheet. Or a team of professionals and specialists. If you could experience something like what Clyde just did – your own numbers, your own life, your own uncertainties held in full and resolved in seconds – would you ever leave that platform behind?

Think carefully about what leaving means. It means losing the complete digital twin fashioned from your life: years of data, simulation history, and advice that proved accurate, a living model of your world that no competitor can reconstruct quickly. Switching to another platform is not an afternoon's admin. It means reconstructing the most comprehensive intelligence anyone has ever applied to your specific life, across all six dimensions of it, from scratch.

Nobody does that voluntarily. And any incentive to switch has all the value of a basket of lollies at the bank branch door.

This is the platform moat. This is why first movers win.

Quantum simulation is not a premium feature for platform banking but the capability that makes the customer relationship permanent. World model architecture makes all of this possible and benefits platform banks that build intelligence rather than merely deploy it.

* * *

9.1.4 Meet Amara, Stretched but Intent

Many readers will recognise Clyde's situation as close to their own. But the case for quantum simulation is not only about managing complexity in a life that has assets but also one that has almost none. Meet Amara, 34, a single parent with two school-age children who works in retail part-time because the hours fit around school pick-up. Her monthly gross income after tax is £1,340 and rent takes £780: 58% of what she has to work with. (Many financial experts recommend a threshold of 30%.) The rest covers everything else. She has £90 in a current account that she tries never to let fall below zero (it is not always possible) and £60 in a savings account she has not added to in eight months.

But Amara is not financially reckless. She is stretched in the same way as roughly a third of the UK population, not in crisis but with no room for error. She makes dozens of financial decisions every week, each consequential, none informed by anything more sophisticated than mental arithmetic and her knowledge of how past money moves worked out.

This evening, Amara must determine whether to run the heating for an extra hour. The mental calculation is complex, more than the unit cost of gas at her current tariff and multiplied by the boiler output rate. To complicate matters, her youngest has had a cough for three days and cold homes worsen respiratory illness. That risks a GP appointment, which risks time off work, which risks her hourly pay. She also wonders whether to take the bus to the discount supermarket two miles away or do the usual shop at the nearby store. The basket savings might be £2, but the return bus fare is £2.40. Unless she walks, which will take 35 minutes each way in the night rain. Three of her coupons expire Sunday and she does not know whether any apply to items she needs this week. Something also nags at her about a government scheme that gives you extra money for saving. But she cannot remember its name or whether she qualifies, and she will not have the time or energy to look it up tonight after she puts her children to bed.

A platform bank with complete six-layer data could do as much for Amara as Clyde—or more, arguably, since her acute needs are greater. Her digital twin knows her income, tenancy, energy tariff and current prepayment metre status. It points to powerful knowledge: Switching to a smart metre would remove her prepayment premium, which would save her about £180 a year. It also grasps her benefit eligibility and that she qualifies for the Help to Save government scheme that offers a 50% bonus on savings of up to £50 a month. That's free money she has never claimed. The digital twin also recognises her children's ages and school status, and that she qualifies for 15 hours of free childcare she does not currently access.

That's not all. The twin knows her local bus routes and fares, regular shopping basket, and the three supermarkets within practical reach with their current prices. It knows that her youngest has had three GP visits for respiratory illness in the past 18 months, a pattern visible in her connected health data, and that cold home exposure most likely contributes to it. What the platform does for Amara as it finds unclaimed benefits, checks coupon value and compares supermarket options, stems from agentic AI and good data integration. Quantum simulation has not yet entered the picture; her problems are solvable with today's classical systems.

Quantum simulation contributes by framing decisions that involve multiple and simultaneous interacting probabilities. The heating question does not stop with a cost calculation; it must incorporate probability distribution over health outcomes, work attendance risk, and downstream costs—all correlated and running in parallel. The platform runs thousands of simultaneous scenarios across these interacting variables.

The platform does not tell Amara to turn the heating on or off, the definitive yes-no, one-zero paradigm of today's computers. Instead, it models a range of scenarios and tells her that an extra hour of heating tonight costs 63p and reduces the probability of a GP visit this week by a meaningful margin given her son's history. And so the simulation presents her with a nuanced answer in service of a smart decision. That is, the total expected cost including health risk is lower with the heating on than off.

Meanwhile, it has also:

- looked up Help to Save, confirmed she qualifies and drafted an application awaiting her approval.
- checked this Sunday's coupons against her usual basket and found that two of the three apply, and that the net saving including the bus fare is 40p in favour of the local store this week. But next week when the fresh offers change, the discount supermarket trip becomes worth making.
- modelled the impact on her monthly outgoings across three available fixed tariffs and the variable alternative, under different scenarios for wholesale energy prices over the next 12 months. It has identified the tariff that minimises her expected cost with the least downside risk given her budget.

Amara does not yet know she needs to make this decision, or others. By modelling her complete financial picture forward 18 months, the simulation has found:

- she is not currently claiming Council Tax Reduction, for which she is eligible, worth approximately £340 per year.
- her employer offers a Cycle to Work scheme she has never used, and that a basic commuter bike would pay back its cost in bus fares within seven months, with net annual savings of £180 thereafter.
- she has a realistic path to £400 in savings that would give her a genuine emergency buffer. *It does not tell her to spend less on things she has already cut to the bone.* Instead, it recommends that Amara recover money lost to things she does not know about: unclaimed benefits, prepayment premiums, the wrong tariff, the missed childcare entitlement.

The platform has given Amara a manageable weekly plan that will produce approximately £1,200 in lower costs and bankable savings.

That is not a simulation of a hypothetical future. The money already belongs to her, unclaimed and invisible, because no single institution has ever possessed enough of her data or information to match her unique situation to financial programs.

Clyde's problem is complexity, Amara's invisibility. Quantum simulation solves both, because both require the ability to hold an entire life in view and find the interactions that no human, working with partial information and limited time, could find alone. The private banker does this for Clyde's equivalent today, but the work is manual, expensive, and available only to wealthy clients who can afford sustained professional attention.

Platform banking with quantum simulation does it for Amara, making it far more inclusive. Does it yield incremental improvements in financial services? No. For customers like Amara, who have never had access to anything remotely like personalised financial guidance, the impact could be substantial. Arguably the most democratising development in retail financial services, since ATMs made banking accessible outside branch hours. Yes, there is always the chance the first companies to build it out will charge a massive premium. The earliest adopters of any new technology (digital recording and editing, for example) will pay a hefty price tag because it gives them front-of-line access to a revolutionary tool that works like nothing before it.

But once the technology becomes more widespread, potent, and cheaper, the marketplace (or even a government agency or financial wellness non-profit) will make quantum simulation via the platform available to all. The historical pattern suggests this trajectory is likely. The price tag part already has, in past generations. That PC I bought in the 1980s? The one that cost the equivalent of £9,000? Today, you can far, far, far outperform it with a £45 Chromebook.

Clyde, Amara, or anyone experiencing some form of financial struggle, psychological or practical, offer flesh-and-blood proof why this technology matters beyond its commercial logic. Every bank's annual report promises to improve customers' financial lives. Thumb through the pages and you'll find buzzwords, sales stats, staged photos of smart-looking men and women huddled around computers with looks of engaged interest. This I know: Quantum simulation is more real than they are. Those carefree climbers do not resemble Clyde, Amara, or most likely you. Our problems are real, too. And for the first time, technology exists to deliver the answers we so seriously need.

* * *

9.2 Quantum Computing's Current State: An Honest Assessment

9.2.1 Where Are We Now?

Clyde and Amara's experiences are grounded in technology that exists today in prototype form and will reach banking production scale within the window this book describes. But before the implementation roadmap, an honest account of where quantum computing actually stands, because the gap between what the technology promises and what it can deliver today is the gap that separates confident investment from expensive disappointment.

Everything described in the Clyde and Amara sections is real in the sense that the architecture exists and the logic is sound. What this book now addresses is the honest question: How far away is this, and what can a bank actually do with quantum today?

It's important not to oversell quantum computing. That has already happened and damaged perceptions in the process. A wave of quantum hype in 2018 and 2019 left many business leaders sceptical after immediate breakthroughs did not materialise. I understand this. Why is a computational marvel capable of going so fast developing so slow? We live in a world that hates to wait for anything, and those in banking already have secure profit margins not under immediate threat. The logic follows mass thinking on climate change in 'red state' America: 'If I cannot see, feel, or detect it, what's there to worry about? Those forecasts are overblown.'

But to conclude that quantum computing bears no relevance to banking strategy is wrong. Here is where things actually stand.

You can access quantum computers in the cloud; you need not build one. You access it via an API, pay per use, and run algorithms on rapidly improving hardware. The machines available today are described as Noisy Intermediate-Scale Quantum devices (NISQ) devices—true quantum computers with true quantum capabilities but also imperfect. Qubits in current machines are fragile; the usable numbers range from dozens to approximately 1,120 on the largest machines depending on the provider, and not all can be used simultaneously for complex calculations because of error rates.

What this means practically is that the full, complex, personalised life simulation I described – with 10,000 simultaneous scenarios for millions of customers, incorporating all six data layers, in real time – lies beyond the reach of what the current hardware can deliver at production scale today. I want to be clear about that. Current quantum computers can solve simplified versions of these problems: optimisation problems with dozens or hundreds of variables that include portfolio optimisation, risk modelling, and scenario generation at reduced complexity. These useful capabilities already outpower what classical systems can do. Google has demonstrated quantum supremacy on specific tasks, proving the fundamental principle works by performing calculations 13,000 times faster than the best classical algorithms on top of supercomputers. But the full vision of quantum simulation that will unfold over this decade is not fully available today.

9.2.2 Trajectory Does Not Undermine the Argument

Quantum computing's improvement trajectory is steep and well documented. IBM's publicly available quantum roadmap shows progression from today's NISQ era towards fault-tolerant quantum computers. Machines that correct errors in real time with the full theoretical power of quantum computation are projected to come on line within this decade. In June 2025 the company predicted (or bragged):

> *'By 2029, we will deliver IBM Quantum Starling—a large-scale, fault-tolerant quantum computer capable of running quantum circuits comprising 100 million quantum gates on 200 logical qubits.* We are building this system at our historic facility in Poughkeepsie, New York.'

The existing gap between current capability and full personalised life simulation is closing quickly. Partial quantum simulation is already valuable and even if today's hardware can run 100 rather than 10,000 personalised scenarios, that still surpasses the classical alternative of working through one or two by hand (let alone my spreadsheet method).

The right analogy here recalls early internet banking. In 1999, when I built the UK's first mobile banking application, it was limited, with slow connections, basic functionality. But it still outclassed the alternative and provided the model that everyone eventually had to adopt. Banks that treated the limitations of 1999 as an excuse to sit tight scrambled to catch up by 2005. The same dynamic will play out with quantum simulation.

9.2.3 Waiting For Maturity Is Fateful Strategy

Waiting for quantum to mature before building is the wrong strategy, and here's why. A quantum simulation's value in banking (or what banking will become) transcends computational firepower. It gives unprecedented potency to once-disconnected data. It cements the customer relationship. It provides simulation history. A bank that starts to run quantum-assisted scenario planning for customers in 2027 with today's imperfect hardware may get flawed simulations. But it will also break ground on building a digital twin of those customers. And accumulate a track record of predictions made and outcomes that followed.

It will earn trust. And as for loyalty, it will establish a relationship that makes switching platforms effectively impossible for most customers in most circumstances. By the time quantum hardware reaches its full capability in 2030 or 2031, the banks that started in 2027 will have three or four years of customer data, simulation history, and trust that their 2029 competitors simply cannot buy. You do not wait to build a relationship until you find perfection. You build the relationship while you improve.

The cost argument often gets overlooked as well. Early adopters of quantum cloud services get access at a relatively modest cost because the market is still developing. As IBM, Amazon, Google, and Microsoft compete for enterprise customers, they offer favourable terms. As quantum computing matures and its value becomes undeniable, these costs will rise. Banks that establish their quantum partnerships and build their technical expertise will lock in advantages in capability, cost, and institutional learning that will leave later movers to pay exorbitant prices.

This same dynamic applies with cloud computing. Banks that adopted it in 2015 are not just technically ahead of those that moved in 2022. They paid significantly less for the same capability over time and today own organisational knowledge gained from years of production experience. Those who leaned on years of evaluation sacrificed this golden opportunity.

* * *

9.3 Banking Applications, Specific and Practical

9.3.1 Life Scenario Simulation: The Core Application

In our quantum simulation scenarios, Clyde and Amara benefited from personalised, multi-variable, simultaneous life scenario modelling. Every major life move, property purchase, career change, family expansion, retirement plan, and aging parent scenario involves dozens of interacting variables with uncertain outcomes. Quantum simulation explores those interactions comprehensively and at life speed. When embedded in a platform bank's customer experience, it enables a quality of guidance no classical systems can provide.

9.3.2 Portfolio Optimisation at Scale

With the second major application – portfolio optimisation – quantum computing is already demonstrating genuine experimental promise. Traditional portfolio optimisation is a well-understood mathematical problem but computationally expensive when the portfolio involves many assets with complex correlations. Today's algorithms solve it approximately and work well for simple portfolios but show constraint as complexity grows. Quantum algorithms – specifically the quantum approximate optimisation algorithm and its variants – can explore the solution space more completely. Goldman Sachs, JPMorgan, and BBVA have published results from early-stage quantum experiments that document potential advantages in simplified portfolio scenarios.

In late 2025 the front widened. HSBC, working with IBM, presented data showing quantum-enhanced models improving predictions in corporate bond trading. Vanguard, also working with IBM, ran algorithms for portfolio construction under real-world constraints: exactly the multi-constraint optimisation that classical solvers handle badly at scale. JPMorgan went further in May 2025, joining Quantinuum, Argonne National Laboratory, Oak Ridge and the University of Texas at Austin to demonstrate quantum speedup using a quantum approximate optimization algorithm (QAOA) on problems spanning financial modelling, logistics and materials science. These are not innovation-team curiosities. They are named institutions, named partners, named results. IBM's own framing is now that 'quantum advantage' (a quantum computer running a calculation more accurately, cheaply or efficiently than a classical computer) should arrive by the end of 2026.

These do not yet exist as production deployments on full operational portfolios. The teams that run these experiments are in most cases research and innovation groups rather than the credit risk or portfolio management desks that oversee the real books. The honest assessment is that current quantum hardware delivers advantage on small, well-structured portfolios, but that advantage becomes harder to sustain as qubit requirements scale.

Further, portfolio optimisation is only as good as the hypothesis it optimises against. If a model assumes the tech stocks Nvidia and AMD move together and that correlation breaks, quantum solves the wrong model faster. Quantum's value does not stem from rescuing flawed correlation assumptions but from exhausting good ones more completely than today's methods.

For platform banking, the direction of travel is clear even if the production timeline unfolds in years rather than months. Quantum-assisted optimisation across all asset classes simultaneously, given a customer's specific tax situation, time horizons, and life event probabilities, marks a qualitative improvement compared to what's possible in banks today.

9.3.3 Risk Assessment That Sees Around Corners

Risk assessment represents the third major application, specifically the kind that matters most for platform banking: life risk rather than just credit risk. Classical credit risk models do a good job at assessing the probability that a customer will default on a loan based on their financial history and current circumstances. But it labours under a backward-looking, narrow model. A quantum risk model works in reverse. It can simulate forward movement across all six data layers, and identify risks not yet materialised but visible in the data pattern. A customer whose health data shows increasing stress markers, whose social data shows reduced engagement, whose spending patterns show early signs of financial pressure, and whose work calendar shows increasing conflict, faces an elevated risk of financial difficulty, even if they boast a currently excellent credit score. Think about them. Credit scores reflect the past via a limited financial dimension. Quantum simulation looks ahead and digests all the dimensions the data will reveal.

Classical systems cannot see this pattern because they lack the data and the ability to process the interactions at the required scale. Quantum simulation, working from a complete digital twin, can see the pattern and prompt proactive, pre-emptive intervention rather than wait for the problem to arrive.

9.3.4 Product Personalisation That Goes Beyond Segmentation

Product pricing and structural innovation – the ability to create actually personalised financial products rather than those selected from a menu – marks the fourth application. Today's banks offer mortgage products in categories: two-year fixed, five-year fixed, variable, and tracker. The categories exist because creating personalised pricing for every customer at present is computationally impractical. Quantum simulation changes this. If you can model a customer's complete financial life across thousands of scenarios, you can price a mortgage specifically for that customer's risk profile, expected life events, asset base and income trajectory. You can structure the product itself around the customer's actual situation rather than the nearest available category. This appears at a level that makes current 'personalised' banking look like mass-market segmentation with a friendlier interface.

These four applications: Life simulation, portfolio optimisation, risk assessment, and product personalisation, represent the quantum banking roadmap. This book sets out the sequence in which to build towards it.

* * *

9.4 What Banks Need to Do, and When

9.4.1 A Practical, Ideal Starting Point

You do not have to build quantum computers, hire quantum physicists, or wait for perfect hardware to begin the quantum banking journey. Instead, engage with existing quantum cloud services and run their algorithms against real banking problems. Start with portfolio optimisation because quantum advantage most clearly presents itself there. Run a pilot with consenting customers. Measure the outcomes against classical systems. Gather organisational knowledge of what quantum computing can and cannot do in practice.

In parallel, start to build the digital twin infrastructure that quantum simulation requires as its input. Quantum simulation is only as good as the data it works with. A bank that starts building its six-layer digital twin now will have the data foundation in place when simulation reaches its full capability. A bank that waits on quantum maturity before it constructs the digital twin will need to start from scratch on the data side at the same time the computational side is ready. *These two investments must happen in parallel, not sequentially.*

9.4.2 The 2027–2030 Arc of Triumph

The realistic arc for a bank that starts in 2027 looks like this.

- **In the first year,** establish quantum cloud partnerships and run pilot programmes on portfolio optimisation and risk modelling.
- Begin digital twin data integration.
- Build internal quantum literacy. Not every banker needs to understand qubits, but technology leaders must grasp the capabilities and limitations well enough to make good investment decisions.

- **In year two,** expand the quantum pilot to life scenario modelling for a limited customer cohort. Though simplified relative to the full vision, they will still contain more personalisation and simultaneous performance than anything now available to ordinary people.
- Assemble the simulation history that makes the advice progressively more accurate.
- **In year three,** broaden the digital twin data coverage and quantum simulation scope as hardware capability improves.
- Embed quantum-assisted guidance into the customer experience at scale. By 2030, when fault-tolerant quantum hardware first becomes available, you'll have accumulated three years of data, customer relationships, simulation history, and organisational experience.

You have not started to use quantum computing but upgraded an already-functioning capability. That separates the first movers from everyone else.

One honest complication is worth naming directly. The boundary between what classical AI will solve and what quantum computing will need to solve is not fixed. AI capabilities are improving rapidly, and some of the simulation complexity that currently requires quantum methods may, over this decade, become tractable for advanced classical systems with sufficient compute. This creates genuine uncertainty about the precise moment when quantum advantage becomes decisive for specific banking applications. The argument for starting now does not depend on that boundary being fixed. It depends on quantum simulation being the direction of travel regardless, and on the data and relationship investment having value whether the quantum component arrives in 2028 or 2032. Banks that build digital twins and begin simulation now are investing in something valuable under either scenario.

9.4.3 The Uncomfortable Truth About Timing

A difficult paradox lies at the heart of the quantum timing question. If you sit on the sidelines until quantum computing matures and the full vision becomes deliverable at scale, expect to wait until roughly 2030 or 2031 for the most ambitious applications. But by 2030, the competitive positions will largely have been established and late entry will be very difficult. By then, first-mover banks will have established their digital twins, customer relationships, simulation histories, and platform moats. They had three years to refine their quantum models. Their customers will have accumulated years of data with the platform. Switching costs will be established. The market will have begun to consolidate.

Starting a quantum banking programme in 2030 is like opening a smartphone app store in 2013 (5 years after Apple): The technology is mature, the standards established, and the market already won. The paradox resolves when you grasp that the goal of starting in 2027 is not to deploy perfect quantum simulation. It is to track its capability as it matures and get your house in order in the meantime. Quantum hardware is improving whether you are ready for it or not. Will you be ready to deploy when the magic moment arrives?

* * *

9.5 Closing: The Question I Cannot Simulate

I still do my monthly spreadsheet. I have not yet experienced the platform bank that makes it unnecessary. But I know how it would feel and sense its value in time saved and the quality of decisions made with comprehensive, personalised, quantum-simulated guidance about my specific financial life and its uncertainties. What weighs heaviest on me is not the financial optimisation question. It's the human one. Like Clyde, I wonder how my wife and children would handle all this complexity if something happened to me.

With 40 years of intuition about these decisions, I understand the interactions between the assets. I know which things to prioritise or leave alone, which risks matter and which are noise. Did I write this down anywhere? No. It is in my head. And it would disappear.

A bank with a complete view of my financial life, powered by quantum simulation that has run scenarios against my situation for years, would leave my intuition and methodology behind in a form that the people I love could actually use.

It would know my risk tolerance not from a questionnaire, but years of observed decisions.

It would understand my priorities, not from a form I filled in, but the pattern of my choices.

It would see my complete financial picture in all its complexity.

And it could guide my family through decisions I'd otherwise leave them to make alone, in grief, with incomplete information.

Quantum simulation makes this possible to the fullest extent: not just better investment returns or a superior tax strategy, but a complete, personalised, continuously updated guidance to navigate the foundational decisions that involve uncertainty, complexity, competing priorities, and consequences that extend decades into the future.

Builder banks will graduate from fickle customers to concrete relationships. Those that lean on incremental improvements via classical computing will get left in the dust.

The Age of the Platform promises a categorically different experience for us all: not just for Clyde, navigating complexity with 40 layers of interacting variables, but also for Amara, for whom the same intelligence finds £1,200 a year she did not know was hers. That is the ***Intelligent Ledger*** in its fullest expression: a complete, living model of a financial life that provides genuine guidance through every decision that actually matters. The ones involving uncertainty, competing priorities, and consequences that extend decades into the future. The Quanvergence is what makes it possible. The platform bank is what delivers it.

* * *

Questions for Your Bank

1. In 2013, JPMorgan Chase CEO Jamie Dimon introduced 'corporate social responsibility' based on the concept of 'doing good' by promoting small business growth, affordable housing and financial health. Whether you agree or not, could you see platform banking as a viable way to improve customers' lives?
2. If your bank has 'secure profit margins not under immediate threat', what force or forces might move you to consider (and build) a Platform? How could those margins provide you with a cushion assuming you take up the challenge?
3. Be specific: What do you see as the stumbling blocks – logistical, technological, political in the bank – that would impede Platform creation?
4. Be honest: Do you think a Platform with quantum simulation capabilities is a good idea or sci-fi fantasy? If the latter, how should customers like Clyde and Amara seek the help they need?

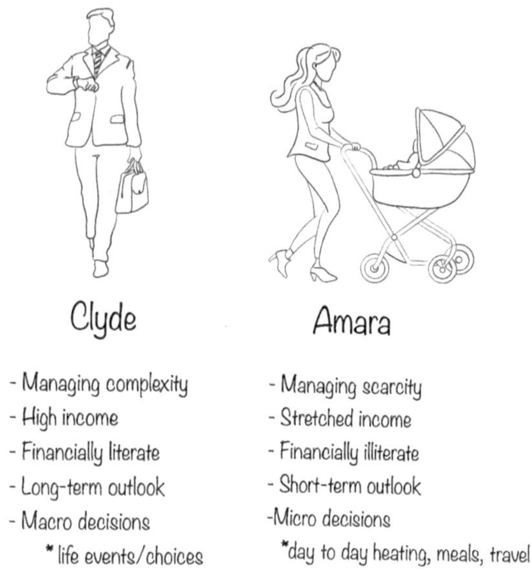
Clyde
- Managing complexity
- High income
- Financially literate
- Long-term outlook
- Macro decisions
* life events/choices
Amara
- Managing scarcity
- Stretched income
- Financially illiterate
- Short-term outlook
-Micro decisions
*day to day heating, meals, travel

10

Execution Realities and Preparation

Clyde and Amara are fictional, but the technology that serves them is not. The previous chapters have established what platform banking requires: A six-layer digital twin, quantum simulation, agentic AI, programmable money, and the strategic clarity to choose Platform over Pipe before the window closes. This chapter is where the argument becomes a programme. Not vision, not strategy: execution. The decisions made in the next 18 months will determine which side of the 2032 predictions table your bank sits on.

The evidence is in: Digital twins, quantum simulation, agentic AI, tokenisation, the six forcing functions, the binary choice between Platform and Pipe all exist as realities. If you have read this far and are a banking executive, the burning question you may have is this:

But how?

In this case, 'how' acts as a two-way sign: Protect the legacy or adopt the technology. To the first path: How does a bank that has spent decades organised around products, governed by committees, measured by quarterly margins, and staffed by people whose entire careers were built inside it, preserve the existing model?

And to the second: How does a forward-thinking bank actually transform into an entity that looks nothing like it does today?

D. Mistry, L. R. Carlozo, *The Intelligent Ledger*,
https://doi.org/10.1007/978-3-032-32842-7_10

We're not talking 'strategy' here, especially the hogwash meant to please and appease shareholders at the quarterly meeting. No. Rather, the specifics of:

- execution,
- decisions,
- sequencing,
- organisational changes (perhaps the hardest to pull off),
- traps, and
- signals that tell you whether you are on track or on rails to nowhere.

Based on my 40 years watching banks attempt to shift gears – and shepherding some of the breakthroughs – I will be honest and tough regarding the hard parts, what kills these programmes, and the difference between transformations that succeed and those announced with a press release and buried two years later in a quiet reorg. We all know what the latter looks like. Maybe you took part in such smoke and mirrors yourself. If so, clear the smoke from the boardroom. Now take a good look at yourself in the mirror. Who do you see? A spearhead or a spectator?

Not only have I erected platforms that succeeded and failed. Dave Wallace, Lou and I have interviewed more than 150 banking and fintech executives on our podcasts. Banks measure 'change' in comfy metrics: milestones, org charts, governance frameworks, and KPIs. Up in smoke, I say. Let's grab hold of a change map you can actually use.

* * *

10.1 Start With a Bracing Assessment

10.1.1 The Decision Tree Nobody Wants to Climb

Before any bank builds a platform, it must answer one question honestly: *Should we?* Not 'Can we?' in the technical sense or 'Do we want to?' in the aspirational sense, but:

> *Should we, given who we are, what we have, and what we are willing to commit?*

It might surprise you, given my strong endorsement of the Platform paradigm, to read here that not every bank should attempt such a transformation.

Some should become excellent Pipe providers and stop pretending otherwise. The decision tree has three branches. The first branch eliminates most banks immediately.

10.1.2 Branch One: Can You Genuinely Let Go of Product?

The first and most important question does not concern technology, capital, or talent. It centres on identity. A platform bank does not sell products. It owns journeys. It consolidates itself around what customers hope to accomplish in their lives, not those products the bank builds to capture margin. Everything that follows – the organisational structure, talent model, metrics, compensation, and culture – flows from this single commitment. Yet most banks lack the will to make it. I have sat in boardrooms where executives nodded enthusiastically at the journey ownership concept and then asked, in the very next breath, 'How would this increase our mortgage sales?'

That question tells you everything.

If your first instinct when someone says 'journey ownership' is to ask what it does for your product line, you lack the readiness to become a platform bank. Just because you say you have it does not mean you can or will prove it.

Lou recalls this story from the Chicago Tribune's change-or-die moment of truth:

> *'Once it was clear the internet was going to eat our newsprint lunch, the Tribune tried in vain to play catch-up ball. Some savants at the paper put their creative minds to it. I heard every manner of idea, from a foldable 'e-paper' people could read on their morning commute that would refresh itself throughout the day, to the formation of 50 or so 'digital garages' where young, web-savvy creatives could work, test-and-learn style, on novel properties to recapture our evaporating audience. A few of us, myself included, talked about building an arts-and entertainment MVP ourselves. And I worked on the first-ever digital native timeline of a world figure, Pope John Paul II, that won a Tribune Innovator Award. Overall, the conversations were exciting to hear but went nowhere. We ran into stalwarts in the C-suite who insisted that if major changes came, they'd initiate them. Better ideas? They didn't have any ideas! And they didn't have the will. They came from old-school journalism and executive MBA programs. So they gave a thumbs-up to transformation during media events at Ivy League schools and industry conferences. But they also kept their heads planted in the sand. They didn't move, though at times they directed resentment at anyone who came forward with an idea that wasn't theirs. On both the professional and personal levels, they saw transformation as a threat. They didn't pass the test. They didn't even know what the test was.'*

* * *

The test is not what leadership says in strategy sessions. You can only understand and pass it through what you measure, reward, and protect during budget cuts. If the journey and product teams fight each other for resources and the product wins because it shows clear P&L attribution – while the journey team cannot – your organisation has answered the question, even if no one states it out loud. Platform transformation requires a CEO who makes a public, irrevocable commitment to measure the bank differently. Not 'might make'. Not 'We're studying it.' And not 'We will view journey metrics alongside product metrics.' 'Alongside' protects the status quo. Journey metrics get trotted out when convenient and product metrics when it counts (literally). True commitment turns this worldview on its head. Journey metrics *replace* product metrics as the primary measure of success. If your CEO delays or defers saying that before the board and the market, you are not building a platform or even a pipe, but a pipe dream. Your expensive innovation programme will get absorbed back into the existing model when the going gets difficult. And if everyone else says 'We tried,' you have the convenient cover of mass industry denial. There is safety – or the unseen peril of the status quo – in numbers.

10.1.3 Branch Two: Do You Have or Can You Genuinely Acquire and Retain the Skills?

Platform banking requires capabilities that traditional banks lack and cannot develop through rejiggering job titles. Journey designers, who think in terms of complete customer experiences across years and multiple touchpoints and not revenue-generating products, work in a fundamentally different profession from product managers. Data scientists who construct and maintain a six-layer digital twin bear no resemblance to the analysts who run SQL queries on transaction data. Quantum algorithm specialists, agentic AI architects, MCP integration engineers: None exist in meaningful numbers inside traditional banks. The question is not whether you can hire a few of these people. It is this: Can you build an organisation where they thrive, their work is valued and resourced, and product-oriented foot soldiers do not overrule them?

To that end, banks consistently underestimate the issue of retention. You can hire excellent technical talent. But if you keep (or cage) them in a traditional banking environment with its committee governance, risk aversion, 18-month project cycles, and chain-of-command hierarchy, they will leave. The moment they feel their work is slowed, diluted, or second-guessed by people who do not understand it, they will leave your Platform aspirations to charlatans who talk a good game. Constructing a platform capability inside a traditional bank requires cultural protection, a ring fence around the team. You must respect the ways the players work and give them the authority to direct and move at the speed that platform building requires. That ring fence is extraordinarily difficult to maintain in the face of inevitable tensions, rivalries, and politics within the existing organisation. Most banks cannot do it. Watch out for the ones that can.

10.1.4 Branch Three: Let the Flywheel Spin Begin

The third question concerns momentum, a variable where many promising platform transformations fall short. A platform flywheel operates via a precise mechanism:

- valuable platform engagement generates data,
- while that data improves insight and simulation quality,
- better insights create customer dependency,
- dependency attracts third-party ecosystem partners who want access to engaged customers,
- third-party services make the platform more valuable,
- which drives more engagement,
- which generates more data.

And away we go.

Before the flywheel starts to spin, it amounts to an expensive machine that requires constant energy to turn. But once it begins, it becomes self-reinforcing and nearly impossible to stop.

What almost always kills the flywheel before it gets going? Launching a platform with a product mindset. Banks that build their so-called 'platform' but still measure success by product sales never generate the engagement data that makes simulation valuable. The stress is on the wrong syllable: They optimise for *transactions* rather than *relationships*. Every interaction designed to sell rather than guide generates less data about what the customer actually needs. Every metric that rewards product conversion rather than engagement depth incentivises the wrong behaviour. Taken to its extreme, you get unbearable pressure on your employees and even plant the seeds of scandal. In 2016, the American bank Wells Fargo was flagged for opening two million unauthorised bank and credit card accounts without customer consent to meet unrealistic sales goals. Leadership set the tone, as since-disgraced CEO John Stumpf infamously coined the cross-selling motto 'Eight is great.' No bank should hijack the headlines this way. But if they build one of the first platform banks, they could make history.

Flywheels need authentic engagement. What does that mean? Simply put, things work when customers use the platform not for purchases but for something priceless: to understand their situation, explore options, and get helpful guidance. That engagement (and encouragement) generates the data, which makes everything else possible. If your bank cannot commit to forging engagement before they extract product revenue from it, the flywheel will never spin.

Among the many things that went wrong and right with AskHomey, the most challenging issue by far was getting the wheel to spin. Decades of product development and management experience did not help me—in fact, it arguably held us back. This lesson for banks is this: Successful product delivery does not equal platform creation ability.

10.1.5 The Unvarnished Verdict

If a bank fails any one of these three tests – willingness to abandon product orientation, ability to acquire and retain the necessary skills, or commitment to engagement before extraction – any attempt at platform transformation will prove fruitless. But is this failure? Hardly, as an alternative exists: Become an excellent pipe bank. Done well, the Pipe model generates sustainable 8-to-20% margins, requires traditional bank capabilities and serves a proven market need. A disciplined bank, acting as an API-first infrastructure provider with world-class reliability, regulatory expertise, and efficient operations, can build a valuable, durable business. By contrast, a bank that half-heartedly attempts Platform or Pipe will achieve neither; it will spend the capital and management attention of a platform programme, meander in pipe territory, and retain the culture and metrics of a product bank, to its own detriment and possible demise.

* * *

10.2 The Three Transformation Killers

10.2.1 Banking Archetypes You Will Recognise

Assuming your bank has moved ahead on the decision tree and committed to platform transformation, the next hurdle will not come via technology or strategy. So what's the roadblock?

Rephrase that: *Who*?

People inside your organisation will, perhaps with the best of professional intentions, ensure your transformation fails. I've repeatedly encountered these three archetypes everywhere, in different banks, countries, and institutions of different sizes. You may recognise them immediately because every large organisation that has ever attempted significant change draws them into the light. But before you blame or scapegoat, practice vigilance. Transformation programmes almost always fail because nobody recognises these patterns early enough.

10.2.2 The Protector

The Protector is typically a senior executive, often a decade or less from retirement, who has built a career and reputation around the existing model. They do not oppose transformation in principle. In fact, Protectors say the right things in strategy meetings, ask intelligent questions, and may have even championed incremental improvements in their time. But when the transformation requires them to give up something they value – budget, authority, headcount, a product line they built, or a process they designed – they obstruct. It's quiet. Effective. Maybe even deceptive. They do not say no, they say 'not yet,' 'we need more analysis,' or 'I'm concerned about the risk to our existing customers.' They request more data, raise legitimate-sounding governance concerns, suggest pilot programmes, and lobby for working groups and steering committees. Every individual intervention sounds reasonable. But together, they decelerate the transformation to a dead stop. The Protector is particularly dangerous because their seniority gives heft and credibility to their concerns. What's more, they are often genuinely liked and respected. Confronting them directly feels like political suicide. Ignoring them is impossible.

To neutralise The Protector, ensure that the transformation programme has a clear mandate from the CEO. Make it explicit that this supersedes the Protector's authority in the areas that matter, and that the CEO will enforce it when tested, which will happen.

10.2.3 The Climber

The Climber is typically a younger, ambitious executive who has identified platform transformation as a career opportunity. Unlike the Protector, they convey genuine enthusiasm, perhaps more than the transformation programme can safely absorb. They want to move fast, make announcements, launch pilots, generate press coverage, and demonstrate impact in timeframes that build their personal profile ahead of any platform. Though in some ways the Protector's opposite, they create equally damaging problems. They over-promise to external stakeholders and create expectations that the programme cannot meet. They prioritise visible wins over foundational infrastructure, because visible wins advance careers and foundational infrastructure does not make good press releases.

They hire people who reflect well on them, or defer to them, rather than the role players the effort requires. They treat the transformation programme as a portfolio item rather than a genuine commitment, which means they will move on to the next opportunity once this one stops generating profile for them. The Climber is hardest to manage because their energy and ambition resemble what transformation programmes need. But what turns out to be a tailwind for their careers and reputation creates nothing but headwind for the effort.

Restore sanity by making The Climber's success metrics identical to the programme's. In the process, ensure that they have enough relevant authority and proper credit so as to reduce the motivation to grandstand.

10.2.4 The Passenger

The Passenger is the most numerous and, in some ways, the most insidious of the three archetypes. Neither obstructive like the Protector nor hyperactive like the Climber, they simply complete their assigned tasks, attend the meetings, produce the outputs, and go home. The expression 'swim in your own lane' was coined just for them. If depicted in a painting, Passengers would resemble the floating men wearing trench coats in René Magritte's 'Golconda'.

Passengers do not question whether the work they do is right, the approach is sound, or the programme remains on track to achieve its stated goals. They are not malicious but comfortable—and comfort is the nemesis of transformation. Transformation requires people who raise uncomfortable truths, flag the unworkable before it becomes a crisis, and challenge assumptions even when senior leadership endorse them.

The Passenger does not do this. They never do this. They complete transformation programme tasks as specified, watch the programme fall short of its goals, and move on to their next assignment without ever having said the thing that needed saying.

Put Passengers in a stimulating, non-status quo culture. Foster a team environment that expects and rewards challenges, rejects comfortable silence, and treats people who raise difficult questions as assets.

* * *

10.3 Getting Budget Right

10.3.1 Two Ways Transformation Budgets Die

Budgets obstruct transformation programmes in one of two ways. Too much money bloats the programme, with Climbers and consultants attracted to the prospect of a free spend. The timeline expands to fill the available resources, accountability diffuses across an ever-growing team, and the programme eventually collapses under its own weight, only producing a great deal of documentation and very little change.

Too little money and the programme bleeds slowly, with insufficient resources to build the digital twin infrastructure properly, hire needed talent, or forge ecosystem partnerships at a pace to meet competitive pressure. The programme survives quarter to quarter by cutting select corners that seem survivable but prove collectively fatal.

Drama surrounds neither failure. In fact, both are common.

The best approach in my experience combines *top-down* and *bottom-up* estimation in a specific sequence. Top-down establishes the envelope, affordability given the bank's capital position and risk appetite, and the required return on investment over the chosen timeframe. This is a CEO-CFO conversation, and it must happen before detailed planning begins, not after. Bottom-up fills the envelope with detailed estimates for each workstream, created by the people who will execute them, stress-tested against realistic rather than optimistic assumptions. The combination reveals the gap: Is the affordable envelope sufficient to build out the programme's required infrastructure? If not, honest options include moves to reduce scope, extend timeline, increase the envelope, or acknowledge that the programme lacks viability in its current form. Most banks skip this reconciliation step and proceed with an envelope that is insufficient for the scope, which guarantees a slow bleed.

Transformation programmes consistently get another budget principle wrong: The allocation between building infrastructure and buying consultants. By instinct and established practice, large organisations overspend on external consultants, particularly established names, on the theory that proven expertise reduces risk. In practice, the opposite outcome often occurs as a result.

Consultants craft recommendations, not platforms. They produce frameworks, not code. They advise on decisions but do not make them. In a programme that leans heavily on consultants, expertise leaves at the end of the engagement and the bank is left with PowerPoint decks and a partially-built system. People matter most for platform building, including:

- those who stay on when the platform goes live,
- engineers who know the architecture they built,
- journey designers who understand the customer experience they created, and
- data scientists who intimately know the models they trained.

Programme directors, rather than those in the finance function, should control a ring-fenced contingency budget reserved for true surprises, not scope creep. This is not a slush fund. It acts as insurance against occurrences bound to hit every programme that even the most gifted directors cannot foresee.

* * *

10.4 Organising for Platform: Your Journey Team

10.4.1 Why Product Teams Cannot Build Platforms

A traditional bank's organisational structure mirrors its product strategy. It has teams for mortgages, credit cards, savings, current accounts, and business banking. Each team has its own P&L, metrics, leadership, and culture. The teams compete for customers, budget, and technology resources; they optimise independently and suboptimise collectively. This structure excels at executing on its design: to manufacture financial products with efficiency and push them through distribution channels. But it cannot create a Platform that owns customer journeys, which requires coordination across every product line at once: A structure and coordination that product teams make impossible. Each fights to maximise its own metrics, which will always conflict with journey-first thinking at the moments that matter most.

At AskHomey, we organised around journeys (buying, living, and moving) rather than products, with the living journey as our primary focus. Within that, we helped homeowners with maintenance, utilities, warranties, contractors, mortgage renewal—not because we had separate teams for each. To us, they belonged to the same customer experience of living in a home. This could not contrast more sharply with how banks organise themselves. A bank's mortgage team would own the mortgage renewal event in the living journey, their utilities partnership team (if it exists at all) the utility switching event, their insurance team the home insurance event.

But who owns the journey as a whole? No one.

Nobody tracks the homeowner's experience across all of those events. The customer feels this as fragmentation and it is—structural fragmentation cemented into the organisation itself.

10.4.2 Journey Teams Up Close

A journey team coalesces around what customers want to accomplish, not the products banks want to sell them. As customers find, buy, occupy, improve, and eventually sell a home, the team tracks with them every step of the way. You might find mortgage specialists, but also:

- data scientists who understand property markets,
- journey designers who map the complete ownership experience,
- partnership managers who interact with third parties that make the journey work, and
- builders of digital twin integrations and agentic workflows that make the guidance seamless: Conveyancers, surveyors, utilities providers, contractors, insurance companies, and technology engineers.

Throw out those mortgage sales KPIs. The team's success metric is customer satisfaction with the complete home experience, as measured by engagement depth, retention, and relationship expansion over the homeownership lifetime.

Attribution constitutes the hardest part of this model. How do teams connect revenue to the journey instead of individual product sales? In a product model, that link is clean: This team sold this many mortgages at this margin. But in a journey model, attribution is diffuse: Through major life events, this journey team serves X customers and the bank earned Y total revenue from multiple products and services over a span of years.

The journey model generates significantly better economics—as the calculations in Appendix A demonstrate, but at a slower, less visible rate than the product model. *This explains why leadership must commit to the new metrics and not waver.* Otherwise, the first quarterly earnings conversation will collapse the journey model back into product thinking. This default mode has an almost irresistible allure: It reflects the language investors, analysts, and boards understand. And speak fluently. They've had more than half a century to learn it.

On 13 Sept. 1970, economist Milton Friedman fired a shot across the bow that financial services has since adopted as gospel. In his New York Times editorial, the Nobel Prize winner contended that companies must concentrate on profits first and foremost:

> *'There is one and only one social responsibility of business, to use its resources and engage in activities designed to increase its profits so long as it stays within the rules of the game, which is to say, engages in open and free competition without deception or fraud.'*

Delighted bank executives read between the lines of Friedman's manifesto and found a glorious loophole. They concluded (wink, wink) that playing 'within the rules of the game' gave them ample latitude to bend or change as many rules as possible to their liking. We know better today. (Back then, ATMs were only three years old.) 'Friedmanomics', if you will, represents short-term thinking – the kind that can deliver instant death to journey teams – because it encourages banks to *maximise* profit rather than *optimise* it. What shareholders want, they get. More mortgage sales. Cool new credit cards with higher APRs. Higher dividends. Put another way, sexy firecrackers that explode and go dark in a flash take precedence over the patient building of a banking lighthouse to lead consumers safely ashore.

Trouble is, 'increase profits' remains the *lingua franca* of sales-obsessed banks. The visionary CEO must instead master and teach their minions a different language. They must find the will to educate the market on new metrics. Most CEOs lack that courage—content to coast, to speak the buzzy dialect of product until it becomes a tongue as dead as Latin.

10.4.3 Transition Tip: You Cannot Flip a Switch

No bank can transition from product to journey teams overnight and any plan that assumes it can is a plan that will fail. Think of this as akin to switching from fossil fuel cars to electric vehicles. As much as the most ambitious environmentalist might wish it so (and it's a laudable wish), no way exists to accomplish this feat in a day, week, year or even two years. The switch requires a thoughtful plan, smart execution, and a reasonable time frame.

So it is for banks: Just because you want to switch does not mean you can flip a switch.

The effort must be phased. Start with a single journey team, properly resourced and protected from the organisation's gravitational pull. Run its developing model in parallel with the existing product structure, prove the model, and then expand it as confidence and capability grow. I recommend the home journey as an ideal starting point for retail banks (as established in Chapter 7).

How long does it take to prove the engagement model works? Give it 18 months. Make sure your newly created flywheel is starting to spin. A comprehensive, positive experience, backed up by proof of concept, creates the engagement that drives the flywheel.

Use that proof to argue for the next journey team. Ah, but practice patience. Do not try to reorganise the entire bank before you demonstrate that the model works. Remember that the journey team model implies who builds the platform and how to organise them. The technology architecture tells you what's built and in what sequence.

* * *

10.5 The Technology Architecture

10.5.1 Building the Stack, Sequence Matters

The platform bank's technology architecture has four layers, and the construction sequence matters as much as the product. Build them in the wrong order and each layer undermines the one above it; in the right order, each layer enables the next. The four layers, in order:

- data infrastructure (the digital twin foundation),
- integration and orchestration (the agentic layer that connects data to action),
- simulation capability (starting with classical optimisation and extending to quantum), and
- customer experience (the interface through which customers find all this useful).

Most banks fumble because they start with the customer experience layer: They build the app, interface, and chatbot, before the underlying infrastructure exists to support it. The result? A sophisticated interface that gives customers access to the same impoverished data and the same product-oriented advice as before. Better packaging, same contents.

Lou relates a common theme he encountered as managing editor at the Bank Administration Institute, and later as creator-host of the Bankadelic Podcast:

> *'The one phrase industry experts beat to death was 'seamless customer experience', inevitably followed by only one example: Amazon. It became such a cliche that in guest column after guest column I had to delete it; the industry experts had no idea how simplistic they sounded. But it wasn't just because they parroted a thousand other bankers. They didn't understand the 'how to do it', or if they did, they failed to explain it. Things they posited as 'seamless' were at best incremental or hocus pocus, from improved automatic bill pay to teller machines with holograms. But all the banks, including the big boys, sent out product offer emails that might as well have been addressed 'Dear Occupant'. Seamless annoyance. Delete delete delete.*
> *Only one person I ever interviewed got it right. We grabbed a quick coffee at a Money2020 conference, and he explained that no bank would crack the 'seamless customer service' code until they mined the data, gleaned the insights, anticipated needs, updated the data continuously and hence knew their customers intimately. Not dandy interfaces but data-based intimacy. His job? Amazon data scientist.'*

Questions for Your Board

1. Can we identify past examples at our bank – or even competing institutions – that might provide a playbook for building a successful journey team?
2. Can our bank let go, even to a small extent, of product-centric thinking? If not, why not? And if so, can we pinpoint the best place to start that would allow time, space and budget to make our first forays into the journey model?
3. Of the three transformation killers – Protectors, Climbers, and Passengers – which ones most often thwart our bank's forward progress? Aside from the suggestions above, can we think of ways to handle them?

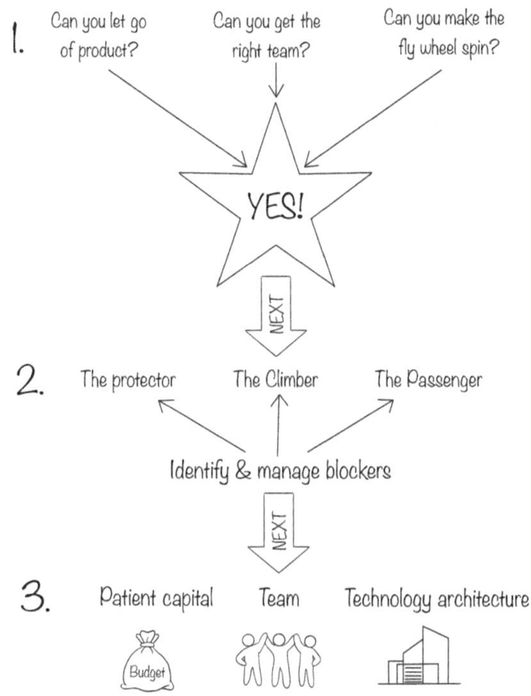
1.
Can you let go of product?
Can you get the right team?
Can you make the fly wheel spin?
YES!
NEXT
2.
The protector
The Climber
The Passenger
Identify & manage blockers
NEXT
3.
Patient capital
Team
Technology architecture
Budget

11

Building the Platform Bank

11.1 Layer 1: The Digital Twin Foundation

Chapter 10 established the decision framework, the budget logic, the team structure, and the transformation killers to watch for. It answered the question: Are we ready to begin? This chapter answers the question that follows: What, exactly, are we building, and in what sequence? The four-layer architecture described here is not a vendor checklist or a technology wishlist. It is the specific construction sequence that makes platform banking structurally possible, as well as the order in which each layer must be built so that each one enables the next rather than undermining it. Get the sequence wrong and the layers compete. Get it right, and they compound. That compounding is where the platform advantage comes from, and it begins here.

The digital twin lays the foundation for everything else, so build it both first and properly. Properly means all six data layers with authentic privacy architecture, consent management, and data governance—not as a compliance checkbox but a customer value proposition. The message to give customers about their digital twin should not be, 'Share your data and we will use it.' That's vague and not quite right. Instead, tell them, 'Share your data and you'll get exactly this in return, with complete control over what you share and how we use it, plus you can withdraw consent at any time.' Do not aspire to that latter statement: Deliver on it, every time, 100%. Privacy architecture needs to enforce it technically, not promise it in two-point type in terms and conditions statements that get universally skipped anyway.

D. Mistry, L. R. Carlozo, *The Intelligent Ledger*,
https://doi.org/10.1007/978-3-032-32842-7_11

Customers who understand and trust the value exchange will share data; we already do. Customers who feel surveilled will not. The quality of the consent design, not the data science, differentiates between the two outcomes.

Open Banking data marks a practical starting point. Banks can access this financial layer right now with customer consent under existing regulatory frameworks. This gives the team a stage of sorts to build on while the bank establishes partnerships for the other five data layers. Start simultaneous partnership conversations with the two or three data providers that matter most for your primary journey. Using the home journey example, talk to location data providers, property market data sources, and home services platforms. Once again, practice steady, forward-moving patience. These partnerships typically take six to 12 months from first conversations to live data integration. Start them in parallel with the technical build, not after it.

11.2 Layer 2: The Agentic Orchestration Layer

The agentic layer upgrades the digital twin from comprehensive to useful. An AI agent with Model Context Protocol (MCP) server access achieves many desirable goals. It can connect to the digital twin data, reason about what the customer needs, orchestrate actions across multiple third-party systems, and deliver personalised guidance, all without a human operator in the loop for routine interactions.

Note that MCP – the open-source intermediary component that acts as a secure, standardised bridge between AI models – does not just replace your API with an equivalent MCP interface. It helps you design a structure that the agent can use. The agent then handles complexity that would otherwise require a team of specialists—and a (very, very helpful) customer willing to compile their own information and schedule multiple appointments.

The technology for this layer exists today, not only with MCP servers but also agentic AI frameworks like LangChain and orchestration tools that can manage complex multi-system workflows. As for build time, you could conceivably sprint through it faster than most banks assume without a compromise in quality. A well-resourced team needs just six months to mount a working prototype and 12 months for a production-ready system that can serve a meaningful customer cohort.

Griffin Bank in the UK has already demonstrated that banking systems can connect to MCP infrastructure. With the kind of fanfare other banks use to announce free jersey giveaways, Griffin declared in May 2025 that its MCP server 'lets agents open accounts, make payments, and analyse transactions, all while maintaining proper safeguards.' The substance of this statement from their CEO, harmonises with the overarching message I've conveyed thus far:

> *'We think there is much further to go ... but to get there,* ***the financial system has to be fundamentally rewired*** *[my emphasis] to accommodate a world in which agents can freely transact, while still retaining appropriate safeguards.'*

Think about that. The challenge is not capability but governance, establishing frameworks for what agents can and cannot do autonomously, where human oversight is required, and how to monitor the system for accuracy, fairness, and compliance. You must lock these governance frameworks into place before the agent goes live. Trying to retrofit them after problems occur could wipe out your agentic efforts on the spot.

The agentic layer also requires a connection to programmable money to reach its full potential. An agent that can only recommend, however accurately or personally, still asks the customer to take an action. An agent connected to tokenised financial rails can act within *pre-approved* parameters: that is, execute transactions autonomously when predefined customer conditions are met. This means, for example, that the mortgage switch happens when the optimal rate becomes available, not when the customer remembers to check.

An agentic layer built without tokenised execution equals a co-pilot that talks but cannot fly. Governance frameworks for autonomous agent action, boundaries, approval thresholds and audit trails apply equally to recommendations and executions. Design these together, not separately. Agents that can act on behalf of customers rank as more valuable in orders of magnitude than those that can only advise. The tokenised rails that make this execution possible are being built right now, regardless of whether your platform is ready to connect to them.

11.3 Layer 3: Simulate, Start Classical, Stretch into Quantum

In Chapter 8, we established the case for quantum simulation with an honest appraisal of where the technology stands today. The practical architecture for 2027 represents a hybrid: classical optimisation for immediate deployment, pilot quantum simulation in use cases where quantum advantage is demonstrable, and a roadmap to expand quantum capability as hardware matures. Of course, we can build the classical simulation layer first, because the technology exists today. It adds value immediately and creates the infrastructure, data pipeline, scenario modelling framework and customer-facing presentation of simulation outputs that the quantum layer will run on when ready. This parallels the single brain concept I developed at Temenos. I envisioned a platform that orchestrated collaborating agents that leveraged individual AI models for risk, fraud and more. But the first implementation utilised a standard rules engine and parameterised rules. A bank that builds classical simulation infrastructure in 2027 still readies itself in a productive way for the quantum age because it will act as a foundation that quantum will enhance. The two will not compete but complement each other.

11.4 Layer 4: Customer Experience

The customer experience layer gets built last because it only functions as well as the layers beneath it. A beautifully designed interface over weak data and no simulation capability disappoints prospective customers. The same interface, undergirded by a complete digital twin and simulation engine, realises startling possibilities. Platform banking's experience design principles differ from those of product banking. The primary question is not, 'How do we make it easy to buy this product?' but '*How do we make it easy for customers to understand their situation, explore their options, and take action on the guidance we have given them?*'That shift may make the sales teams fidget.

But when it guides every design decision, magic happens.

The question is so important it bears repeating: 'How do we make it easy for customers to understand their situation, explore their options, and take action on the guidance we have given them?' The paradigm shift this produces cannot be overstated. It changes:

- the information that gets surfaced,
- how options are presented,
- what constitutes a successful interaction, and
- what the customer leaves with that they did not have before.

Journey designers (who think in terms of the complete experience over time) should lead this work, not UX designers (who evaluate how customers will react to the screen in front of them). Meanwhile, financial services is transitioning away from graphical UI design towards conversational interfaces anyway.

* * *

11.5 The Flywheel Goal: Get It Spinning, Keep It Spinning

11.5.1 The Mechanism

Banks that understand and establish a platform flywheel will distinguish themselves from those that mount infrastructure, then watch it sit idle. The flywheel has five stages that must occur in sequence.

Stage One: Genuine Engagement. Customers use the platform to understand their situation. They explore their digital twin, examine options, ask questions, and use the simulation capability to think through decisions. Using it for marketing or short-term offers distracts from and defeats these benefits.

Stage Two: Data Accumulation. Every engagement generates more data: about what the customer thinks about, information they found useful, decisions made, next occurrences. Fed back into the digital twin, the data renders a clearer picture that emerges with better personalisation and guidance. The twin grows smarter.

Stage Three: Increasing Dependency. As digital twins blossom, their guidance becomes richer. Years of data not only accumulate but differentiate. As stated earlier, competitors cannot possibly catch up. For customers, the switching cost establishes itself not as friction, but as the prospect of losing an immensely valuable guide.

Stage Four: Ecosystem Attraction. Partners with ancillary services – insurers and investment managers, for example – vie to engage the platform as well. They know invested, data-rich customers trust it enough to act on its guidance. The platform's customer engagement attracts these partners, who remain otherwise inaccessible to the bank.

Stage Five: Platform Value Multiplication. Each partner that joins the ecosystem increases the platform's value to customers. This drives more engagement, which generates more data, which improves guidance, which deepens beneficial dependency. The flywheel accelerates.

11.5.2 The Flywheel Killer: Lack of Engagement

Flywheels die at stage one if the bank fails to generate bona fide engagement. If this book repeats the sales element to a level of stridency, it's because the mentality is so entrenched in banking operations that an overwhelming number of executives can only see the world through that lens. Platform banking, in this sense, implies a 'vision' of a second kind. You will never see the tremendous opportunity and industry transition with blinders on.

The customer who opens the platform to an immediate presentation of product recommendations has experienced the same-old same-old. They've been offered nothing in the way of guidance but plenty in terms of being treated like a number, calculated in pounds and pence.

Call this a sophisticated sales funnel driven by unsophisticated thinking and better graphics. Customers looking for a truly transcendent banking experience will use it once, find it no different from their banking app and not return. Your competitor who builds the flywheel and delivers its unprecedented value will coax them instead. Customer attrition, at least, is a metric that sales-hungry bankers can attach to this. Will it compel them to reframe their thinking? Probably not—unless someone in the company (certainly not a Climber or Protector) can make the case.

The engagement that drives the flywheel appears when the customer receives valuable insight about their situation, clarity about their options, guidance that helps them make better decisions *before* any product is mentioned. That sequence – value first, product second – diametrically opposes how product banking works and why the product mindset kills the flywheel before it starts to spin. Organisations that nail the correct sequence commit to the journey model and hold fast to it. Product models always revert to product first.

11.5.3 The Ecosystem Is Not Optional

Banks that try to build the platform all by themselves set a trap for themselves. They see an ecosystem of third parties from a loss-aversion vantage point. 'Why should all those profits go to partners when they should come to our bank?' And so, they adopt a platform mentality that obsesses about owning the full stack. This is woefully invalid thinking.

Platform means *orchestrating* the full stack on behalf of the customer. No bank can excel at serving every customer need at once: from insurance and investment management to mortgage shopping and pension consolidation. The attempt to build all of this in-house yields mediocrity across the board and destroys the speed of execution that platform building requires. The ideal ecosystem partners – specialist providers who excel at each journey component – make the platform useful and desirable. The bank's roles? Own the relationship, aggregate data, provide simulation intelligence, and orchestrate the experience. The partners provide the *services* that fill the journey and add capability, not subtract profits. Banks that refuse to recognise this value exchange and disintermediate their ecosystem partners will throw up their hands as customers head to the specialists instead. By contrast, banks that make their ecosystem partners more successful will have grasped the wisdom that a rising tide floats all boats. They win, the partners prosper, and customers flock to the platform, staying there until their presence becomes permanent.

* * *

11.6 The bunq Lesson: A Look at Getting It Right from Day One

Here's the hard truth and I encourage you to prove otherwise: In Western markets, no traditional bank has fully executed the transformation this book describes. The digital twin, the quantum simulation, the complete journey ownership model: The capabilities exist. Now. Proven. Available. But one attribute cannot possibly be programmed, manufactured, or otherwise fabricated: Successful deployment.

That noted, examples exist of banks that shed legacy thinking from day one and organised themselves in a way that makes platform transformation achievable, even if they have yet to complete the journey. Europe's clearest example is bunq (spelt with a small b).

What makes bunq special? To find out, let's start at the start. Ali Niknam founded bunq in Amsterdam in 2012. It was not easy. The fresh-faced Niknam – who resembles a fashion model with his short dark brown hair, winning smile, and snug black T-shirt and jeans – self-funded bunq in the early years because not a single prospective investor believed in a bank without branches, legacy infrastructure, or conventional product architecture. Still, he believed the bank could compete.

bunq built its entire technology stack from scratch without the processes or legacy systems that constrain traditional banks. And so bunq racked up an impressive array of distinctions. Among them: first newly licensed European bank in more than 35 years and first EU neobank to reach structural profitability. By March 2017, Niknam had a sandbox live and by 2025 had 17 million users across Europe. bunq reported a net profit of €85.3 million, a 65% increase year on year, and filed for a broker-dealer licence in the United States as the first step towards full US banking expansion. (Perhaps as a foreshadowing, bunq's 'Bank of The Free' tagline resembles the 'home of the free' lyric from America's national anthem.)

bunq's progress should not have surprised industry observers and certainly turned heads in the challenger bank community. Niknam outlined his banking worldview in a 2019 interview with The Banking Scene. See if you can spot the parallels to the clarion call I've conveyed thus far.

> *'To me, everything [in banking] would be real-time, everything would be intertwined with each other. We would have a lot more insights into our spending behaviour and a lot more insights on how to reduce spending. There would be a lot less friction, there would be a lot less time spent on administrative tasks. This is just the stuff that you can predict.'*

* * *

bunq's relevance to this chapter and this book has little to do with its growth or profitability, impressive as both are. Rather, its build demonstrates the emergence of a true Platform in progress. It offers a subscription model where customers pay for the platform rather than individual products, which immediately aligns the bank's revenue with customer value rather than product sales volume. ('Bank of the Free' indeed.) It allows customers to open up to 25 IBAN accounts, link cards to any account, and manage money across multiple sub-accounts for different purposes, a financial architecture that treats complexity as a feature rather than a problem to simplify and shunt aside. Its construction aims to work for customers with complex, multi-country financial lives: digital nomads, expats, international entrepreneurs, and people whose financial lives do not fit neatly into the one-current-account product model traditional banks serve. In doing so, bunq has generated a deeply engaged subscriber base that generates significant data and maintains a high tolerance for the platform fees that make the economics work.

Certainly, bunq does not exemplify the fully realised platform bank this book describes. It lacks a six-layer digital twin and does not employ quantum simulation. Its journey ownership thus remains partial. It tracks one's financial life well, but has not yet expanded into any number of complete journeys for home, business, or wealth. But I find it thrilling that bunq's foundation prepares it to capitalise (in every sense of the word) on banking's near future. I encourage you to see what I do: clean tech architecture, subscription economics, an engaged customer base, and a true ecosystem that includes third-party integrations. When quantum simulation deploys at scale in 2029 and

2030, bunq stands more than ready to add it to an infrastructure built to support it. Then, those journeys described above will verge on realities.

Meanwhile, traditional banks will try to retrofit quantum simulation onto product-centric networks. That puts them conservatively at five years of competitive disadvantage.

They'd be better off starting from scratch, if only they could or would. bunq proves the irrefutable wisdom of starting clean. Traditional banks cannot do this as they lack the will, courage, or hyperfocus on sales, among other things. But they can choose to create the cleanest possible foundation for what comes next.

* * *

11.7 The 18–24 Month Transformation Roadmap

11.7.1 Milestones Matter, Not Time

A transformation roadmap expressed primarily in calendar time has already succumbed to a fundamental error. Governance committees love this as a way to assess progress. Milestones and specific, verifiable capabilities governed by the stopwatch matter most—an offshoot of the expression 'If it can be measured, it can be managed.'

But to what end? An on-schedule programme that lacks *meaningful capability milestones* merely fails on schedule: the most expensive kind of failure. The following roadmap is organised around milestones, with calendar time as a rough guide rather than a commitment. Timing will vary significantly; this depends on the bank's starting point, capital position, existing technology infrastructure, and, most importantly, the quality of the team that executes it.

11.7.2 Months 1–3: Foundation and Commitment

The first three months? Do not worry about building anything. Instead, ensure that everything that follows rests on genuine foundations, not comfortable assumptions. The CEO makes a public, specific, irrevocable commitment—not platitudes that salute 'digital transformation' or (ugh) 'innovation'. They must point to a named journey, team structure, metrics, and named accountability. This specific and targeted commitment implies responsibility and commitment: 'We will launch a home journey team with journey metrics that replace product metrics for that customer segment by month 18.' Beware of out-of-focus press releases such as 'We are committed to being a platform bank.' In other words: Clarity, not vagueness.

The next step is to appoint a programme director, not a chief digital officer with a broad remit. You must enlist, without question, a specific person with a specific mandate and direct CEO access. Decision tree assessment is complete and authentic, with the three archetypes identified across the leadership team and organisational programme protections established in writing. That acts as a safeguard against political pressure to compromise or kill them. (Look out for the Protector, who can do this with a wan smile, chuckle, and dismissive wave.)

11.7.3 Months 3–9: Infrastructure Before Experience

Months three to nine determine whether the transformation succeeds or fails. This period ranks as the most rushed because it yields nothing visible. This compares to a garden where seeds germinate but produce no sprouts. And without fruit on the tree to pick, let alone the tree itself, old-school execs and sales teams get judgmental and impatient.

But this precise spot marks where composure and commitment win the day. With quietude and stealth, savvy organisations build the digital twin foundation, establish data partnerships, design consent management architecture, and complete Open Banking integration. They also contract, from the outside, the first two or three additional data layer partnerships.

Next, the agentic orchestration layer prototype emerges. Momentum gathers as the project fosters autonomous agent operation, establishes MCP server connections, designs and tests first agent workflows, and creates governance frameworks. The time has now come to assemble the journey team and set it free to start its work. Ready, steady, go!

Customer experience, though important, does not come next. The team maps the journey in detail, pinpoints the data gaps, identifies ecosystem partners, and introduces metrics to prove the model works. Though customers will not see this, all of it is essential. Programmes in month six that rush this phase to appease the board will spend the next 12 months retrofitting the foundational work they supposedly skipped. This will create technical debt, and what's worse, technical nooses in the form of tactical decisions that strangle an architecture.

11.7.4 Months 9–18: The First Cohort

By month nine, the infrastructure should serve a limited customer cohort. This does not equal a mass launch, but a solid pilot with real customers who consent to share data across multiple layers and want to experience the platform in its early form. At this point, the cohort constitutes the programme's most critical asset:

- **They generate the engagement data** that refines the simulation.
- **They provide feedback** that improves the customer experience.
- **They build the simulation history** that creates palpable switching costs.
- **They demonstrate to the bank's leadership that the model works**—showing off actual customer behaviour rather than the faked pose of nattily dressed models on slide decks.

How large a cohort, then? Shoot for a minimum of 10,000 customers: large enough to generate statistically meaningful data, but small enough that you can fix problems before they impact the broader customer base. The journey team manages this cohort with intensity. They treat every interaction as an opportunity to learn, every piece of feedback as programme-critical intelligence.

11.7.5 Months 18–24: Proof and Expansion

By month 18, the programme should produce a proof of engagement model, with data that shows cohort customers engage more deeply, stay longer, expand their relationship, and generate better economics than comparable customers outside the programme. This proof justifies expansion to the next stage that broadens the cohort, deepens digital twin data coverage, introduces the quantum simulation pilot for life optimisation, and kicks off the case for the second journey team. The proof also justifies organisational changes once promised but possibly delayed: the metric shift from product P&L to journey economics, budget reallocation from product development to journey infrastructure, and talent changes the programme needs but were politically difficult to make before results appeared. Among many crossroad moments, month 18 marks when the transformation either stalls or sustains itself. The former almost always encounters a lapse in organisational commitment, even if proof of concept exists. The CEO who initially made the public commitment cannot waffle. They must now guard against institutional resistance that 18 months of change has generated.

Phase	Months	Key Milestones	Critical Success Factor
Foundation	1–3	CEO public commitment. Programme director appointed. Authentic decision tree completed. Journey team structure agreed. Archetypes identified and managed.	Commitment specificity. Vague commitments equal broken commitments.
Infrastructure	3–9	Open Banking integration goes live. Two additional data layer partnerships contracted. MCP orchestration layer prototyped. Ecosystem partner pipeline established. Governance framework for agentic AI documented.	Resist the pressure to reveal visible progress before the foundation solidifies.
First Cohort	9–18	10,000+ customer pilot goes live. Engagement metrics tracked. Simulation outputs used by real customers. Feedback loop established. Switching cost indicators emerge.	Treat the cohort as the programme's most important asset.
Proof and Expansion	18–24	Proof of engagement model documented. Quantum simulation pilot launched. Metric shifts from product P&L to journey economics. Second journey team case made.	CEO enforces commitment against institutional resistance.

* * *

11.8 Financial Modelling, Honest Economics

11.8.1 What You Actually Invest In

Make no mistake: You are not investing in a product or system in the first two to three years. This concerns the capability to build and maintain relationships with customers at a depth and quality that the current banking model cannot achieve. That new capability generates revenue, but at a slow pace and in ways traditional financial models struggle to capture. Customer lifetime value, relationship expansion, reduced churn, and improved acquisition economics through word of mouth comprise real economic benefits, but never appear in quarterly product P&L reports. The financial model for platform transformation requires a different accounting framework. Getting board and investor buy-in for it represents one of the hardest tasks the CEO will ever have to tackle.

The investment magnitude varies significantly by bank size, geographic scope and starting point infrastructure. Rather than provide fuzzy numbers for general scenarios, let me describe the economic shape. In years one and two, the investment runs materially ahead of revenue from the new model. You cannot avoid this. Not only do building infrastructure and assembling skills the bank needs amount to costly work; customers cannot yet access an end product.

The break-even point for a well-executed programme – where journey-model revenue exceeds programme costs – typically falls in years three to five. Banks that try to accelerate past this break-even point, especially via infrastructure investment cuts, will not achieve break-even earlier but create a weaker model that takes longer to generate real returns. If it ever does.

The three-to-five year timeline is borne of patience and practicality, not pessimism. To recognise this amounts to grasping the honest shape of capability investment: Build first, extract next. Scale signals that the model works via enthusiastic customer response. They return to the platform voluntarily, spend meaningful time with the simulation capability and act on guidance that improves their financial decisions. That engagement serves as the lead indicator. Everything else follows.

* * *

11.9 Closing: The Transformation You Are Actually Choosing

It may sound strange to hear a former coder and tech executive say that transformation does not boil down to a technology project. It first and foremost presents a choice about what kind of institution you want to be. Technology acts as the means. The choice is obvious. Does your bank exist to sell products to customers or to serve them through complete life journeys? It's easy to choose the latter by way of lip service or sounding like the smartest banker in the room. That noted, no less a figure than British suffragette Emmeline Pankhurst declared: 'Deeds not words.' The only winning vote for change turns voice and vision into action: Strong, sustained, and committed.

Get the choice right and clear decisions will transcend the blather bandied about by executives, boffins and TED Talkers striding across a stage. Get the choice wrong, or descend into hazy planning, and all the technology in the world will not save you from the institutional gravity that pulls every large organisation back towards what it already knows how to do. Former Duke and Columbia professor Dorie Clark – author of 'The Long Game: How to Be a Long-Term Thinker in a Short-Term World' – puts it exceedingly well: 'The real reason people resist change... is uncertainty.'

The corollary here is that the perfect is the enemy of the good. bunq built something worth studying—not because it hit every mark, but it made the first choice clearly. To eliminate legacy systems, they eliminated legacy thinking. No branches meant no branch economics to protect. No product teams meant no product metrics to defend.

Starting clean offers an advantage that traditional banks cannot replicate. It would be like turning 1,000 bank vaults and 10,000 mortgages into a data repository for 100,000 permanent customer journeys. But they can approach success by assembling a journey team shielded from the existing organisation, the Protectors and Climbers especially. A CEO who defends the new metrics can wield plenty of power to amplify the team's efforts.

Those who posit the correct choices will encounter politics, resistance, perhaps even sabotage from within. Press on anyway. If the profit mongers wish to trot out the Friedman Doctrine at all costs, tell them this about shareholder value: By the 2030s, bank consolidation will come to mean something entirely different. In one corner, platform banks will dominate in their markets. And in another, the rest will spend the decade explaining to upset shareholders why the other cohort demoted their banks to commodity infrastructure providers.

You'll have to make quite a case for it, even if you win enough converts. It will get hard. It always does. That in large part explains why this book exists. Do not just read it: Use it. Apply it. Then, stick to it.

Questions for Your Board

1. Do the time segments for transformation make sense for us? Or would we tweak them based on our own unique circumstances?
2. Does our CEO (or a powerful proxy) fit the description of someone who can make 'a public, specific, irrevocable commitment' to change? If you're not the CEO (or even if you are!), feel free to keep this answer confidential.
3. Does the example of bunq inspire envy, disdain, or dismissiveness at our institution? Approached from a positive vantage point, how might bunq inspire us in concrete ways to embrace the future?

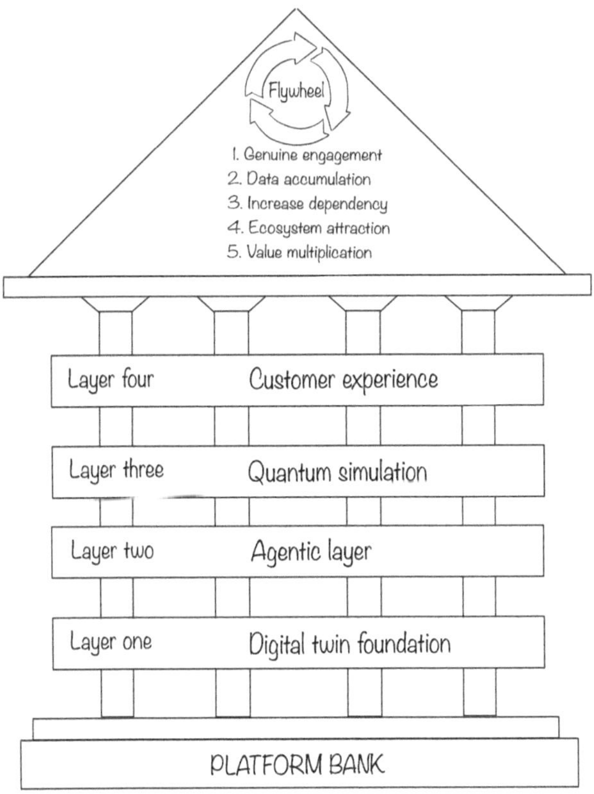

12

The Winners and Losers 2032

Of the future fintech predictions that never came to pass, one sticks out as *prima facie* evidence of hubris-meets-financial myopia. Remember when Sweden announced with much fanfare in 2018 that it would achieve cashless status by 2025? Some experts rolled their eyes and called it an empty boast. Turns out they were right. Instead, 2025 marked the year when Sweden's central bank, the Riksbank, called for 'urgent legislative action' to safeguard the role of cash due to risks that included cyberattacks, power outages, and war. (Some would call it a fitting retreat, given that Sweden gave Europe its first paper banknotes in 1661.)

So making a fixed forecast about banking's future, complete with a target date, amounts to risky business. I get this; so does my co-author. To the extent that we have experience in financial services (mine four decades long, his roughly half that), this chapter marks where reputations get put on the line.

What follows are specific predictions about what the banking landscape will look like in 2032: Specific names attached to specific outcomes, and a section at the end where I reflect on where I could miss the mark. That said, I refuse to hide behind 'scenarios' and 'possible futures.' That would run counter to the thrust and spirit of this book. Here's the what and why behind what I believe will happen and what it would take to prove me wrong.

I divide the observations below into confident horizon views and mere predictions, two disparate things we should not confuse so as to water down this future view.

* * *

D. Mistry, L. R. Carlozo, *The Intelligent Ledger*,
https://doi.org/10.1007/978-3-032-32842-7_12

12.1 Setting the Scene, 2032 from Today

12.1.1 What We Know With Confidence ...

By 2032, digital twin technology will be mature, affordable and deployable at banking scale. The six-layer data architecture this book describes in Chapter 3 is not speculative: It represents an engineering challenge and engineering challenges get solved. I expect that quantum simulation will have reached early production capability for the banking applications listed in Chapter 8, based on IBM, Google, and Microsoft's published hardware roadmaps and the trajectory of error correction research.

Agentic AI, already in production at scale at Lloyds and other banks in 2026, will contain enough sophistication to orchestrate complete, autonomous financial life journeys.

Clarity in the regulatory environment for stablecoins and DeFi will emerge in the US, EU, and UK by 2027 at the latest, and this will trigger the next wave of structural change in banking.

12.1.2 ... and What We Predict

These Platform-Pipe predictions are based on several generations of watching this industry move. Though willing to be wrong on the record, I refuse to hedge. The window closes in 2027 not because I say so, but because the market arithmetic this chapter sets out leaves no other conclusion. My personal window closed when I started writing 'The Intelligent Ledger'.

12.1.3 The Shape of the Market in 2032

These numbers form the foundation of my predictions. There are approximately 8,700 commercial banks globally. Their revenue has grown to $3.9 trillion over the last five years, according to IBIS World. Of those, around 1,000 are large enough to appear in The Banker's annual ranking.

Of those 1,000 banks, perhaps 100 have the customer scale, capital position, and data assets to make a definitive choice between Platform or Pipe. The rest will fall, over time, in line based on what those 100 do. They will be acquired or serviced by them, or quietly wound down as customers migrate to platforms they cannot compete with. This will resemble the long-standing trend of bank consolidation, but along a markedly different path.

I predict ten to 20 platform winners globally, which follows this book's argument that roughly 10% of banks that attempt platform transformation will complete it. Applied to the 100 institutions with a genuine shot, that gives you 10 at the floor.

Add neobanks and non-bank platforms that enter from adjacent industries and a realistic ceiling allows for 15 to 20. A forecast of 50 to 100 Pipe providers reflects the deliberate choosers from that same top 100, plus specialist institutions from the next tier down: trade finance, custody, and cross-border payments. Their depth makes each an ecosystem necessity rather than a residual institution.

* * *

The banking market in 2032 will have consolidated into three distinct tiers, more clearly separated than anything we see today:

The first tier, platform banks, will be small in number and enormous in influence. These 10 to 20 will own the primary financial relationships of their customers across complete life journeys, operate at 40+% margins on their platform businesses, and establish switching costs so high that their customer base is effectively permanent unless they catastrophically fail. These institutions will not resemble banks in the 2026 sense but look more like the operating systems of their customers' financial lives: present at every significant decision to invisibly orchestrate the ecosystem of services the decision requires, even as it continuously learns and improves from every interaction.

Not every platform winner in 2032 will be a full-spectrum platform bank in the DBS or Lloyds sense, owning multiple major life journeys across tens of millions of customers. Alongside those full-spectrum winners will emerge a cohort of 'micro-platform' banks. These institutions will penetrate a single specific journey so deeply that they find themselves effectively unchallenged within it: the kind of 'blue ocean' pioneers that strategists W. Chan Kim and Renée Mauborgne (authors of the bestselling book) would single out as original thinkers.

Examples include:

- a specialist who owns the later-life financial journey – care funding, equity release, estate planning, lasting power of attorney – for the over-70s demographic that mainstream banks consistently underserve.
- a bank that owns the agricultural finance journey end-to-end for farming businesses, whose financial lives look nothing like those of urban retail customers.

- a platform that owns SME international trade: FX, letters of credit, supply chain finance, cross-border compliance for businesses operating across multiple jurisdictions.

These are not Pipe banks. They own customer relationships within their domain, due in large part to prohibitive switching costs. They operate on platform economics within their niche. But they succeed because they go deeper than any full-spectrum or generalist platform player would bother to go, and serve lower-priority customers marginalised because of their complexity. Add the micro-platform tier to the '10 to 20' Platform pioneers and the total winners globally could skyrocket. I flag this not to soften the urgency of the main argument – the full-spectrum window is no less narrow for it – but because some executives may read '10 to 20' and conclude the odds are too long for their institution to bother. But they are not. For them, the micro-platform route is real, viable and demanding in its own right. It's not necessarily easier to own one journey completely versus many journeys partially. Organisational commitment and data discipline apply across the board. The difference lies not in the scope of ambition but in the required depth of execution.

The second tier, Pipe banks, will be more numerous, perhaps 50 to 100 significant players globally. They will function as the infrastructure that platform banks and other financial services businesses run on. Lower margins, more transactional relationships, diminished or absent customer-facing presence will characterise them. But they will still excel at what they do – custody, settlement, regulatory compliance, capital management, specialist lending – and serve as an essential component of the ecosystem. They will not own customer relationships but will service them, invisibly, through the platforms above them.

This is not a failure. Deliberate choice and peerless performance guarantee them a sustainable and valuable role. But if done by default because the bank failed to choose the platform approach in time, it will fade into acquisition or irrelevance: A broken Pipe, you might say.

The third tier will succumb to various stages of distress. Platform banks or Pipe consolidators will acquire some for their customer base or infrastructure. Some will merge with peers in a bet that scale solves the strategic problem (except that it never has). Others will enter managed wind-down, their balance sheets slowly shrinking as customers flock to platforms that serve them better and regulators quietly manage the exit. A small number will fail outright, triggering the kind of government intervention we saw in 2008. This time, however, careless planning will replace reckless lending as the trigger.

Strategic paralysis and overanalysis will characterise the endgame: a transformation they understood intellectually but could not execute politically.

* * *

12.2 The Winners, Five Profiles

12.2.1 The Benchmark DBS

Every Western banking executive should study one institution before they dismiss platform transformation as attractive in theory but impossible in practice. Development Bank of Singapore (DBS), Southeast Asia's largest bank, has made quiet, measurable progress on fronts where Western banks have neglected to see the urgency. Their location should come as little surprise to digital experts and observers. With its population of 6 million, Singapore exemplifies smart city technology – in mobility, health, safety, and productivity – like no other metropolis on Earth.

DBS began its efforts in 2016 with what it called Digital Value Capture, a rigorous framework that measured AI-generated economic value against control groups rather than to forecast it in theory. Its AI capability has compounded year on year with a discipline that makes most bank innovation programmes in Europe and America look like hobby projects. From S$180 million (about £105 million) in measured AI value in 2022, DBS snowballed to S$1 billion (£580 million) by 2025, a growth rate of 556%. That year, its 430 use cases ran more than 2,000 models, with nine operating model transformation programmes completed. The bank rebuilt workflows, flattened structures and reskilled staff rather than simply layering AI tools over existing processes. CEO of DBS, Tan Su Shan, frames this in no uncertain terms. Under her leadership, the goal for DBS's generative AI is to become a trusted, personalised and agentic financial adviser for every retail customer. As she told McKinsey & Company in late 2025:

> *'AI is eating the world. You've got the birth of data centres and the demise of other industries, for example. Just being ahead of these trends requires a fair amount of open-mindedness, agility, and nimbleness. Having that sort of constant eye on the future – "What's cooking now?" – requires that ambidextrous leadership.'*

DBS has not distilled some committee report into a vague vision statement. Its 'constant eye on the future' has materialised as a programme already underway at production scale. At roughly ten times the measured AI value that

Lloyds Bank reported for 2025, DBS answers the question sceptical banking executives would rightly ask when they read this book: Has any traditional bank actually done this?

Yes. DBS. And the lesson for Western banks is not to copy DBS's specific use cases but to understand the commitment behind the accomplishment: a decade of patient, disciplined, measurable investment – started before anyone deemed it fashionable – governed by a framework that required purpose and reasoning behind every AI initiative, all tied to tangible business impact. Lloyds Bank has the data position and AI infrastructure to follow this path. But can they muster the equivalent of a decade's worth of patience and compress it into the five years the competitive window allows?

12.2.2 Lloyds Banking Group, the Incumbent That Chose

Among the world's traditional banks, I watch Lloyds Banking Group most closely as a potential platform winner. I do not write this as flattery to a former employer but because objective evidence supports the argument. What's more, Lloyds' strategic choices in the past two years bear more significance than the market currently appreciates.

By 2026, Lloyds had become the first UK bank to deploy agentic AI at scale. Its financial assistant can reach 21 million customers across its Lloyds, Halifax, and Bank of Scotland brands. Rather than buy from a vendor, the bank built its proprietary generative and agentic AI framework in-house. This matters because any bank that creates its own AI infrastructure owns the data architecture, whereas a bank that runs on a third-party platform does not. Lloyds hired its AI director, Dr. Rohit Dhawan, away from Amazon Web Services, and the bank migrated its AI framework to Google Cloud's Vertex AI platform. Their agentic system processes natural language, executes multi-step financial tasks, and retains conversational memory across sessions. In 2025, this generated £50 million in measurable value. In 2026, Lloyds targeted £100 million. The trajectory is steep and ambitious, but with proactive investment to match.

The infrastructure has a name now. In January 2026, Lloyds unveiled Envoy, an agentic AI marketplace and governance hub built with Google Cloud, that includes the responsibility framework built into the stack rather than bolted on later. Alongside it, the bank committed to putting all 67,000 of its employees through a new AI Academy by year-end 2026. The technology is the easy part; Lloyds is doing the hard part too.

What makes Lloyds a platform candidate rather than just a digitally competent traditional bank? The combination of its AI capability and data position. Its 28 million customers comprise the largest retail customer base of any UK bank. As a whole, they generate transaction data across current accounts, mortgages, savings, investments, car finance, and insurance: a formidable foundation for Layer 6 of the digital twin, at a scale no neobank can match.

Nor has this financial institution stood still as they adopt and create technology that will define banking's next decade—even as they expand their real estate footprint in a related (and novel) way.

In 2021, Lloyds began to invest in property at a clip that made it one of the largest commercial landlords in the UK. Starting with around 7,500 properties, they aim to own and manage 50,000 by 2030. But their home journey ambition extends well beyond any property portfolio. Lloyds recently announced trials with the Open Property Data Association (OPDA). I know this organisation well, as I participated in it early on. Today, Maria Harris leads it and has defined its mission thus: to make property data open, standardised, and shareable across the entire home buying process with key industry stakeholders in collaboration. CEO Charlie Nunn posts regularly about Lloyds' property work and with good reason: The home buying journey serves as an example of the complex, multi-party, emotionally charged life event that platform banks will exist to own. A simultaneous major landlord, mortgage lender, and force to open property data infrastructure does not equal a bank that wants to dabble in the home journey. I posit that Lloyds is assembling the complete picture, layer by layer.

In January 2026, Lloyds completed the UK's first gilt purchase using tokenised deposits, issued them on the Canton Network public blockchain, and used them to buy a tokenised gilt from the Archax regulated crypto exchange. This demonstrated 'atomic settlement' (where asset transfers and payments occur simultaneously and instantly) between blockchain and traditional banking systems in a single, seamless transaction. It proved far from a standalone experiment. Lloyds is one of six major UK banks (alongside Barclays, HSBC, NatWest, Nationwide, and Santander) that participated in the Great British Tokenised Deposits pilot led by UK Finance, running until mid-2026 to test three real-world scenarios: person–to–person payments to reduce marketplace fraud, remortgaging processes to speed up conveyancing, and digital asset settlement that links tokenised commercial bank money directly to on-chain assets.

In April 2026, Lloyds completed the first-known experiment to use quantum computing to identify money mule networks, running on IBM's

Quantum Heron device across anonymised transaction data to detect fraud patterns that overwhelm classical systems at scale.

Behind all of this sits a design capability most banks can only dream about. More than 400 experienced staffers span UX, UI, service design, inclusive design, and design research to build and own customer journeys across millions of customers.

Now, see whether you can grasp the strategic tension at the heart of Lloyds' position. A bank that owns 400-plus designers quite possibly has a design of a different sort in mind: to control the customer relationship end-to-end at every swipe, every journey, every touchpoint. But that describes the mechanics of a Pipe bank, not a Platform. A true platform bank would open those journeys to third parties and compete on infrastructure, not experience.

Whether Lloyds becomes a platform winner, or an extremely well-capitalised and well-designed product bank, centres on the yes-or-no decision to make the journey team commitment described in Chapter 7—and resolve that tension in favour of openness rather than control. Their AI assistant is powerful, their quantum and tokenisation investments tangible. So what are they aiming for exactly? More efficient product sales? Or more complete ownership of customer journeys?

By 2032, their market position will tell the story. My prediction is that they make it: not easily, not without political cost inside the organisation. But their combined data position and AI infrastructure give them a head start. Add to that the competitive pressure from neobanks and Big Tech forces, and Lloyds is forced to choose—correctly in this case, I believe. Put another way, they will own the journeys, not just the infrastructure beneath them.

And so Lloyds in 2032 re-establishes itself as a platform bank, starting with the home journey and finishing with the wealth journey.

12.2.3 Nubank, the Scale That Proves the Model

If Lloyds proves that a traditional incumbent can transform, Nubank demonstrates that the platform model works at a scale that puts the entire Western banking industry to shame. Founded in São Paulo in 2013 by David Vélez, Cristina Junqueira, and Edward Wible, Nubank set out to do something that every Brazilian bank told them was impossible: build a digital-only, fee-free credit card that ordinary Brazilians could access without branch visits, paperwork, and the exploitative charges traditional Brazilian banks had normalised.

By the end of 2025, Nubank claimed 131 million customers across Brazil, Mexico, and Colombia. That's more than any neobank in the world or the individual customer bases of most G7 national banking systems. It ranks as

Brazil's third-largest financial institution, serving 61% of the country's adult population. It reached full-year profitability in 2023, one of the very few neobanks globally to do so. It provided first-time credit card access to 21 million Brazilians excluded by the existing system. Its cost-to-income ratio of 36% in 2023 was better than most Western incumbents that had optimised operations for decades. If you think a high-powered marketing firm, branch networks, or inherited customer relationships from a century-old institution made all this possible, do not. Between 80 and 90% of Nubank's customer growth came through word of mouth: Pure platform flywheel in motion.

Impressive as all this sounds, Nubank has an AI strategy with resources to deliver on the Platform promise. In June 2024, Nubank acquired Hyperplane, a Silicon Valley 'AI-for-banks' start-up. This data intelligence company builds proprietary foundation models on first-party financial data, specifically to accelerate its AI-first platform ambition. The goal, stated plainly by Nubank CEO David Vélez, is to give every Nubank customer access to the kind of sophisticated financial guidance previously available only to wealthy individuals with private bankers:

> *'Consumers globally will access not only the very best financial products but also receive truly customised financial advice that empowers them to live a better life.'*

Their AI assistant already handles more than two million monthly customer conversations, resolving 55% of tier-one inquiries without human escalation. Their agentic money transfer system reduced transaction time from 70 seconds across nine screens to under 30, via a single natural language interaction. Their real-time event AI predicts customer needs based on app behaviour and transactions, improving service interactions by more than 50%. Far from a chatbot bolted onto a traditional banking system, this embodies an AI-native financial platform, built from scratch. It operates at a major national bank scale and improves continuously thanks to the data 131 million customers generate – 60% of whom now consider Nubank their primary banking relationship.

Six years ahead of the 2032 finish line, Nubank has surpassed any Western bank in its platform journey. The scale validates the economics in markets where the forcing functions this book describes arrived earlier and hit harder. Brazil's incumbent banks had no consumer trust to show after they spent decades charging ordinary Brazilians exorbitant fees for services they needed. And the absence of an incumbent moat meant Nubank could move at a speed enviable to Western neobanks, which operate in markets where incumbents are trusted and established.

Western banks must build the model Nubank has proven. But they will have to work quickly as Nubank is moving West. In January 2026, Nubank received conditional approval from the US Office of the Comptroller of the Currency for a *de novo* national bank charter, the first step towards full US banking operations. By 2032, Nubank is on track to achieve global platform bank status, unless Western regulators find reasons to slow its US entry that go beyond the technical requirements of a *de novo* charter. Will banks in the US, UK, EU, and elsewhere stand ready to compete? Or merely serve as Nubank's commodity infrastructure providers?

12.2.4 Bank of America, the US Parallel

Bank of America represents the Lloyds story played out in the US market, with a five-year head start – but on a scale that makes even Lloyds look modest. Their Erica virtual assistant, launched in 2018 and iterated continuously since, had accumulated more than two billion customer interactions by 2025. That activity generated an extraordinary volume of conversational data concerning how American households think about and manage their finances. To be sure, Erica is not yet a quantum-powered simulation or complete digital twin. But it showcases the most mature AI-to-customer financial relationship in traditional banking, and no competitor can quickly replicate the learning embedded in two billion interactions.

Bank of America's strategic position in 2032 mirrors Lloyds' in the UK: A large, data-rich incumbent whose AI investment gives it a genuine shot at platform leadership if it makes the necessary organisational commitment. All of these factors point towards strong platform potential:

- a customer base of 66 million consumers and small businesses,
- investment management capability through Merrill Lynch, and
- one of the highest technology investments in US banking.

Given their unique position thanks to Merrill Lynch, BOA will own the wealth management journey by 2032. In doing so, I believe they will integrate everyday banking with investment management, retirement planning and estate planning, delivered through AI guidance knit from the complete financial picture of each customer. Of course, organisational commitment is a prerequisite. But that could come by way of the same competitive pressure that will force Lloyds' hand in the UK. By 2032, Bank of America steps up as a platform bank in wealth and business banking, with retail as the data foundation that powers both.

12.2.5 bunq, the Clean-Sheet Winner

Because of their clean strategic logic, bunq stands out as the most straightforward prediction here. As I described in Chapter 7, bunq rose up without legacy baggage from day one: No inherited architecture, product teams to defend product metrics, or branch network economics to protect. By early 2026, it boasted:

- 17 million users across Europe,
- €85.3 million in net profit (up 65% year on year),
- Structural profitability achieved before any major Western neobank competitor, and
- a US expansion underway through its broker-dealer licence filing.

With its subscription model, customers pay for the platform rather than individual products. This means bunq's revenue already aligns with customer value, not product sales. Traditional banks would find that feat nearly impossible to pull off. Starting from square one would be the only way to erect what bunq has possessed from the beginning.

bunq's customer base sets it up for platform success: A unique mix of digital nomads, expats, international entrepreneurs and people with complex multi-currency, multi-country financial lives. With more data to share, scenarios to simulate, decisions to navigate – and a higher willingness to pay for specialised insight about their complete financial picture – these financially complex customers represent ideal candidates for the quantum-simulated, digitally-twinned financial guidance this book describes.

What's more, bunq finds itself as ready as any bank on my prediction list. They've served this customer for more than a decade – a critical fact in that bunq understands their needs in a way that traditional banks cannot. bunq's paradigm makes for three-dimensional finance, so to speak, whereas legacy banks trade mostly on a single-country, single-currency model, inched forward (if at all) by product-by-product strategy. By 2032, bunq wins as a platform bank with a blue ocean clientele: The internationally mobile customer. They will not rank as the largest Platform by customer count, but potentially the highest margin and technically sophisticated – a natural fit, given the sophistication of its on-the-move customers.

12.2.6 Kraken, the Wild Card with a Fighting Chance

I'll admit it: London-based Kraken, until recently part of Octopus Energy, may not seem like it belongs on this platform list. If its inclusion surprises you, know that I feel confident about its platform prospects. But why?

Kraken began as the technology platform that Octopus Energy built to run its own energy supply business. It included customer management, billing, smart metre integration, demand response, and renewable energy optimisation. In December 2025, Kraken completed its first standalone investment round at a valuation of £6.43 billion ($8.65 billion US). And at the start of 2026, it raised about £745 million ($1 billion) from D1 Capital Partners, fast off the heels of a formal spinoff from Octopus Energy Group.

As the Kraken team announced with fanfare:

> *We've come a long way in a short time: 70+ million accounts globally, 6GWs daily optimised power, 4x growth in three years, $500m+ in contracted annual revenue. None of this would be possible without our incredible customers and brilliant team.*

Note that phrase: *Incredible customers.* Hmmm.

Its contracted annual revenue comes from licensing agreements with EDF, E.ON, National Grid US, Origin Energy, Tokyo Gas, and more than 30 global utilities. It processed 15 billion new data points every day across more than 75 million household and business accounts in 27 countries. And in September 2025, Octopus Energy overtook British Gas as Great Britain's largest household energy supplier. How did a challenger founded in 2015 displace an incumbent with decades of market dominance?

Here's how: The Kraken platform.

Though Kraken occupies a different business space, it still owns what no bank has built: A real-time data platform at industry scale that processes the complete energy life of tens of millions of households. This comes with a proven track record of customer satisfaction and operational efficiency, with cost reductions of 30 to 40% for its utility clients. Energy data resides in Layer 2 of the digital twin: Environmental and consumption data that tells you how a household actually lives, not just how it spends. Energy consumption patterns reveal dozens of signals about the reality of their domestic life: When people are home, how many live there, their appliances, whether they possess an electric vehicle and/or solar panels, and the energy efficiency of their home. Now, how many banks own this transaction data, let alone can glean anything from it?

That's right: Nil. Meanwhile, Kraken can process in real time the data from 75 million accounts: A figure more than eight times the population of Greater London.

In my FinTech Futures columns, I've posed this question: Could Kraken leap into banking? Organisational will, interestingly, probably comes behind organisational interest. Regardless, the logic of platform economics makes a strong case for it. Given not just its data volume and resiliency but also its financial strength following its December 2025 demerger, Kraken could easily depart or explore beyond the energy sector.

Kraken already partially owns the home journey from the energy side. Now, add (in AskHomey fashion) the complete financial picture of home-ownership: Mortgage, insurance, maintenance, and the like, with counsel and proactive cost-savings moves to accompany, and Kraken already knows how each home actually functions. So this is not so much speculation as extrapolation: The logical next step for an evolving platform that has already scaled and captured customer trust.

I predict that in 2032, Kraken – whether banking partnerships or its own new banking licence – will run the dominant home journey platform in the UK and several European markets. Banks cannot see it coming because this disruptor does not resemble a bank. Which is exactly the point, come 2032.

Revolut: Let's Revisit This

Every banking executive reading this chapter watches Revolut in anticipation of what comes next. With £1.7 billion in pre-tax profit in 2025 (up 57% year on year), revenues of £4.5 billion, and 68.3 million retail customers, Revolut cannot be ignored. A chapter about banking winners in 2032 that excludes them stands accused of oversight, ignorance, or perhaps both. Moreover, the numbers tell one powerful story.

In Spain, France, and Italy, roughly one in three newly opened bank accounts land at Revolut. And in March 2026, they finally secured a full UK banking licence after five or so years of regulatory friction. That unlocked a spectrum of opportunities – lending, mortgages, and FSCS-protected deposits – in their home market. That same month, Revolut filed for a US national bank charter. Its £55.7 billion valuation ($75 billion) places it on a credible path towards an IPO of roughly £74 billion ($100 billion or so).

So why deliberately leave Revolut off my confirmed winners list? Because even though 'the numbers tell one powerful story,' the climactic chapters that count have not yet materialised. That is, Revolut's model is not necessarily *the* model.

The fintech operates as a multi-product super-app, with 11 separate revenue lines that each exceed £100 million annually. The company calls it a 'multi-engine platform.' That framing reveals much. So does this quote from then-Revolut US CFO Max Lapin, who described the company's ambitions in March 2025 to CFODive:

> *'Lapin is proposing the term 'banktech' to help describe the shift; 'banktech', as Lapin defines it, is "a fully regulated bank, but [one] that is keeping [its] agility as a tech company."'*

And so, bank first, tech company second. 'Banktech' may be just the term to coin. But nothing about it, or Lapin's description, captures the spirit and thrust of platform building. The fintech/banktech's vision may be poised for growth, but pun intended, it's not revolutionary.

Multiple products on a single app does not imply or equal owning a customer journey. Revolut understands the gaps banks and other fintechs have left and filled them with products. That places them in a powerful competitive position. But the orientation does not point them to the future as we've described it in The Intelligent Ledger: Journey ownership.

Revolut serves customers via currency exchange, crypto, savings, and a credit card. But in turn, those customers do not give Revolut their complete financial life. Revolut has consolidated several products in one place. Those products may in turn offer tremendous deals and appeal. But banking customers, reserving their right to be fickle, will still depart once a better deal comes around. The term for this is 'customer attrition.' Banktech, no matter how sexy, still allows for it. But not a platform. By 2032, switching costs for its customers will simply run too high.

The three-year licensing saga raises structural questions. Revolut moved fast, hit regulatory walls, and only now has begun to operate as a full bank in its primary market. Revolut in the UK and Europe lacks the data advantage that Brazil's Nubank built over a decade of solidifying primary banking relationships. Revolut's customer acquisition numbers, while extraordinary, do not add up to a corresponding depth of relationship.

The genuine question for 2032 is whether (and then how) Revolut uses its data position, its now-licensed banking infrastructure and its NVIDIA-backed AI investment to pursue journey ownership, or continues to optimise the product model. If it chooses the latter, Revolut may turn out to be successful and profitable, yet still miss out on the transition that matters most: From excellent product bank to pioneering platform banking. If they make the shift, they belong atop the winners' table and my prediction misses the mark badly. And if they do not, they will own a remarkable business but a Pipe-adjacent one that nonetheless leaves them vulnerable to Platform bank ascendancy.

I watch Revolut more carefully than any other institution in this chapter. The numbers demand it – but the model does not clinch it.

JPMorgan Chase: The One and Only Exception

JPMorgan Chase fits the Pipe-or-Platform binary least comfortably and deliberately so. Their Kinexys wholesale payments platform amounts to the most credible Pipe infrastructure play built by any incumbent, while their Chase retail operation gives them a simultaneous platform option no other bank could afford to run alongside it. They also carry more than $4.42 trillion in total assets in the US alone, an amount greater than the forecasted GDP for the UK in 2026. Thus, they cannot serve as an industry model: Their sheer scale makes them an outlier. Except for JPMorgan Chase, no traditional or challenger bank can afford to run both plays.

* * *

12.3 What Good Looks Like on the Pipe Survivors' Side

Not every bank that winds up a Pipe provider in 2032 will have failed. The banks that will survive and thrive in the Pipe tier will choose deliberately, early, and completely, and will conclude – *not concede* – that platform transformation does not suit them. After they analyse their capabilities, market position, and culture, and then apply the Chapter 10 decision tree consciously, they will drive towards Pipe excellence with the same energy and investment platform banks put into journey ownership. A viable, sustainable, valuable business awaits them on the other side of that choice.

These attributes will characterise the Pipe banks that matter most in 2032:

- authoritative regulatory expertise,
- world-class technology reliability,
- efficient capital management, and
- deep specialist capabilities in areas where platform banks will require partners: Trade finance, structured lending, cross-border payments, custody, and derivatives.

None of this comes easy. It requires years of expertise, regulatory relationships and operational discipline that no platform bank will want to build in-house. And why should it when a Pipe partner can provide it? The Pipe bank matters as a specialist infrastructure provider that reigns over the functionality platform banks need and have no desire to run themselves. That amounts to a real business worth a dedicated buildout.

By contrast, the Pipe banks that struggle in 2032 will arrive there through any number of mishaps. Perhaps by default, or attempted platform transformation that lacked genuine commitment. Maybe they spent five years and significant capital on a programme that produced a better app and a worse balance sheet – only to learn too late that half-hearted platform building yields the worst of both worlds. Without the data-rich customer relationships of a Platform or the operational excellence of a committed Pipe provider, they will land in an inevitable position: Caught between two markets, competitive in neither, and facing a choice that stems from all they avoided in 2027: Acquire, be acquired, or wind down.

* * *

12.4 Bank Failure Then and Now, Fast to Slow

Bank failure in the 21st Century rarely looks like what it did in 2008. The 2008 crisis was acute. It involved institutions that made specific, identifiable mistakes in mortgage underwriting, structured products, and leverage ratios. They collapsed in a rapid, conspicuous fashion when asset price assumptions that underpinned those miscues collapsed. The 2027–2032 'failscape' period will look nothing like that – the opposite, in fact, in terms of speed. Their collapse will be slow, structural, and at first almost invisible, so long as the revenue still exists, the balance sheet remains sound, and the quarterly reports pass muster. The crisis will grow out of strategy, not finance, and strategic crises take longer to emerge. It's much harder to ferret out of a glowing or adequate quarterly report.

The pattern I expect to see follows every previous transformation cycle in every sector where incumbents faced acute platform disruption: Consolidation. The strong acquire the weak. Regulators facilitate mergers not likely to pass in a more competitive market. The alternative – a significant deposit institution's outright failure – leaves everyone worse off: Customers, the financial system, and those caught in the political intrigue or perceived inaction. When the financial crisis forced the Lloyds-Halifax merger of 2009, it created the UK's largest retail bank. The mergers of 2029–2032 will stem from a different kind of crisis, but the force mechanism will be similar. A bank caught without a viable path forward will land in the hands of one that can. This may preserve the customer base for a time, but important unknowns will remain.

In other words, it's right back to the Pipe-or-Platform drawing board.

Then there is the *other* human question: What about the tens of thousands of bank employees who may get trapped in the consolidation landslide? I think about this a lot. These people went to work for institutions that seemed stable and built their careers there. They must now watch those structures crumble, through no fault of their own, faster than the banks can adapt.

Leaders then have a responsibility to either guide a proper transformation or own the failure, should it come to that. They need to deliver straight communication about strategic direction, invest in reskilling, and make hard decisions early rather than comfortable ones late. This rarely gets discussed in banking but deserves more attention. Those who tell their people everything is fine amidst a strategic collapse may think they're protecting their people. They're not. In fact, they deny them the time to prepare a post-bank Plan B.

Some banks will even compound failure by applying a spit shine on the inevitable. In a sector smitten with its numbers, charts, and jargon, it's not uncommon to hear phrases such as '10,000 right-sized positions.' It turns incompetent decision-making and an avoidable human toll into a sound bite that impersonates shrewd business strategy, meant not to acknowledge or admit to a crisis but to navigate a temporary bump.

Some institutions – but not many – will get cast adrift in the upcoming consolidation. Regulators treat outright bank failure as a catastrophe for depositors and the broader economy, which explains why they intervene well before failure becomes unavoidable.

But the smaller regional banks and building societies that lack the scale to become meaningful Pipe providers and the differentiation to carve out a platform niche will reach a critical point. That arrives when no acquirer wants to pay a meaningful premium and a winddown becomes the managed outcome. Do not confuse this with a prediction of widespread collapse. The forecast of structural consolidation at the lower end of the market assumes that it will happen gradually enough so as to create a series of manageable ebbs. Only in retrospect will any aggregate effect emerge.

* * *

12.5 Putting It All Together: The Predictions Table

Prediction	Confidence	Possible Complications
Lloyds Banking Group is a platform bank in the UK home and wealth journeys by 2032, with journey metrics replacing product metrics as primary performance measures.	High	If Lloyds' AI assistant remains a product sales tool rather than a genuine journey guide, or if leadership reverts to product metrics under market pressure before the platform moat is established.
Bank of America is a platform bank in US wealth and business banking by 2032, leveraging Erica's conversational data and the Merrill Lynch relationship.	High	If the organisational separation between Bank of America and Merrill Lynch prevents the integrated journey model, or if a new CEO reverses the AI investment trajectory.
bunq is the dominant platform bank for internationally mobile customers in Europe by 2032, with the highest per-customer margins of any Western neobank.	Very High	If bunq's US expansion fails and forces a retrenchment that consumes the capital needed for platform capability investment.
Kraken enters the UK home journey banking market by 2032, either through a banking licence or through deep partnerships with a licensed bank, and becomes the dominant platform for homeowners.	High	If Kraken's focus remains exclusively on utilities and it does not pursue the adjacent home journey opportunity that its data position makes available.
At least three significant UK bank mergers occur between 2028 and 2032, driven by strategic failure rather than financial crisis.	Very High	If regulatory intervention creates a protected environment that allows strategically weak banks to survive independently longer than market logic would suggest.
Fewer than five traditional banks globally complete platform transformation, full journey ownership, digital twin, and quantum simulation by 2032.	High	If the development acceleration from agentic AI makes platform building faster and cheaper than I have assumed, enabling more banks to complete the transformation in the available window.

Prediction	Confidence	Possible Complications
At least one major bank globally announces a partnership with a quantum cloud provider for production banking applications by the end of 2028.	Very High	If quantum hardware development stalls significantly beyond current projections, possible but not consistent with IBM, Google, and Microsoft's published roadmaps.
Quantum simulation is in production at one or more platform banks by 2031, for portfolio optimisation at minimum.	High	If quantum error correction takes longer than expected, the most plausible scenario under which this prediction fails.

The table above represents my best judgment with the information available in 2026. Section 12.6 now does the thing that honest prediction requires: Names the scenarios under which the whole thesis could break down.

* * *

12.6 What Could Possibly Go Wrong (with My Predictions)?

12.6.1 This Fear Keeps Me Honest

Forty years of presaging the direction of change but not the timing make me cautious. I truly believe we will witness the kind of tectonic shift that will reconfigure banking as we know it. But am I confusing history being made with history rewriting itself – especially given my fintech bias?

Of this much I'm certain: The history of banking transformation contains few if any examples of banks themselves leading change. Quite the opposite: Banks spanning the generations have reacted to shifts (usually late) that started somewhere else: In technology, customer behaviour, regulation or adjacent industries.

- Customers forced Internet banking on financial institutions after they had already adapted to the Internet in every other part of their lives.
- The smartphone forced mobile banking.
- Regulation forced Open Banking.

The destination? This book represents my wager on being correct (with my reputation as table stakes). But the catalyst? That's harder to say.

That long list of possibilities – forcing functions, technology convergence, first-mover advantage, DeFi, regulatory catalysts, changed customer behaviour, collapsed development barriers – might not include the first domino to fall. The transformation could also originate from an unexpected direction: A Chinese or Southeast Asian platform company, for example, that penetrates Western markets faster than anyone anticipated. Or a regulatory intervention that changes the rules of the game in ways that nobody predicted. Or a technology breakthrough that makes quantum simulation available five years earlier than expected. Would that compress the transformation window to a point where the banks I've dubbed winners cannot execute in time?

12.6.2 The AI Guardrail Risk

AI's regulatory environment also concerns me. I have assumed in this book that the regulatory trajectory – the EU AI Act, the UK's principles-based approach, the emerging US framework – will create a predictable enough environment that fosters confident investment by banks in AI-powered platform banking. But AI's regulatory environment has evolved faster than any previous framework I have experienced, and in an environment of considerable political uncertainty.

If significant financial harm comes from an autonomous AI system that makes wrong decisions for large numbers of people, a regulatory overcorrection could ensue. As a result, the agentic AI deployment that platform banking requires could be constrained in ways that render my 2032 timeline a non-starter. While not likely, it is possible. Any banking executive who reads this book – even just this section – should invest now in the explainability and human oversight architecture that make their AI systems defensible, even in a more restrictive regulatory environment.

12.6.3 Geopolitics and the Risk to AI Access

The third risk, specific to the UK, troubles me more than perhaps it should. Because the UK lacks a domestic foundational AI model of significance, the nation depends on superpowers to fill the void. With every major AI capability a UK bank deploys – the large language models, agentic frameworks, and quantum cloud infrastructure – an American tech company controls the same (or, to a lesser extent, a Chinese one).

When geopolitical relationships remain stable, the dependency is manageable. But the events of 2026 have proven just how much the stability assumption no longer applies. In a world of strained relationships, where access to American AI turns into a negotiating chip in trade or security disputes, UK banks could find themselves in an impossibly tough spot. What happens when you depend on technology you cannot access, replicate or replace quickly? This structural vulnerability ranks as a red flag that the UK banking industry should take seriously. Without a domestic foundational AI capability, the UK has reached a strategic full stop that someone in government should lose sleep over.

12.6.4 Breaking Down Where the Thesis Breaks Down

Here's one possible scenario where my entire thesis falls apart: Banks neither lead nor lag in the transformation effort. Instead, the Big Tech platforms – Apple, Google, and Amazon – move into banking after stablecoin regulatory clarity emerges in 2027 and 2028. If they move at light speed, then the platforms that win are not banks at all. Every bank becomes a Pipe provider because the platform moat originates from the other side: Apple Pay becomes Apple Bank, and Google Pay becomes Google Financial Life. While not the most likely outcome, banks should consider it, lest they become lost in Apple's convergence wave 2.0.

* * *

12.7 The Reason for Hope

12.7.1 What Banking Transformation's History Actually Shows

Despite the many ways I've harped on banks for not getting it – products over Platform and all that – I want to raise a point that the evidence supports and a relentless urgency focus sometimes obscures:

Banking institutions are more capable of transformation than they appear from the outside or believe themselves to be from the inside.

Throughout my career, I've seen the banking industry adapt and change when the times demanded it. The bank I joined as a young technologist in the early 1990s – a physical network of branches, paper-based processes and human-mediated everything – had largely remade itself by 2010. On the whole, change happened inside ancient institutions by commercial standards, staffed by people who had fashioned careers inside the old model, governed by change-cautious regulators. It happened because the evidence became undeniable, the competitive pressure irresistible. Enough people inside those institutions chose the difficulty of adaptation over the certainty of irrelevance.

But the transformation this book describes will prove harder than what preceded it, as it demands a more fundamental reimagining of traditional banks – with capabilities they currently lack. It also requires the willingness to be measured, organised and valued in a whole new way.

But banks that completed the internet transformation in the late 1990s also began without the capabilities they needed. They constructed and hired them, or partnered with vendors. The same scenario played out in the 2000s with apps and mobile. They learnt or bought companies that knew. The pattern repeated. It may repeat this time around, too.

With the capabilities in place to kick off a new age of transformation, the question returns to the fortitude banks exercise, or do not, to acquire and deploy what they need. The mounting evidence could not be more straightforward: Platform banking generates better customer outcomes and better economics. By 2027, disputing this will become difficult, and by 2028, the banks that watched evidence turn to proof without acting will most likely get featured in the losers column of this book's next edition. For now, time remains to act, with the history of past success as precedent.

12.7.2 A Tough Love Letter for Executives

Dear Banking Executive: Take note but Take Heart. Your situation is serious but not hopeless.

The prospective platform winners of 2032 still have building left to do, while some have barely started. What will separate the finishers from the also-rans? Not capital. Not tech. Not talent. At its most basic level, the differentiator costs nothing but means everything.

Commit. Embrace the truism that the destination is worth the struggle. That decision is yours to make. The technology will be available, your customers ready. That window you see from a distance? It's real and open. The only question is whether you approach it, enter, and remain 'open' to what's next.

Make no mistake: The window is narrow as well. Not everyone will gather the courage to squeeze through. Others will waver and back off. And a good number of your colleagues will take note of what they see and remand it back to a committee. They might as well hope to still the march of time.

I stake four decades' experience, my reputation, and standing among my peers on the reality I see: The institutions that win in 2032 are committing right now. Some know it. Most do not.

For a few more years, you have the chance to take the banking road less travelled, but indeed will make all the difference. Take it. Commit.

Sincerely and in financial security (yours),

Dharmesh Mistry (and Lou Carlozo)

Questions for Your Board

1. Which of the eight predictions in section 12.5 align with our competitor analysis?
2. The chapter qualifies its arithmetic to calculate 10–20 platform winners globally, and 50–100 pipe winners that choose the latter role on purpose. Which outcome will we target? Or can we pivot successfully to a micro-platform role?
3. Lloyds and especially DBS have clearly articulated value capture from AI investments. Does our bank have similar measurements and targets defined?

13

The Big Tech Threat: Why Apple, Google and Others May Beat Banks

Chapter 12 mapped the competitive landscape bank by bank: Who will win as a Platform, who will survive as a Pipe, and who will fail. That analysis assumed the primary competition is between banks, though that is not necessarily true. The winners' table in 2032 will not be populated solely by institutions that started as banks. The Big Tech threat does not serve as a subplot to the Platform or Pipe story. For some banks, it constitutes the main event.

February 2026: Santander bolstered its US presence with a $12.2 billion Webster Bank deal. Payoneer applied for a national trust bank charter for PAYO, its proposed stablecoin-focused digital bank. And with the continued march of artificial intelligence, Wall Street's financial firms ended the month awash in red ink.

Yet amidst those weighty headlines, another story broke that escaped the notice of most Western banking executives. It involved Grab, the Southeast Asian super-app that serves 50 million monthly users across eight Southeast Asian countries with ride-hailing, food delivery, and financial services. It acquired Stash, an AI-powered financial guidance platform in the US, for $425 million.

Stash boasted more than a million paying subscribers, $5 billion in assets under management, and an AI Money Coach it launched in late 2024. Talk about a winning record: That coach drove half of its users to take a positive financial action *on the same day they engaged with it.* Goal!

Now let's say you did catch that story and thought, 'Interesting fintech acquisition,' then moved on to your morning coffee. If so, you missed the

D. Mistry, L. R. Carlozo, *The Intelligent Ledger*,
https://doi.org/10.1007/978-3-032-32842-7_13

point. Grab is not a fintech but a platform company. It started in transport and expanded into every adjacent service that platform economics made available. Now it's moving to build out financial services. With existing digital banking licences in Singapore and Malaysia, Grab already operates in lending, insurance, and payments across its user base. These customers use Grab to assist with tasks throughout the day, from commuting in the morning to ordering dinner at night.

You could call this the ultimate 'Stash and Grab'. As a result of the purchase, Grab now owns AI financial guidance technology, a stronger subscriber base, and the talent to accelerate its financial services ambitions beyond Asia and into the United States. Another institution might wait for permission of some sort, whether from the C-suite or some puzzled regulator. Not Grab. It wants to execute.

No isolated event, the Grab-Stash deal signals a process already underway: the convergence of platform companies, AI platforms, and emerging market super-apps staking out the financial services territory banks have treated as exclusively their own for a century or more. (Remember that banker who remarked to me, 'We own our customers'?) Here I want to detail the nature of that threat. Who ranks as the most dangerous and why? What have banks (and the threats, for that matter) waited for? And what do banks possess that the technology giants do not? To be certain, a narrow but real set of advantages makes a bank response possible. But with 2032 in sight, and the Grab deal a present-day reality, it must happen fast.

* * *

13.1 New Rails, New Ride

13.1.1 What's Happened Since the Last Time Someone Said This?

For most of the 2010s, I predicted, along with others, that fintech piranhas and Big Tech sharks would take bites out of banking. The threat was real – who would want to mess with such toothy brutes? – but the timing early. Circumstances have changed since then.

Chapter 5 established some salient facts. First, the nature of money itself is changing. Stablecoins, for example, solve for 'issues with efficiency, access and timing with money in settlement,' Anthony Vassallo, Silicon Valley Bank's Senior Vice President of Crypto, told my co-author at Money2020 in 2025.

What's more, stablecoins, central bank digital currencies (CBDCs) and tokenised deposits do not represent incremental improvements to the existing payment infrastructure. They comprise a new infrastructure unto itself: open and programmable, these elements operate at a fraction of the cost of legacy rails. The infrastructure also removes the single most effective defence banking has leveraged against Big Tech disruption for the past decade.

Throughout that period, the four tech giants most equipped to disrupt banking – Apple, Google, Amazon, and Meta – have conspicuously restrained themselves. Each entered financial services in specific but limited ways: Apple Pay and Apple Card; Google Pay and Google Wallet; Amazon-branded credit cards and loans to its marketplace sellers; Meta Pay within its messaging platforms. Substantial moves? Yes. Full-on assaults on the banking industry and its customer relationships? No.

You could chalk up the cautious treading to any number of reasons, from a wait-and-see attitude to a perception that the task simply amounted to too much. In reality, infrastructure explains why. The existing payment rails, settlement systems and correspondent banking networks operate in a proprietary nature. They're heavily regulated, extraordinarily expensive legacy architecture took decades and hundreds of billions of dollars to build. To compete on those rails, a technology company would either have to build its own version or negotiate access to the existing one through today's banks. Neither option presents itself as attractive. In fact, the existing infrastructure acts as one of banking's most effective defences against Big Tech disruption. The barriers to entry, or to replicate something from scratch, simply presented too many obstacles—especially cost in the latter case.

A stablecoin infrastructure turns this circumstance on its head.

Consider that a stablecoin running on blockchain rails does not require access to SWIFT. Or correspondent banking relationships. Or the decades of regulatory relationship building that traditional banking infrastructure access demands.

Nope. It only requires a stablecoin licence. The US, EU, and UK should have licensing frameworks in place by 2027 and 2028. And when they arrive, the infrastructure barrier that has protected banking from Big Tech dissolves. As noted in Chapter 5, the banking licence itself becomes an optional 'infrastructure' rather than the competitive moat.

One technology executive has already said the quiet part out loud. In October 2023, Elon Musk was reported to have told X employees exactly what he meant by payments. Not a wallet. Not a peer-to-peer transfer. 'You will not need a bank account,' he said. 'When I say payments, I actually mean someone's entire financial life. If it involves money, it'll be on our platform.' X has since struggled to execute on that vision, and Musk's credibility as a technology forecaster has taken its share of hits. But the ambition he articulated was never uniquely his. It is the ambition of every platform company in this chapter. He was simply the only one senior enough, and unguarded enough, to say it.

13.1.2 A Compelling Cost Efficiency

A straightforward economic case explains why Big Tech could move to stablecoin-based banking. A payment on SWIFT, for example, costs somewhere between 25 cents and $45, depending on the route. Multiple intermediaries collect a fee, while settlement takes one to five business days and generates fragmented data across every institution in the chain.

Compare that to a payment on stablecoin rails, which:

- settles in seconds,
- costs fractions of a cent,
- involves no intermediaries, and
- generates complete, auditable transaction data in a single place.

For Apple, which processed an estimated $6 trillion in payment volume through Apple Pay in 2024, the difference represents an annual financial opportunity measured in billions of dollars. The motivation is straightforward economics. The new rails dramatically outperform the old ones, and the companies best positioned to build on them do not include legacy banks resting on a comparatively ancient architecture. It represents the difference, to extend the rail metaphor, between a system built for locomotives versus bullet trains.

Thus, stablecoin regulatory clarity will trigger Big Tech's full entry into banking. Yes, Apple or Google could build bank-like services on existing rails—and have, in limited ways. But doing this requires deep entanglement with a legacy banking system that, in essence, runs the railroad. The system controls and encompasses the costs, constraints, and regulatory dependencies. Stablecoin rails offer a clean break. No incumbent owns them. Anyone with a licence can access it. And it operates at a fraction of the cost. For any tech company that has spent its existence building clean architectures rather than inheriting obsolete ones, the stablecoin moment marks not just a regulatory event. It equates to an architectural invitation.

* * *

13.2 The Four Giants, What Each Actually Has

13.2.1 Apple, The Most Dangerous Competitor

I consider Apple the most dangerous of the four major technology giants to banks for this reason: Apple is the only one whose relationship with banks is characterised as competition rather than cooperation. Google, Amazon, and Microsoft all generate significant revenue from cloud services sold to banks, and because of this, banking disruption would also unsettle their own enterprise customers, which would create genuine strategic tension. Apple sells hardware and services directly to consumers. Its revenue does not depend on bank relationships. It benefits from uncomplicated incentives: own the customer and source the infrastructure from whoever offers the best terms.

Moreover, banking analysts consistently underestimate how far along Apple has travelled on that journey.

It only took Apple Pay ten years from its 2014 launch to hit the $6 trillion annual payment processing mark. That makes Apple one of the largest payment processors in the world *without holding a single banking licence.* When Apple Card launched in 2019, the company tapped Goldman Sachs to provide the regulated infrastructure, which allowed Apple to own the customer interface, relationships, and consumer data. Then came Apple Savings in 2023, which attracted $10 billion in deposits within its first year—a savings product, FDIC-insured, that lives in Apple's Wallet app. When Apple Pay Later launched later the same year, Apple took on the role of lender for the first time, which allowed it to make credit decisions without a bank partner in the loop. And in 2024, Apple terminated its partnership with Goldman Sachs. Did the products fail? No. In fact, Apple had extracted enough from the partnership to know it wanted to own more of the stack for itself.

Review that sequence carefully. Each move followed the same logic: source the regulated infrastructure from whoever offers the best terms, own the customer experience, accumulate the financial data, then reduce dependence on the partner once the data and trust become established. Chapter 5 describes this precise model as a path to make the banking licence optional—and Apple has executed it, product by product, for a decade. The Goldman exit was not a retreat but a graduation. Goldman was the training partner, a mentor of sorts. The next exam arrives with the stablecoin era.

Apple occupies an equally formidable data position across the non-financial layers, and once again, bank analysts underappreciate this in favour of a transaction data focus. Consider what Apple already holds through the iPhone and Apple Watch:

- continuous location and behavioural data (Layer 2),
- fitness and health data via HealthKit (Layer 1),
- communications and social patterns via messages and FaceTime (Layer 3),
- stress and emotional proxies via wellness features (Layer 4), and
- detailed cognitive and decision patterns through the App Store from every digital service consumers install, along with how they use them (Layer 5).

This constitutes Layers 1 through 5 of the digital twin: Assembled across more than two billion active devices, updated continuously, with customer consent and trust levels no other company can equal. Given how effectively it manages customer data, Apple benefits from an authentic 'privacy-first' marketing message as well. Customers share data more willingly with Apple than perhaps any other technology company on earth. It makes for a precise, elegant cause-and-effect: The company that most stresses privacy as a brand value has become the world's most trusted data collector.

Since 2014, Apple has acquired Layer 6 financial data via Apple Pay transaction history, Apple Card spending data, and Apple Savings behaviour data. Stablecoin regulatory clarity sets the stage for Apple to own Layer 6 completely. No longer will the tech giant need to route transactions through bank rails or adhere to the data-sharing constraints bank partnerships impose. Rather than shift from outside banking to inside it, Apple can move from partial to complete ownership of its financial relationships and maintain them at a fraction of the current infrastructure cost.

A fully stablecoin-enabled Apple does more than deprive banks of product revenue: Their position in that customer's financial life evaporates. How could they possibly compete with a digital twin assembled across 15 years of daily device use, five complete non-financial layers, and a financial layer no competitor can reconstruct from scratch? The switching cost amounts to the accumulated intelligence of a customer's life.

13.2.2 Google, The Intent Engine

Though it differs from Apple's, Google's advantage in banking ranks as equally profound. Where Apple knows what you *do*, Google knows what you *think about doing*. All told, its search intent data – inclusive of 20 years of inquiries on mortgages, insurance, loans, investments, financial difficulty and life events – offers the most direct window into financial decision-making of any data set in the world.

How does this play out on a day-to-day basis? When someone searches 'How much can I borrow for a mortgage?', 'What happens if I miss a credit card payment?', or 'What are the best savings rates for retirement?', they do more than ask a question. They reveal a financial decision-making moment that any bank would pay significant money to witness. Google has collected these signals for two decades and every bank's marketing department knows it. This explains why banks make some of the largest Google advertising buys. But an enormous difference exists between a bank that pays Google to reach customers at moments of financial intent versus Google's power to use those moments of financial intent to serve those customers directly.

Google's cloud business creates the strategic tension: It generates significant revenue from banking clients that include HSBC and Deutsche Bank. But Google has demonstrated on many occasions that it will compete with its own enterprise customers when a large enough consumer opportunity presents itself. It built Android's dominance of the smartphone market partly at the expense of the handset manufacturers that also happened to be Google's distribution partners. YouTube competed directly with Google's media advertising clients. When Google spies a large enough consumer financial services opportunity to justify the enterprise relationship tension, it will move. Stablecoin regulatory clarity will mark the moment that calculation manifests again, freeing Google to leverage 20 years of financial intent data that no bank possesses—or could hope to possess.

13.2.3 Amazon, The Prime Commerce and Lending Machine

Amazon's banking position most immediately threatens one specific segment: small business lending. Amazon already lends billions of dollars annually to the merchants who sell on its marketplace. Its data on transactions, inventory, customer review, and fulfilment performance inform credit decisions that traditional banks simply cannot make with the limited information available to them. An Amazon seller who applies for a traditional bank loan provides financial statements and credit history. But Amazon already knows the seller's daily revenue, return rates, customer satisfaction scores, inventory turnover, seasonal patterns, and business performance trajectory. By comparison, the bank's underwriting is a guess. As a result, Amazon can lend to merchants that banks would decline—and at competitive rates, with fewer defaults, because its information advantage results in better credit decisions.

In consumer banking, Amazon mounts its data position around consumption behaviour: what people buy and how often, what they pay for it, and what they subscribe to and return. This provides a rich signal about household economics, lifestyle, and financial capacity that complements but does not replicate the data positions of Apple or Google. Amazon's specific banking entry point will likely target the complete commerce journey. Through it, they can help customers finance purchases, manage household spending, optimise subscription costs, and plan for major expenditures. All this takes place within an Amazon ecosystem that already handles a substantial fraction of Western consumer commerce: just shy of 38% of all US ecommerce, according to Forbes.

When Amazon can execute all this on stablecoin rails – without bank partnerships that reduce its margin and constrain its data use – a compelling incentive to build a full banking product will follow.

13.2.4 Meta, The Social Graph and Consent Lesson

Meta's position easily qualifies as the most complex of the four major players, because it holds the most data but inspires the least trust. It boasts the richest social layer of the digital twin that any company possesses.

Think about this (which you may not do consciously, even if you're a regular Facebook or Instagram user). Meta knows who you know and how well; how you communicate; which life events you share; what you celebrate; and what you worry about. It records births, deaths, marriages, divorces, new jobs, redundancies, house moves, health challenges, and financial struggles through the patterns of what information users share and how they interact. This social and relationship data – Layer 3 of the digital twin – exists at a scale and depth no other company can approach. Combined with Meta's payments infrastructure across WhatsApp Pay, Facebook Pay, and Instagram, it possesses, in theory, a significant banking capability.

The way Meta explicitly telegraphs its data-for-services model has clarified the value exchange. When Meta introduced its subscription option for European users – pay for the service or consent to data use for advertising – it defined a fundamental model that customers had accepted implicitly for years. Interestingly, this clarity did not cause the mass exodus that privacy advocates predicted. When millions of users chose the data-sharing option, they made the calculation out of free will that the service was worth the data. Data exchange normalisation makes platform banking possible: The shift from 'I do not know what they do with my data' to 'I understand the exchange and accept it because I get something valuable in return.' Uncomfortable as this makes privacy advocates, Meta's explicit data model could actually serve as a rehearsal for the consent architecture platform banking requires.

When Meta's financial services ambitions become as explicit as its data model, it will stand ready to monetise a customer base that understands and has accepted the value exchange.

* * *

13.3 The Second Wave, Emerging Market Platforms Moving West

13.3.1 The Threat Beyond Western Big Tech

The Grab-Stash acquisition offers the clearest signal yet that the competitive threat to Western banking extends beyond the four technology giants headquartered on the American West Coast. Platform companies from Southeast Asia, Latin America, and China have spent the past decade building integrated financial services into super-app ecosystems that serve hundreds of millions of customers with a completeness no Western bank has achieved. These companies have begun to move West: not tentatively or experimentally, but with the capital, technology, and ambition of companies that, having won their home markets, now seek the next frontier.

Grab's acquisition of Stash represents the template. Why build Western financial services capability from scratch if you can acquire it? Stash had one million paying subscribers, $5 billion in assets under management, an AI Money Coach with proven engagement metrics, and a regulatory relationship with the SEC as a registered investment adviser.

Grab acquired all of that for $425 million, a fraction of the cost to build it from scratch or the required spend for any Western bank to develop comparable AI financial guidance capability. The acquisition gives Grab a US financial services presence, regulatory credibility, and customer relationships. Combine this with Grab's platform data from Southeast Asia and its proven ability to build super-app financial ecosystems, and you get a combined entity more capable of platform buildout than either part alone. And others will replicate the model.

As described in Chapter 12, Nubank has filed for a US banking licence. A company that serves 60% of Brazilian adults and has built an AI-native financial platform for 131 million customers will not stop at Latin America. In fact, its Brazil customer acquisition playbook – zero fees, genuine AI guidance, word-of-mouth growth, no branch costs – better suits the American market than the Brazilian one. The US already has the smartphone penetration and digital banking comfort that Nubank needed to build from scratch in Brazil. The US market's main protection against Nubank comes from an odd place: navigating the regulatory complexity to obtain a US banking charter.

But consider that protection as both finite and time-limited. When Nubank obtains its US licence – and their application trajectory suggests a matter of years, not decades – it will enter the US market with a proven model, better AI than most US banks, and a track record. After all, they've already redefined a major market on an enormous scale.

13.3.2 Why Western Banks Do Not Get Super-App Logic

While Western banking executives often obsess about competition, super-app companies concentrate on *expansion*. This explains why banks consistently underestimate the competitive threat from emerging market platforms. For Western banks, it's about products and markets: 'Who else offers mortgages in our geography or a current account product that competes with ours?' Super-app companies flip the switch by viewing competition in terms of customer time and problems: 'What do they want to accomplish, and how do we become the place they come to accomplish it?'

When Grab expands into financial services, the calculus does not equal 'We should add a banking product to our app.' Instead, it follows this thesis: 'Our customers manage money as part of living their lives, and use us every day for transport, food, and digital services. Financial management? That's the next logical dimension of our evolving life platform.'

Every service Grab adds to its platform increases the stickiness of every other service. The more customers use it, and for more purposes, the more data Grab collects. Behold the righteous circle: More data across more services enables Grab to better serve customers across all the things they do, which makes them use Grab for more things. This is the super-app flywheel, and it is more powerful than the banking flywheel because it starts from a broader base of customer life engagement. Consider that a bank that builds a platform starts from financial data and tries to expand outward. But a super-app that adds banking starts from complete life engagement and adds financial intelligence to what it already knows. The starting position, originating from that opposite pole, drives the flywheel via the benefit of momentum that's already established.

* * *

13.4 The AI Platform: No Longer a Wildcard

13.4.1 The Threat Nobody Is Talking About Yet

The first draft of this chapter was called 'AI Platforms as a Wildcard.' Then on 13 April 2026, that description became obsolete.

OpenAI acquired Hiro Finance, an AI-powered personal finance start-up built specifically to give users verifiable, mathematically precise answers to financial planning questions. Hiro founder Ethan Bloch – who previously built and sold the automated savings app Digit for more than $200 million – joined OpenAI with his team. That previous October, OpenAI acquired the personal finance app Roi. Hmmmm. Two consumer personal finance acquisitions in six months. Combined with the PayPal-powered digital wallet already integrated into ChatGPT for in-chat purchases, the strategic intent has emerged. OpenAI's assistant will not just talk about your finances: It will manage them.

Bloch's own framing on joining OpenAI is worth reading carefully:

> *'For decades, personalised financial guidance has been too expensive, too generic, or too hard to access. ChatGPT is finally changing that.'*

A technology company merely out to build a productivity tool does not use (or choose) that kind of language. Instead, we hear the language of a financial services company focused on a primary relationship. He highlights a crystal-clear mission: To improve people's financial well-being at scale. Notice how this aligns with the mission statement of every platform bank this book describes. Intuit, parent of TurboTax and Credit Karma, read the signal correctly: Its stock hit a four-year low on the news.

The distinction here is subtle but profound: A progression from 'I help you think about your finances' to 'I help you manage your finances.' For OpenAI, this constitutes a natural evolution of a forming relationship, driven by genuine utility, now deliberately accelerated by specialist talent acquisition.

And so banks must address the question of where other AI platforms will position themselves. The answer reveals a competitive dynamic that banks need to understand clearly.

Anthropic launched Claude for Financial Services in July 2025, with deep integrations into FactSet, Morningstar, S&P Global, and other professional data providers. Claude leads financial reasoning benchmarks; institutions including Bridgewater, Citi, and NBIM, the world's largest sovereign wealth fund, now deploy it. In February 2026, Intuit partnered with Anthropic to introduce Claude within QuickBooks, TurboTax, and Credit Karma. Google's Gemini now integrates into Google Finance, embedded in Wells Fargo, HSBC, and Deutsche Bank's internal workflows, and deployed as Gemini Enterprise across professional financial institutions.

This critical distinction reinforces this chapter's argument. As Claude and Gemini move into financial services on the B2B and professional side, they serve banks and financial institutions as tools. This improves analyst productivity, automates compliance, and accelerates due diligence. In the language of this book, this strengthens the Pipe layer. Meanwhile, OpenAI has targeted the consumer side. Rather than just serve as the origin point of a clever LLM that answers detailed questions, writes resume drafts, or designs PowerPoint presentations, they now strive to acquire personal finance talent, develop consumer-facing financial guidance, and integrate payment capability. Such are the beginnings of a Platform layer that bypasses the bank entirely.

Meanwhile, most banking executives have failed to grasp or articulate this crucial, competitive dynamic in the AI financial services landscape. At present, AI companies do not pose a monolithic threat. They fall into two groups: those that work *with* banks and those that work *around* them. A bank that deploys Claude for its analysts gains capability. A bank that ignores OpenAI's consumer financial guidance ambitions accumulates risk.

What's more, the regulatory path for any AI platform to graduate to a licensed financial services provider remains complex. Important liability questions around AI-generated financial advice, and specifically the absence of fiduciary duty in AI systems, remain unresolved. OpenAI has neither announced nor pursued a banking licence application. But OpenAI has opted not to wait for answers before hiring people who will answer them. Hiro's verifiable financial mathematics, which addresses the accuracy problem that heretofore constrained AI in financial advice, filled OpenAI's product need—and OpenAI recognised it. Hiro solves the trust problem that stands between an AI assistant and a primary financial relationship.

Days before this book went to press, OpenAI moved from talent to product. On 15 May 2026, ChatGPT Pro subscribers in the US gained a Finances tab in the sidebar. Through a Plaid integration covering more than 12,000 institutions – Chase, Schwab, Fidelity, Robinhood, American Express, and Capital One among them – they can now connect bank accounts, credit cards, and investment portfolios directly to a chatbot running on a new GPT-5.5 Thinking model, benchmarked by OpenAI alongside more than 50 financial professionals. Intuit integration is on the roadmap. Read-only access, *for now* ... *For now.*

Notice what OpenAI disclosed about its own customer base in the launch post: More than 200 million people were already asking ChatGPT financial questions every month *before* the product existed. Two hundred million. That is the latent platform-bank customer base no traditional bank has access to, accumulating the kind of intent data Google has spent 20 years harvesting but with a conversational interface that makes acting on it natural rather than awkward.

Hiro was the talent. The May launch is the foundation. The next step, when stablecoin clarity arrives, is the bank.

Banks misread the situation – and do so at a profound level – when they treat AI companies as technology suppliers rather than competitive threats. Will AI platforms enter consumer banking? That's the wrong question. Better to pose this: Will they choose to partner with or replace banks? Based on the passage you've just read, consider the answer you think fits best.

* * *

13.5 Fear Not, Banks: You Do Have Advantages

13.5.1 Four Things Big Tech Cannot Buy Quickly

The competitive situation for banks, while serious, is not hopeless.

I do not want to present an incomplete or dishonest picture, so let's account for what banks possess that tech giants do not. Banks enter the platform race with three bona fide yet time-limited advantages. When traditional financial institutions grasp them, they will fathom the length of time they have to act and what they must do with it.

The first substantial advantage combines regulatory experience and trust in financial data. Over decades, banks have fostered relationships with a host of global regulators—the PRA, FCA, Federal Reserve, OCC, and ECB among them. The banks and these parties mutually understand what financial services organisations require and what they risk. They operate within compliance architecture, risk management frameworks, and institutional knowledge of safe operation in a regulated financial environment. To be precise: Just because a fintech or aspiring platform can acquire talent or buy advantageous properties does not mean they can replicate what banks have built here. They're not even close.

For example: When Apple launches Apple Banking, it will require a banking licence, which requires a clear demonstration of regulatory maturity for which no shortcut exists. It takes years to create that. Not just a competitive barrier, the regulatory relationship amounts to a competence that banks own and tech players lack. Yes, this advantage erodes as they invest in regulatory relationships and acquire licensed entities. But it does not disappear overnight. Even the formidable Revolut took five years to get a UK banking licence, and that's with a focus only on banking.

The second advantage involves the financial data relationship itself. Banks hold the transaction history, credit relationships, savings patterns, and liability information that constitute the financial layer of the digital twin. More importantly, customers have a specific and different money relationship with their bank than with any technology platform. If they did not, Apple, Meta, Google, and Amazon would have surpassed banks long ago—assuming they had regulatory heft to begin with. Meta in particular must overcome the stigma that it manipulates user relationships and data for its own gain: a characteristic that more resembles a direct transactional model than one suited for a platform. (In this case, the 'product' comes indirectly through targeted advertising.)

Third, consumers trust banks with their money. Apple Pay, for example, has not yet replicated this psychological dimension. Even if a customer shares health data with Apple, location data with Google and social data with Meta, they may still hesitate before giving an AI platform the same access and authority with financial data and the same authority over their financial decisions. Regarding trust gap issues, Meta stands as the prime example. Its unethical (and arguably immoral) manipulation of toxic content aimed at teenage girls, along with its gaffes in allowing Russian bots to post false information in the 2016 US presidential election, does not speak well in terms of why consumers should offer them their financial information.

But the narrow trust advantage erodes as technology platforms establish financial credibility. Even Meta could likely overcome its challenges with effective marketing.

Fourth, banks have time on their side – for now. The hesitation that exists today among consumers to hand over their financial data gives banks a window of opportunity. But it will not stay open indefinitely, and most banking executives do not appreciate this. Traditional banks still have time while regulators iron out the frameworks for stablecoin-based banking. While legislative trajectories in the US, EU, and UK gain traction, banks can establish digital twins, AI guidance capability and quantum simulation pilots. By then, their platform flywheels will cement customer relationships with prohibitive switching costs and beat tech competitors dependent on stablecoin infrastructure. A note to banks: If you use the period that leads to 2028 to study, evaluate, pilot, govern, and form committees, your analysis may prove excellent. But the race could already be lost.

13.5.2 Banks: Asymmetry Does Not Equal Safety

I constantly hear a dangerous misreading from banking executives. The argument goes: Big Tech has threatened to disrupt banking for 10 years, but it has not happened yet. The regulatory and cultural barriers, as well as the customer trust in banks, are real. The threat? Perennial. Survivable.

This argument misreads the past decade, though. It mistakes pulling the trigger – a one-time action – with the patient process of assembling the cannon while Quanvergence takes shape. The infrastructure, data positions, customer relationships, and regulatory knowledge continue to gain traction. Names be damned, Apple Pay did not fail to become Apple Bank. It established the payment habit and trust relationship while it harvested valuable data. Google Wallet did not fail to become Google Finance. It collected financial behaviour data and reinforced interface habits that make Google Finance compelling. Amazon Lending did not fail to become Amazon Bank. It proved the credit model, built the merchant relationship, and demonstrated that technology-driven lending beats bank lending on information quality, all while using criteria that transcend the FICO score or old-fashioned balance sheets.

I hope this corrects some common misperceptions. In real (but not complete) ways, Big Tech has displaced banking over a decade of preparation. The full-on assault begins when the new rails open. The main event has not yet commenced, making its likelihood easy to ignore. But when the big reveal arrives, will banks be ready?

* * *

13.6 The Competitive Map: Who Threatens What, and When

Competitor	Primary Data Advantage	Banking Entry Point	Likely Timeline	Bank Response Window
Apple	Device behaviour, health, location, payment (2B+ devices)	Full retail banking on stablecoin rails; Apple Banking app replacing Apple Card	2027–2029: Post-stablecoin clarity	Now to 2027: Establish digital twin and platform moat before Apple moves
Google	Search intent, location, Android behaviour, 20 years of financial queries	Financial guidance via Google Assistant; payments on stablecoin rails; AI-powered financial planning	2028–2030: Cloud enterprise tension slows entry	2026–2028:Buildjourney engagement that makes Google guidance less appealing than bank guidance
Amazon	Commerce data, lending track record, merchant relationships, consumption behaviour	Consumer finance around commerce journey; expanded SME banking; household financial management	2027–2028 for commerce-linked products; 2029–2030 for full banking	Immediate: SME banking is already under threat from Amazon Lending
Meta	Social graph, life events, relationship data, messaging behaviour	Payments via WhatsApp/Instagram expanding to banking; financial services within social context	2028–2030: Trust deficit slows consumer banking entry	2027–2029: Social data partnerships before Meta builds them into competing products

Competitor	Primary Data Advantage	Banking Entry Point	Likely Timeline	Bank Response Window
Grab / Southeast Asian super-apps	Super-app ecosystem data, daily life engagement, Southeast Asian financial model	US market via Stash acquisition; Western markets via further acquisitions	Already on record: Stash acquisition Feb 2026	Immediate: The acquisition has happened
Nubank / LatAm platforms	131M customer primary relationships, AI-native platform, proven model	US banking licence in progress; Western markets following Brazil model	2027–2029: US banking launch	2026–2027: Build the platform moat before Nubank's US licence is granted
OpenAI (consumer)	Conversational relationship, personal finance acquisitions (Hiro, Roi), PayPal wallet integration	Consumer financial guidance; AI personal CFO bypassing bank entirely	Already underway; full banking 2028–2030	Immediate: OpenAI is acquiring fintech talent now; treat as competitive threat, not technology supplier
Anthropic / Gemini (B2B)	Financial reasoning benchmarks, professional data integrations (FactSet, Morningstar, S&P Global)	B2B tools strengthening bank analysts and workflows; Pipe layer reinforcement, not consumer threat	Ongoing; not a direct consumer banking threat	Deploy as productivity tool; monitor OpenAI separately as the consumer competitive threat

* * *

13.7 A Race, Not a Foregone Conclusion

13.7.1 A Straightforward Assessment

At the start of this chapter, I promised to refrain from unnecessary confrontation but not to soften my read on the threat. Here's what I believe: If banks fail to act decisively in the next two to three years, Big Tech will beat them.

Notice how I couched that outcome as conditional, not inevitable. The distinction matters. So take heart, bankers: Forward motion rooted in action, not rumination, merits a different, hopeful, and honest assessment.

Take a good look at that window I described above and leverage it without delay or boardroom chart gymnastics. The time to study the threat is over, so begin. Now.

In the meantime, as they say in American football, do not play a prevent defence.

Instead, embark on the journey to build your platform. The pieces already exist, and your colleagues at Lloyds and Bank of America have already begun to assemble some of them: the complete digital twin, AI-powered guidance, quantum simulation, journey ownership and ecosystem partnerships. Establish (or leverage) relationship depth and switching costs to manage or even sidestep that when it arrives. Let's look at the existing bank customer who gets a crack at its inaugural platform. Like never before, that consumer would reap substantial benefits, including (but not limited to):

- home journey navigation,
- simulation history, based on a treasure trove of bank data, and
- a digital twin that no competitor can reconstruct without monumental effort.

Combine all that and you wind up with a happy account holder who's far less likely to defect to a newly launched Apple Bank. They may use Apple Pay for convenience. They will not use Apple Bank for the financial decisions that matter.

13.7.2 Platforms Are Not Impregnable

The above highlights a crucial point: The average consumer has at least five to seven financial accounts with different providers, according to MX. These include banks, credit unions, and fintech leaders. Credit unions in particular enjoy an advantage no platform can supplant. The platform may deliver an unprecedented level of *data intimacy*. But this does not equal *personal intimacy*. They cannot sit across the desk from you, take a drive out to your small business, and collect the kind of 'data' – or offer the compassion – of a banker with a 20-year personal relationship. A certain percentage of people will insist on doing things the old-fashioned way, just as some writers, designers, and healthcare professionals eschew the use of LLMs.

There is more. If consumers already cross-pollinate credit cards and accounts from several banks, along with niche financial providers such as PayPal and Venmo, and bonehead-simple investment apps such as Acorns, they could mix things up in an age of platform providers. 'Switching costs', I must note, can work two ways. Consumers who resist entering a new credit card number into online platforms after a breach may decide, without evidence, that the leap to a platform simply is not worth the (perceived) headache, no matter the overwhelming advantages. This fits the definition of friction, assuming the platform provider cannot guarantee – and demonstrate – that the switch will prove far easier than they may think and produce error-free results. Overcoming the cultural and media perception that AI hallucinates, at least in the present day, amounts to one tall order.

13.7.3 Get a Financial Life

The credit union example should give platform builders pause. In all aspects of life, relationships matter. The most resilient banks will construct the Intelligent Ledger's financial life *relationship* based on *long-standing trust* as well as data. That goes deeper and matters more than anything a technology company can build from the outside in.

Even marketers can get in on the act, for perceptions trump reality in a great many instances. Imagine an ad campaign that features Mark Zuckerberg, a universally loathed tech baron, with the headline: 'Would you trust this man with your money?'

Banks thus have an inside position in the financial relationship. They can keep it if they use it. They will lose it if they do not.

The race is real, but the outcome is not yet determined. The window remains open, but for a shorter duration than most banking executives now believe. Banks with decades of accumulated history and a rock-solid foundation in times of crisis could prevail as the safest choice, but also portray the stodgy institution that refused to change with the times.

And so we reach the crossroads. Down one path, banks raise platforms that make them irreplaceable. And down the other, bumbling banks with blinders on pursue false security, only to become the buggy whip makers of tomorrow.

For a few more years, the choice remains open. At the crossroads, where do you stand? And in which direction will you start to walk?

Questions for Your Board

1. Have we performed a risk assessment based on the section 13.6 table? If so, what has it revealed to you?
2. Do we have an accurate picture of Big Tech capabilities and acquisitions in financial services over the last ten years? At what level do you understand this as thoughtful and deliberate planning over time?
3. Do we understand the various plays AI platform companies have made? Are we partnering when we should consider them as future competitors?

14

Conclusion: The Monday Morning Question

Ludwig van Beethoven took roughly six years to compose his Ninth Symphony. We are six years from 2032. The parallel fascinates me for this reason: Beethoven composed for instruments and a chorus altogether unique in that configuration—and in the process made history. As institutions build the first platform banks, the Ninth Symphony serves as a useful analogy. The score does not yet exist.

The question for everyone who has read this far is whether you intend to rank among the groundbreaking composers or the passive audience.

To get to this point in the book, you transcended the role of a casual browser and took this question seriously. This brings us to the final question, the only one that matters as you read this penultimate chapter:

What will you do on Monday morning?

Before you answer that, we want to name the elephant in the room dressed in its smart Armani or Ann Taylor suit. In four decades on the tech side of things, and then in C-suite roles, I have watched bank executives mistake motion for action, presentations for proactivity, and visuals for vision.

There's a good chance you know someone like this—or, to be blunt, maybe this sounds just like you. You read the reports, attend conferences, nod thoughtfully at keynote presentations, and return to the office to do broadly

D. Mistry, L. R. Carlozo, *The Intelligent Ledger*,
https://doi.org/10.1007/978-3-032-32842-7_14

what you did in the first place. The cycle is well-established: Insight arrives, is acknowledged and discussed. Then the institution absorbs, neutralizes, and files it under 'strategic considerations for future review.' I have delivered those insights more times than I can count. I know, and now so do you, how that story usually ends.

So we will not pretend that reading this book is sufficient—not when it could wind up in your institution's 'strategic considerations' cardboard box. Other fates likewise spell 'graveyard': discussions, strategy reviews of the implications, working groups that never work. Platform banking gets added to the next retreat agenda, reduced to sloppy squiggles on a dry-erase board as attendees anxiously count the minutes to lunch break. None of this will answer the Monday Morning Question. None. It's a financial paradox that this question proves simpler and harder to answer. To that end, all the gesticulation and note-taking in the world by the company Climber may impress the CEO, but it proves fruitless.

Meanwhile, the Monday Morning Question lies in wait for an answer:

Who in your organisation is accountable – by name, with a budget and timeline – to build the capabilities this book describes?

If you cannot answer right now with a name and a number, then the book perhaps piqued your interest but was not useful. And interest without utility captures the fate that awaits the losing institutions described in Chapter 12.

In Chapter 10, you met the archetypal people who will determine which column your institution lands in. The Protector, with too much to lose, will never champion something this disruptive. The Passenger will support the initiative in meetings and quietly deprioritise it everywhere else. And the above-mentioned Climber will attach their name to it if it looks like a winner and distance themselves from it the moment it starts to fail. You know these people because you work with them. Or perhaps some part of them tugs within you – all of you, even – in the name of minimising personal risk.

But if you've read every chapter up to this point, then I believe (or at least hope) that you seek a fourth option. We cannot name it because it does not qualify as an archetype: It demands a choice. Go back to your organisation on Monday and make it.

* * *

14.1 About Those Chapter-Capping Questions

What were those questions for your board at the end of every chapter designed to do? Not test your reading comprehension. Nor condense each chapter's argument. They were meant to diagnose, direct, and perhaps course correct.

If your board can answer these summarised Chapter 2 questions – have we identified convergence, do we agree with the timescale, and have we stress-tested the forcing functions? – then your board operates at a strategic awareness level that this moment requires. And on the other side, if you've avoided the conversation or batted it around long enough to conclude a lack of urgency exists, then you still possess valuable if cautionary intelligence: The problem rests not with the technology but leadership. You'll need a different book to rectify that.

Return to the questions in each chapter now and consider them from your executive role. Do not nail down 'the right answer' *but what your board would actually say*. If you cannot see the point of the exercise, then I've fallen short in my efforts to persuade you based on decades of experience and witnessing similar dilemmas where financial institutions did not grasp moments of convergence or wholesale change.

Lou and I contend that such a moment has arrived again, but with the force of a gathering tsunami as opposed to any other wave. The gap between that so-called right answer and what your board would actually say reveals much: where you are versus where you need to be. You can measure and close that gap but only if you name it first.

The six forcing functions in Chapter 4 will not wait for your board to agree with them. The 2027 start window referenced throughout this book does not boil down to a negotiation. The Quanvergence decidedly lacks a 'park this and look later' option. Nor will it ask for your kind permission, no matter the marketing campaign and working capital at your disposal. You might as well beam back to June 2007 and try to stop the first iPhone dead in its tracks. (Steve Jobs and his fans would've had you for lunch.)

Chapter 4 established a bedrock fact, one heard in too many conversations among banking execs and thought leaders in the past few years: Institutions that treat the changes as medium-term considerations are late to the party. And those convinced the Quanvergence exists as a long-term consideration – assuming they can name its components to begin with – have signed the figurative contract to exit from relevance and perhaps existence.

* * *

14.1.1 The Choice You (Yes, You) Will Make

Chapter 7 presented the Platform-or-Pipe binary as a strategic choice. Now let's reframe it as something more personal and beyond the temptation – always present – to defer the decision to a committee.

Beyond Platform or Pipe, the poignant choice centres on whether you, within your organisation, will identify the situation, act on it with courage and conviction, and build something that truly serves the customers your institution claims to serve. Otherwise, will you hide in the safety that comes with intellectual understanding but stops at the door of carefully managed politics? That preserves the existing structure, and leaves transformation to whoever comes next?

Two paths, both available today. Without doubt, the second one promises more comfort in the short term. It carries a lower personal risk profile and stands out as easier to defend in board meetings. But once the 2032 scenario in Chapter 12 arrives, only the first choice will guarantee a fighting chance for your institution.

AskHomey failed because it amounted to the right model at the wrong time, a tough but ultimately necessary fate to accept. That said, this book stands as our testament to alert banks to the inevitable choice that lies ahead in the next six years. Past that point, the timing will prove wrong for every traditional financial institution – but stem not so much from delays or avoidable circumstances as hard-headed leadership.

* * *

14.1.2 The Intelligent Ledger Defined

The book takes its name from an idea worth revisiting one last time. It's easy to misread the future as a pure function of technology such as a platform (small p) or stack. Nor does it represent a product, analyst category, vendor vision, or transformation programme. Rather, banking blossoms into The Intelligent Ledger when it moves from past tense to future tense: from what occurred to customers to what happens next for them.

Every bank in existence knows at some level that it exists to improve the financial lives of its customers. Every annual report says so, every brand campaign implies it, and every CEO speech at Money2020 or Sibos reaffirms it. Reality, however, overrules every pretence of appearance. Even a bank C-suite member may carry in her purse a credit card with a nosebleed-high APR.

These institutions inevitably exist to make shareholders and owners happy: to sell (and push) products, manage margins, and optimise quarterly numbers. The gap between stated mission and actual operating model creates a black hole that exercises an inevitable pull on customers. The death of trust is slow, incremental, and invisible. But for how long will consumers put up with this state of affairs? The first platform that offers a far better experience will tug customers in the opposite direction. No bank will be able to counteract it. Former clients will scramble for the exits without looking back.

The Intelligent Ledger embodies this sea change: not with better products, improved customer service, or a digital transformation programme and bright shiny new app. Instead, it forges a fundamentally different relationship between a financial institution and the people it serves. The Intelligent Ledger works continuously on behalf of the customer and not periodically on behalf of a quarterly target.

Streaming money makes that possible; tokenised money provides the programmable infrastructure. Quantum simulation supplies the analytical power to look ahead at every possible outcome. Agentic AI contributes the orchestration to make the bank – not just money – flow in real time. Digital twins furnish the deep customer understanding banks never boasted. And the platform model creates the commercial logic and business model that sustains it all. Not a single one of these components amounts to science fiction. In varying degrees of maturity, all of them exist. The only thing missing? The will and knowledge to assemble them.

Do you own that will?

The Monday Morning Question encapsulates this. Not, 'Do we believe this is coming?' It is. The question is whether your institution shapes what it becomes, with you taking an active leadership role, or watches from the wings while someone else runs the show before you.

* * *

14.1.3 Winners Use the Window

I have used the phrase 'the window is open' many times. I want to conclude by driving home the specific urgency. While it *remains* open, banks can still forge platform capability and use it as a competitive differentiator rather than a desperate catch-up play.

But not for long. By 2030, the first platform banks will have established flywheel effects that render competition effectively impossible. How could any bank hope to compete with customer data moats, partner ecosystems, AI models trained on years of platform data, and brand associations with financial intelligence as opposed to financial products? (Customised credit cards with your favourite sports team's logo certainly will not cut it.) At that point, the choice for banks no longer amounts to Platform or Pipe: It's Pipe or exit.

By 2027 – a year chosen deliberately based on evidence and arguments in every preceding chapter – banks can still unveil an 'MVP' (minimum viable Platform). Nor is a 2028 start impossible. But your competitive position weakens as more non-banks begin to mount their efforts.

I have been wrong about timing before. Chapter 2 documents that honestly. But early does not equal wrong. And Lou does not believe I am early this time, based on hundreds of interviews on his Bankadelic podcast. The forcing functions described in Chapter 4 are already in motion. Regulatory frameworks and Platform infrastructure are being fleshed out. The first platform banks are finding their footing. The institutions that will define the 2032 landscape will not wait for permission. Right now, they have moved into the early stages of composing an entirely new work without precedent.

Composing a Financial Symphony

Beethoven was paid £50 by the Royal Philharmonic Society to write the Ninth Symphony, roughly £7,100 in today's money. This adds up to a pittance for what became one of the most performed pieces of music in history. The economics of platform banking are far, far more favourable than that. But it still requires an analogous creative act: to compose for instruments in an entirely new way for an audience unprepared for what it will witness. From the first notes, those people will erupt in rapturous applause, never to return to what came before.

The Intelligent Ledger promises transformational banking that works continuously for the people it serves. For every unclaimed benefit it finds, consumers will wonder what made this so hard in the first place—and why their banks never offered anything like it, though exorbitant late fees never seemed to go out of style.

Those who create The Intelligent Ledger with courage and conviction might recognise their magnum opus by a slightly different moniker: The *Emotionally* Intelligent Ledger. Money is an ever-emotional topic for us all, often charged with stress, scarcity mentality and irrational behaviour. No bank that charges 25% APR on a credit card (with your favourite sports team logo on it) can pretend for a second to understand this.

But the Platform providers will get it. Petty as it might seem, consumers given a chance to leave behind the financial avarice of banks might see it as the ultimate example of how 'Living well is the best revenge,' to quote 17th-century English poet George Herbert. Let me emphasise this: Lou and I are not out to bash banks (nor was Herbert, even if poets made less than composers). I built my career at Lloyds; Lou has interviewed executives at institutions from Citi to Citizens Bank of Edmond, so integral to Oklahoma that it predates statehood. Many fine people within the banking sphere have changed lives for the better. Banks have a chance to make untold amounts of money simply by showing the courage, vision and *financial intelligence* to act on the risk-reward opportunity. They also have the ultimate opportunity to make good on the promise, too oft unrealised, of doing well – extremely well – by doing good: a tremendous amount of good.

The Ninth Symphony closes with the 'Ode to Joy'. We like that as a parting metaphor. We cannot think of a single reason to exclude anyone from a joyful banking denouement. All consumers who can access a Platform will get their chance. Every non-banking entrepreneur who assembles the parts can compose their own masterpiece. And yes, banks have every opportunity to join the performance.

But not all will choose to do so. Some will refuse to do so. Still others will mistake today's environment for a time of deliberation when dress rehearsals are already underway. The debut?

Not in five years . . .

Not in three years . . .

Not in a year.

The curtain parts today.

Which side are you on?

15

The Monday Morning Answer: Your Guide to True Forward Motion

While many of tech's most monumental achievements followed the framework of 'test and learn,' here it's time to do the opposite: Learn and test. The 14 chapters of information here have put you in a position to grasp the changes that will reshape financial services over the next six-plus years. Yet 'The Intelligent Ledger' does not represent an exercise in academic argument or a series of talking points for your mental file cabinet to trot out at the next board meeting. The authors prefer that you view it, ultimately, as a flight manual. The Quanvergence is real, not theoretical. Many financial institutions today will become footnotes tomorrow: Set your watches for 2032. Or maybe stopwatches are more appropriate. Assuming the maturity of quantum computing, the moment of truth for all banks will arrive sooner than most think.

So now that you've finished exploring, let's get to scoring. The C-suite and the executive layer can complete the tasks below in as little as 30 minutes. This will yield a starting point to assess where your institution stands. The goal is to determine whether you can achieve platform transformation—and if so, on what timeline. Accuracy here depends on honesty. An institution that scores itself accurately at 14 has a realistic path forward. But another that inflates its score to 22 when it deserves a 14 will waste the next 18 months doubling back. Though both institutions may start at the same place, the one that inaccurately assumes itself further along will discover knowledge and operational gaps the hard way.

D. Mistry, L. R. Carlozo, *The Intelligent Ledger*,
https://doi.org/10.1007/978-3-032-32842-7_15

This scorecard is broken down into six categories or dimensions:

- Strategic Clarity
- Data Foundation
- AI Capability
- Organisational Readiness
- Ecosystem and Partnerships
- Leadership and Culture

Score your institution from 1 to 5 using the descriptors provided. Then assess your velocity, which ties these dimensions together. It's crucial to examine not just how much progress you make but also at what clip. A score of 3 advancing is a different situation from a score of 3 static. Forward progress, you could say, depends on the speed of forward motion.

* * *

15.1 Dimension 1: Strategic Clarity

Is the Platform or Pipe choice explicit and public enough to survive institutional pressure?

Score	Description
1	• No explicit choice has been made. • The institution describes itself as 'committed to digital transformation' without specifying what that means in structural terms. • The words Platform and Pipe are not in active use in leadership conversations. • The institutional strategy remains tied to product ownership and existing end customer relationships.
2	• There is a general direction towards platform thinking, articulated in strategy documents, but no specific commitment to journey teams and metrics or named leadership accountability. • The existing product structure is unchanged.
3	• A platform direction has been communicated internally with some pilots underway. • However, the commitment is not public, metrics are still primarily product-based, and the programme has not yet been stress-tested by a significant budget or priority conflict.

Score	Description
4	• A specific, public platform commitment has been made with a named first journey, named programme director and an explicit statement that journey metrics will replace product metrics. • The commitment has survived at least one serious test.
5	• The choice is irreversible, public and operationally embedded. • Journey metrics are in use alongside (and beginning to replace) product metrics. • The CEO has communicated the strategic direction to investors, regulators and staff with enough specificity to be held accountable.

Your Score (1–5): _____ **Velocity:** Advancing/Static/Retreating

15.2 Dimension 2: Data Foundation

How complete is your digital twin today, and how quickly is it being built?

Score	Description
1	• Financial transaction data only, held in siloed systems across product lines. • No Open Banking integration. • No consent management architecture. • No data partnerships with non-financial data providers.
2	• Open Banking integration exists or is in progress. • Some data unification across internal product lines. • Basic consent management is in place. • No significant non-financial data layer partnerships.
3	• Financial layer (Layer 6) is substantially complete with Open Banking, with plans for Open Finance. • One or two additional data layer partnerships are active (likely property data or energy data). • Consent architecture built. • Transaction categorisation and enrichment running. • Strategy for building customer trust and driving engagement for more data has been defined.
4	• Three to four data layers live with real partnerships, consent architecture and real-time updating. • Environmental data (Layer 2) and social data (Layer 3) are active alongside financial. Data quality governance in place. • Pilot cohort experiencing multi-layer digital twin. • Trust and engagement strategy being executed.

Score	Description
5	• Five to six data layers active for pilot cohort. • Health data (Layer 1) integrated via wearable partnerships. • Behavioural patterns (Layers 4 and 5) derived from platform interaction data. • Real-time updating across all active layers. • Consent management fully operational with customer-facing transparency.

Your Score (1–5): _____ **Velocity:** Advancing/Static/Retreating

15.3 Dimension 3: AI Capability

Where is your institution on the journey from chatbot to agentic AI platform?

Score	Description
1	• AI in production is limited to rule-based chatbots and basic fraud detection. • No generative AI in customer-facing applications. • No agentic AI capability. • AI governance framework is minimal or absent.
2	• Generative AI in pilot or limited production (internal tools, FAQ handling, basic customer queries). • No agentic AI, though AI governance framework being built. • Some AI talent in-house but mostly vendor dependent.
3	• Generative AI in production for customer-facing applications at meaningful scale. • Agentic AI in pilot, capable of multi-step task execution in controlled scenarios. • AI governance framework operational. • Proprietary AI infrastructure being built alongside vendor tools, enterprise architecture and roadmap design.
4	• Agentic AI in production to handle customer financial queries, execute transactions, and orchestrate simple journeys autonomously. • MCP server integration with at least one external data source live. • Human oversight framework operational. • AI generates measurable customer value. • Enterprise architecture for agentic AI in place.

Score	Description
5	• Agentic AI orchestrating complete journey interactions autonomously for a significant cohort. • Multi-source MCP integration across digital twin data layers. • AI guidance demonstrably better than non-AI customer interactions on measured outcomes. • Quantum simulation pilot running alongside classical AI.

Your Score (1–5): _____ **Velocity:** Advancing/Static/Retreating

15.4 Dimension 4: Organisational Readiness

Are you organised around journeys or products, and is the structure changing?

Score	Description
1	• Pure product organisation. • Mortgage, credit card and savings teams, each with its own P&L, metrics, and leadership. • No journey thinking in organisational structure. • Transformation is managed as a separate programme reporting to a CDO or CTO without authority over product lines.
2	• Journey thinking exists in strategy documents and some working groups but the organisational structure and metrics remain product-based. • A 'customer experience' function exists but does not own product decisions or budgets.
3	• A journey team exists for at least one journey (pilot), operating alongside the existing product structure. • The journey team has a protected budget and some authority over the customer experience within its journey scope but attribution remains primarily product-based.
4	• Journey team model is operational for at least one journey with genuine authority: It owns the customer experience end-to-end, controls relevant partnerships, and is measured on journey metrics. • Product teams still exist but their relationship to the journey team is defined and governed.
5	• Two or more journey teams operate, each with true journey ownership/ metrics and a protected operating model. • Product teams repositioned as capability providers to journey teams rather than independent P&L owners. • Attribution model for journey economics is operationalised and reported to the board.

Your Score (1–5): _____ **Velocity:** Advancing/Static/Retreating

15.5 Dimension 5: Ecosystem and Partnerships

How built out is the third-party ecosystem that makes the platform genuinely useful to customers?

Score	Description
1	• No meaningful ecosystem partnerships beyond core banking infrastructure providers. • Third-party relationships are primarily vendor relationships (technology, compliance, outsourcing) rather than ecosystem partnerships that create customer value.
2	• Some partnership conversations are in progress across relevant journey areas (property, insurance, utilities, investment management) but no live integrations generate customer value. • Partnership framework and commercial model not yet defined.
3	• Two to four live ecosystem partnerships embedded in at least one journey area, generating some customer value (referrals, data enrichment, or basic service access). • Commercial model defined. • A partnership framework is operational but not scaled.
4	• Active ecosystem across at least one complete journey: Multiple partners covering different journey touchpoints, generating measurable customer engagement. • Partner data flowing into digital twin (with consent). • Revenue sharing model is operational.
5	• Rich ecosystem across two or more journeys. • Partners actively building on the platform API rather than being passively integrated. • Ecosystem data meaningfully enriching digital twin. Platform attractive to new partners because of engaged customer base it provides access to. • Flywheel beginning to self-reinforce.

Your Score (1–5): _____ **Velocity:** Advancing/Static/Retreating

15.6 Dimension 6: Leadership and Culture

Honestly: Which archetypes dominate your leadership layer, and is the programme protected?

Score	Description
1	• Protectors in key seats relevant to the transformation. • No explicit programme protection. • Transformation is managed through existing governance structures that the Protectors control. • The CEO has not tested their own commitment against institutional resistance.
2	• CEO commitment is genuine but not yet tested by significant institutional resistance. • Some Protectors identified but not managed. • Climbers present and energetic but not yet aligned to programme success metrics. • Programme governance exists but is not ring-fenced.
3	• CEO commitment has survived at least one meaningful test. • Key Protectors identified and either managed around or brought into alignment. • Programme director has direct CEO access. • Climbers' incentives partially aligned to programme outcomes. • Cultural challenge to the status quo is permitted and occasionally rewarded.
4	• CEO commitment is robust and publicly demonstrated. • Protector obstruction has been addressed explicitly in at least one case. • Programme team has genuine operating authority within defined scope. • Climbers are generating momentum in the right direction. • Passengers are being actively managed towards genuine contribution.
5	• Transformation has survived multiple serious tests of institutional commitment. • The leadership culture around the programme genuinely rewards challenge, flags problems early, and holds accountability for outcomes rather than activity. • The programme is self-reinforcing: Early successes have created genuine believers who are now advocates rather than passengers.

Your Score (1–5): _____ **Velocity:** Advancing/Static/Retreating

* * *

15.7 Scoring and Interpretation

Total Score	Velocity Profile	Interpretation	Recommended First Actions
6–12	Any	• The Platform or Pipe choice has not been made clearly. • The organisation is in the drift zone Chapter 7 describes as the most dangerous position, neither committing to Platform nor accepting Pipe.	• Complete the decision tree in Chapter 7. • Make the binary choice. • If Platform, apply Chapter 7's foundation phase immediately. • If Pipe, begin the deliberate Pipe excellence investment.
13–18	Static or Retreating	• Platform intent exists but execution is stalling. • The institutional gravity towards the existing model is winning. • Without active intervention, the programme will not reach first cohort before the competitive window closes.	• Diagnose which dimension is the binding constraint. • Almost always Dimension 1 (strategic clarity) or Dimension 6 (leadership and culture). • Address the root cause, not the symptoms.
13–18	Advancing	• Genuine early-stage platform build underway with real momentum. • The risk is pace; the 2027 window requires first cohort live by end of 2026 or early 2027 at the latest. • Assess whether current pace delivers that timing.	• Map the critical path to first cohort launch. • Identify the three to four decisions or investments that would most accelerate arrival at cohort launch. • Make them.
19–24	Advancing	• Solid platform execution in progress. • The risk shifts from 'whether' to 'how well': Whether the flywheel will generate engagement or merely compliant usage, and whether the ecosystem is building fast enough to make the platform valuable.	• Focus investment on Dimension 5 (ecosystem), the dimension most likely to be lagging relative to the technical build. • Ecosystem richness determines whether the platform is genuinely useful or merely technically impressive.

Total Score	Velocity Profile	Interpretation	Recommended First Actions
25–30	Advancing	• Executing well. • The primary risks are complacency, the institutional gravity of the existing model never fully disappears, and programmes that stop actively managing the culture and leadership dimensions often see regression when the early momentum fades.	• Protect the programme's success. • Ensure the metrics, governance, and CEO engagement that drove the early build are sustained as the programme becomes 'established'. • The moment transformation feels routine is the moment the Protectors find their opening.

* * *

15.8 The Velocity Question

As noted above, two institutions with identical scores can find themselves in completely different positions. The velocity assessment for each dimension – advancing, static or retreating – is as important as the score itself because it tells you whether the gap between your position and target has closed or widened.

An institution that scores 2 on Data Foundation but that actively builds, designs consent architecture, moves on Open Banking integration, and contracts two data partnerships ranks just 12–18 months from a score of 4. An institution that scores 3 on the Data Foundation category but sits static – the pilot ran 18 months ago, the results were positive, the next phase is 'under review' – may actually be moving backward as the competitive context shifts and the relative position deteriorates.

You can find the most dangerous velocity signal in a retreat on Dimension 1 or Dimension 6. A programme that lacks strategic clarity or leadership commitment cannot usually recover without a significant external catalyst, a competitor move, board intervention or CEO change. If your velocity assessment on either of these dimensions shows a retreat, you must address this before any other dimension on this scorecard.

* * *

This scorecard marks a starting point—not a destination. Complete it and share it with your leadership team. If you disagree about scores, that is because disagreement can promote dialogue; it reveals divergent views within the organisation about its own readiness and willingness. Then use it to address the question that Chapter 7 asks – 'Platform or Pipe?' – and act on that answer before the window to 2032 closes.

Appendix A:

Home Ownership Journey Value Calculation

Total Value Over 10–15 Years: £500,000+

This appendix provides a detailed breakdown, referenced in Chapters 6 and 7, showing why home ownership represents £500,000-plus in total value over a typical ownership period.

Assumptions

Property: £350,000 purchase price (UK average first-time buyer, 2024).
Ownership period: 12.5 years (midpoint of the 10–15-year ownership period).
Mortgage: 90% LTV (£315,000 loan, £35,000 deposit).
Average mortgage rate: 3.5% over the period.

Purchase Phase Costs

Item	Amount
Property purchase	£350,000
Stamp duty	£5,000
Legal fees	£1,500–2,000
Survey/valuation	£500–1,000
Moving costs	£1,000–2,000

D. Mistry, L. R. Carlozo, *The Intelligent Ledger*,
https://doi.org/10.1007/978-3-032-32842-7

Item	Amount
Mortgage arrangement	£1,000
Subtotal	£359,000–361,000

Ongoing Costs (12.5 Years) Utilities and Services

Item	Annual	Total (12.5yr)
Gas heating	£800	£10,000
Electricity	£1,000	£12,500
Water	£400	£5,000
Council tax	£1,800	£22,500
Internet/TV	£600	£7,500
Subtotal		£57,500

Maintenance and Repairs

Item	Cost
Boiler services (annual £100 × 12)	£1,200
Boiler replacement (once)	£3,000
Plumbing repairs	£2,000
Electrical work	£2,000
Roof repairs	£3,000–5,000
Painting (internal/external)	£5,000
General repairs and maintenance	£5,000
Subtotal	£21,200–23,200

Home Improvements (Variable)

Improvement	Cost
Kitchen upgrade	£15,000
Bathroom upgrade	£8,000
Extensions/conversions	£20,000
Landscaping/garden	£3,000
Flooring	£3,000
Windows/doors	£5,000
Conservative (minimal)	£10,000
Mid-range (typical)	£30,000
Higher-end (major)	£54,000

Insurance

Item	Annual	Total (12.5 yr)
Buildings insurance	£300	£3,750
Contents insurance	£200	£2,500
Subtotal		£6,250

Appliances and Service Contracts

Item	Cost
Washing machine/dryer replacement	£1,000
Fridge/freezer replacement	£800
Oven/hob replacement	£600
Dishwasher	£500
Various small appliances	£500
Appliances subtotal	£3,400
Boiler/heating cover (£300/yr × 12.5)	£3,750
Home emergency cover (£150/yr × 12.5)	£1,875
Service contracts subtotal	£5,625

Sale Phase Costs

Item	Amount
Estate agent fees (1.5% of £450K)	£6,750
Legal fees	£1,500–2,000
EPC certificate	£100
Removal costs	£1,000–2,000
Subtotal	£9,350–10,850

Total Journey Value Calculations

Category	Conservative	Mid-Range	Higher-End
Purchase	£359,000	£359,000	£359,000
Utilities	£57,500	£57,500	£57,500
Maintenance	£21,200	£22,000	£23,000
Improvements	£10,000	£30,000	£54,000
Insurance	£6,250	£6,250	£6,250
Appliances	£3,400	£3,400	£3,400
Service contracts	£5,625	£5,625	£5,625

Category	Conservative	Mid-Range	Higher-End
Sale costs	£9,350	£10,000	£10,850
TOTAL	£472,325	£493,775	£519,625

Value Capture Comparison

Metric	Traditional Bank	Platform Bank Opportunity
Mortgage interest margin	~£2,000	£2,000
Insurance commissions	£500–1,000	£1,500
Utility switching commissions	–	£400–800
Contractor referrals	–	£2,000–4,000
Appliance/service referrals	–	£500–1,000
Journey subscription (£150/mo × 120)	–	£18,000
Sale service commission	–	£1,000–2,000
TOTAL	£2,500–3,000 (0.4–0.6% of journey)	£25,400–29,300 (5–6% of journey)

Banks currently capture less than 1% of the total home ownership journey value despite having the trust, capital, and brand to own the complete relationship. Platform thinking shifts the model from £2,000 lifetime margin on one product to £25,000-plus lifetime value across the complete journey. This proves why journey ownership beats product ownership.

Appendix B: Data Layers Implementation Guide

This appendix is written for CTOs, chief data officers, and senior technology architects responsible for building the digital twin infrastructure described in Chapter 3 and operationalised in Chapters 10–11. It covers the practical implementation of each data layer: what data is included, where it comes from, the technical integration approach, the consent and privacy architecture required, and the realistic timeline for getting each layer to production quality. It does not assume a greenfield architecture; most banks reading this will be working with existing core banking systems, data warehouses, and API infrastructure that the digital twin must integrate with rather than replace. The data sources are UK-specific unless there are global options available. As such this appendix only serves as a guideline/outline plan for non-UK countries.

* * *

Architectural Principles

Before detailing each layer, four architectural principles apply across all of them and should be established before any layer-specific build begins.

Consent-first architecture means every data integration is designed around explicit customer consent from the outset, not retrofitted after the data pipeline is built. The consent management system is Layer Zero, the infrastructure that enables and governs all six layers, and it must be built before any data collection begins. Customers must be able to see exactly the data held about them in each layer, understand specifically

D. Mistry, L. R. Carlozo, *The Intelligent Ledger*,
https://doi.org/10.1007/978-3-032-32842-7

what that data enables the platform to do for them, and withdraw consent for any layer independently without losing access to the platform. This is not a compliance requirement dressed as architecture. It is the value proposition: Customers share data because the value exchange is explicit and genuinely in their favour. Banks in countries with Open Banking regulations should be familiar with this approach. In the UK, industries outside financial services are using Open Banking as a model for their own smart data initiatives.

API-first integration means every data source is integrated through documented, versioned APIs rather than batch file transfers or direct database connections. This is essential for the real-time updating that makes the digital twin genuinely useful, a digital twin that updates monthly from batch files is not a twin; it is a slow snapshot. Open Banking provides the template: Near real-time API access to financial data is already standard. The same approach applies to every other layer. As agentic AI grows in impact these APIs will get replaced by Model Context Protocol interfaces for agents to interact more easily and intelligently.

Privacy by design means data minimisation, purpose limitation, and retention controls are built into the architecture rather than applied as governance overlays. Collect only what is needed for the specific guidance purpose. Retain only as long as the guidance purpose requires. Log every access and every use. This architecture makes regulatory compliance easier and customer trust easier to earn and maintain.

Federated storage with centralised reasoning means the physical data for different layers may reside in different systems, health data in a health data vault, financial data in the core banking system, location data in a location service, but the reasoning layer (the agentic AI) has a unified view across all layers through a secure orchestration API. This avoids the single massive data lake that creates both security risk and governance complexity, while still enabling the cross-layer reasoning that makes the digital twin valuable.

* * *

Layer by Layer Implementation

Layer 6: Financial, Start Here

Despite being the sixth layer in the conceptual model, financial data is where implementation begins, for two reasons: Banks already have it, and Open Banking regulation has already established the API infrastructure to aggregate it across institutions. The implementation work is not data collection, it is data unification, enrichment, and real-time accessibility.

Component	Data Included	Integration Approach	Timeline to Production
Internal accounts	Transaction history, balances, product holdings across all bank products	Direct core banking API integration; real-time	Month 1–3
External accounts (Open Banking)	Accounts at other institutions: Current, savings, mortgages, credit cards, investments	Open Banking API (FCA regulated in UK, PSD2 in EU, emerging in US); customer-consented	Month 2–4
Investment and pension data	Investment portfolios, pension values, ISAs, fund holdings	Open Finance API where available; direct provider partnerships where not	Month 4–9
Credit data enrichment	Credit score trajectory, credit utilisation, credit applications across market	Credit bureau API (Experian, Equifax, TransUnion); consented pull	Month 3–6
Transaction categorisation	AI-enriched spending categories, merchant intelligence, recurring pattern detection	ML categorisation layer over raw transaction data; continuous improvement	Month 2–5

Health and Fitness (Layer 1)

Health data is the most sensitive layer and requires the most careful consent architecture, but it is also among the most valuable for the financial guidance use case. Stress indicators, sleep patterns, and activity levels are directly relevant to financial decision quality and life planning. The integration is via customer-consented data-sharing from existing health platforms rather than direct collection.

Component	Data Included	Integration Approach	Timeline to Production
Wearable device data	Heart rate variability, sleep quality, activity levels, stress indicators	Apple HealthKit API, Google Health Connect, Garmin Connect, Fitbit API; customer-consented OAuth	Month 6–12
Health app data	Nutrition, medication, mental health app data where customer shares	Health data aggregator partnerships (e.g. Validic, Human API); customer-controlled sharing	Month 9–15
Insurance health data	Health insurance claims history, wellness programme data	Direct insurer API partnerships; customer consent required; data minimisation essential	Month 12–18

Environment (Layer 2)

Location and environmental data provide the contextual layer that makes financial guidance genuinely situational, knowing that a customer commutes two hours daily, lives in a high property-value area, or has recently moved changes the relevant financial guidance significantly. This layer is built through partnerships rather than direct data collection.

Component	Data Included	Integration Approach	Timeline to Production
Home and property data	Property value, energy efficiency rating, local property market trends, mortgage-to-value	Land Registry API, Zoopla/Rightmove property data API, EPC Register API; Land Registry and planning portal, Open Property Data Association	Month 4–9
Commute and mobility	Regular commute patterns, transport costs, travel behaviour	Customer-shared location data via platform app; transport API integrations, GPS	Month 9–15
Energy and utilities	Energy consumption patterns, utility costs, efficiency opportunities	Smart metre data via SMETS2 API (UK); utility provider partnerships; Kraken-type platform integration	Month 6–12

Social (Layer 3)

Social data is the most partnership-dependent layer and the most sensitive after health data. The implementation approach prioritises customer-provided relationship context over third-party social platform integration, both for privacy reasons and because customer-provided data is more accurate and more trusted.

Component	Data Included	Integration Approach	Timeline to Production
Family and household structure	Household composition, dependants, life stage, caring responsibilities	Customer self-declaration via platform onboarding; updated through life event detection	Month 3–6
Life events	Marriage, divorce, birth, bereavement, job change, house move	Transaction pattern detection; customer-reported; social media signal (with consent) where available	Month 4–8

Component	Data Included	Integration Approach	Timeline to Production
Social platform data	Public social signals relevant to financial life stage	Optional customer-consented social API connection; treat as an enhancement, not a foundation; aggregators like Sprinklr	Month 15–24

Emotional and Cognitive (Layers 4 and 5)

These layers are the most nascent technically and should be treated as second-generation capabilities, valuable enhancements to the digital twin once the foundational layers are established, but not prerequisites for the initial platform launch. Emotional data (stress indicators, decision patterns under pressure) is partially available through Layer 1 wearable data and through behavioural signals in platform interaction patterns. Cognitive data (decision-making style, risk tolerance revealed through behaviour) emerges from platform interaction data over time. Many banks will have explored emotional detection in areas like fraud.

Component	Data Source	Integration Approach	Timeline
Stress and decision context	HRV from wearables, platform interaction timing, query patterns under financial stress events	Derived from Layer 1 data plus platform behavioural analytics	Month 18–30
Risk tolerance revealed	Actual financial decisions made versus options presented; simulation choices	Platform behavioural data; A/B analysis of option selection	Month 12–24
Decision pattern analysis	Deliberate versus impulsive decision patterns, seasonal patterns, event-triggered behaviour	Platform interaction analytics; transaction pattern analysis	Month 15–24

* * *

Consent Management Architecture

The consent management system is the most important piece of infrastructure in the entire digital twin build, because it is the foundation on which customer trust is built and maintained. A consent management system that is technically sound but experientially poor, where customers cannot easily understand what they have consented to, cannot easily change their consent, and cannot easily see what their data has been used for, will undermine the trust relationship that makes the digital twin valuable. The following are the non-negotiable requirements.

Requirement	Why It Matters	Implementation Approach
Granular per-layer consent	Customers must be able to consent to financial data-sharing without consenting to health data, and vice versa	Independent consent records per layer; withdrawal of one layer does not affect others
Plain-language consent presentation	Customers must understand what they are consenting to in order to genuinely consent	Plain English explanations of each data type and its specific use; no legal boilerplate as primary consent language
Real-time consent audit trail	Every data access must be logged against the consent record that authorised it	Immutable consent audit log; customer-accessible view of every data access
Instant consent withdrawal	Withdrawal must take effect immediately and result in data deletion within regulatory timeframe	Real-time consent flag propagation across all systems; automated deletion workflow
Value exchange transparency	Customers must be able to see specifically what capability each layer of consent enables	Consent management UI shows: 'Sharing health data enables stress-aware financial guidance'; not abstract permissions
Third-party consent governance	Customer consent for data use extends to third-party ecosystem partners	Partner data access governed by same consent framework; partners access via API not raw data

* * *

Data Quality and Governance

A digital twin is only as useful as the data it is built from. Data quality governance is not a post-launch concern; it is a continuous operational requirement from the moment the first layer goes live. The specific risks to manage are: Staleness (data that was accurate when collected but is no longer current), incompleteness (gaps in data that create blind spots in guidance), inconsistency (conflicting data across layers that produces contradictory guidance), and inaccuracy (data that is simply wrong, either through collection error or customer mis-declaration).

Risk	Detection Approach	Remediation Approach
Staleness	Timestamp monitoring per data element; alert when refresh cycle exceeds threshold	Automated re-pull where API allows; customer prompt where manual update required
Incompleteness	Completeness scoring per layer and per customer; cohort-level monitoring	Targeted customer prompts for missing high-value data; ecosystem partner data to fill gaps
Inconsistency	Cross-layer consistency checks; flag contradictions for human review	Customer confirmation workflow for material inconsistencies; audit trail of resolution
Inaccuracy	Customer feedback loop; comparison with third-party data sources; anomaly detection	Customer correction workflow; source reliability scoring; third-party validation

* * *

Realistic Implementation Timeline

Phase	Months	Layers Active	Capability Enabled	Key Milestones
Foundation	1–6	Layer 6 (Financial) core	Basic digital twin: Financial picture across all accounts; spending intelligence; basic simulation	Consent management live; Open Banking integrated; internal data unified; transaction categorisation running

Phase	Months	Layers Active	Capability Enabled	Key Milestones
Environmental and Social	6–12	Layers 6, 2, 3	Home journey guidance: Property intelligence, energy data, family structure, life event detection	Property data partnerships live; energy API integrated; household onboarding flow; life event detection in transaction patterns
Health Integration	12–18	Layers 6, 2, 3, 1	Stress-aware guidance: financial decisions contextualised by health indicators; Life planning across health trajectory	Health platform partnerships; wearable API integrations; stress-financial correlation models trained
Behavioural Layers	18–30	All six layers	Complete digital twin: Full simulation across all life dimensions; cognitive and emotional context for guidance	Behavioural analytics platform; decision pattern models; full simulation capability; quantum pilot on portfolio optimisation

Appendix C:

Quantum Computing Primer for Banking Leaders

This appendix is written for CTOs, chief architects, and technology leaders evaluating quantum computing for banking applications. It covers essential concepts, the current hardware landscape, the most relevant algorithms, realistic deployment timelines, and the build-versus-partner decision. I intend for it to be technically substantive without requiring a background in quantum physics. Chapter 8 explains the why; this appendix explains the how.

Core Concepts

Qubits and Superposition

A classical bit stores exactly one value at any time: 0 or 1. A qubit stores a quantum state that represents a probability distribution over 0 and 1 simultaneously, a property called superposition. Until a qubit is measured, it exists in both states at once. This is not a metaphor but the physical reality of quantum systems. A system of n qubits in superposition can represent 2^n states simultaneously. In practical terms: 10 qubits represent 1,024 states simultaneously (or the number 2 doubled to 4, 4 to 8 and so on up until 1,024); 50 qubits represent approximately 10^15 simultaneous states; 300 qubits represent more states than atoms in the observable universe. Quantum computing does not deliver an advantage for all problem types. Classical computers remain superior for most sequential, linear tasks. Quantum advantage emerges specifically for problems that involve large solution spaces simultaneously, which includes optimisation, simulation, and certain cryptographic problems directly relevant to banking.

D. Mistry, L. R. Carlozo, *The Intelligent Ledger*,
https://doi.org/10.1007/978-3-032-32842-7

Entanglement

When two qubits become 'entangled,' their quantum states become correlated such that measuring one instantly determines information about the other, regardless of physical distance. Entanglement allows quantum systems to process correlations between variables at the same time rather than in sequence. For banking applications, where every variable in a customer's financial life affects every other variable, entanglement allows the quantum system to explore the complete web of interdependencies at once, rather than compute each pairwise relationship separately. This makes quantum simulation of complex life scenarios qualitatively different from classical simulation.

Interference

Quantum algorithms use interference to amplify the probability of correct answers and suppress incorrect ones. Without interference, a quantum computer would generate all possible states simultaneously with no mechanism to extract useful results. Interference serves as the design principle behind all quantum algorithms: They are structured so that the quantum state evolves to constructively reinforce correct solutions (like waves adding together) and destructively cancel incorrect ones (like waves cancelling out). This explains why quantum algorithms do not simply dictate, 'Try everything at once.' They employ carefully designed procedures that use interference to guide computation towards correct results.

Measurement

Measurement is what collapses a quantum system from its superposition of possible states into a single definite classical result that can be read and used. This is necessary: Without measurement, quantum computations produce no usable output, but it is also the fundamental constraint that makes quantum algorithm design genuinely difficult. An unmeasured quantum system exists in all possible states simultaneously. Measurement forces it to one. Without carefully designed interference patterns amplifying correct answers before measurement, you would simply sample a random outcome from the distribution of possibilities. This is why quantum algorithms are not 'try everything and pick the best': They are structured procedures that use interference to concentrate probability towards correct answers before measurement collapses the system. Measurement is also why quantum computing is not a silver bullet. The need to extract classical information from a quantum system means that not every problem benefits from quantum treatment, only those where good algorithms exist to exploit interference before measurement. For banking practitioners, the implication is that quantum advantage is problem-specific and algorithm-dependent, not a general capability that applies to any computation.

The NISQ Era: What Current Hardware Actually Delivers

Current quantum computers are described as Noisy Intermediate-Scale Quantum (NISQ) devices, Noisy Intermediate-Scale Quantum. This means two things practically. First, they work at an intermediate scale: Current machines contain between 50 and approximately 1,120 physical qubits, depending on provider and architecture. Not all can be used simultaneously for complex calculations due to error rates.

Second, they are noisy as qubits are fragile. It remains technically difficult to maintain quantum coherence and keep qubits in their quantum state long enough to complete a calculation. Environmental interference from temperature fluctuations, electromagnetic noise, and vibration can cause qubit errors. Current error rates range from approximately 0.1% to 1% per gate operation, limiting the length and complexity of circuits that can run reliably. NISQ devices deliver real quantum advantage on specific, well-structured problems. But fault-tolerant quantum computers that will deliver the full vision of quantum simulation at banking scale do not yet exist. That transition is expected to begin between 2028 and 2032, depending on progress in error correction.

The Quantum Insider's March 2026 analysis of quantum AI puts this distinction plainly. It categorises 'quantum-enhanced AI' that uses quantum computers to accelerate AI workloads; full-life simulation requires this. This is because fault-tolerant hardware does not yet exist. 'AI for quantum computing' uses classical machine learning to calibrate, optimise and operate quantum hardware, as already actively deployed in labs with high current impact. Earlier chapters describe this asymmetry. The intelligence layer that makes quantum simulation useful is buildable now, while quantum hardware that runs the full simulation matures through 2029 to 2031.

Quantum Algorithms Most Relevant to Banking

Quantum Approximate Optimisation Algorithm (QAOA)

The most deployable quantum algorithm for banking at present, QAOA addresses combinatorial optimisation by finding the best combination from a large number of possibilities. Portfolio optimisation is the canonical banking application: Given a universe of assets with complex correlations, what combination maximises expected return for a given risk level? QAOA explores this solution space quantum-mechanically. Where classical algorithms struggle, it identifies near-optimal solutions for constrained problems. Goldman Sachs, JPMorgan, and BBVA have published results from quantum experiments that demonstrate potential advantages in simplified portfolio scenarios. These results, it must be noted, represent early-stage experiments on small, structured portfolios, not production deployments on the full operational books that those institutions run.

Current QAOA implementations also face legitimate constraints, including the 'barren plateaus' problem (a mathematical dead end that has plagued variational quantum computing for years) and a classical bottleneck in the backpropagation step where the algorithm's speed advantage is bounded by its classical component. (In backpropagation, the computer recycles information, allowing it to learn from its mistakes and produces cleaner outcomes.) These boil down to engineering problems with solutions in progress, not theoretical objections.

From a practical standpoint for banks today, QAOA delivers demonstrable advantage on well-structured optimisation problems within current qubit and error-rate constraints, and that advantage will grow as hardware matures. This algorithm is well-suited to NISQ-era pilots and a recommended starting point for banks that wish to explore quantum advantage today, with clear eyes about what 'advantage' means at this stage.

Quantum Monte Carlo Simulation

On a wide scale, banking risk management already runs 'Monte Carlo simulation', where thousands of random scenarios estimate probability distributions. Quantum Monte Carlo achieves a quadratic reduction in the number of scenarios required: A problem that requires 10,000 classical scenarios can theoretically be solved by approximately 100 quantum scenarios with equivalent accuracy. However, this does not translate directly into a practical speedup on current hardware. Each individual quantum scenario currently takes roughly 1,000 to 100,000 times longer to compute than its classical counterpart, because quantum gates are significantly slower than classical operations at this stage of the technology's development. The net practical advantage, whether the reduction in scenario count outweighs the per-scenario slowdown, is genuinely debated and depends on how quickly quantum hardware speeds improve. The theoretical case for eventual advantage is sound; the practical timeline for this speedup to become decisive in real-world banking should not be overstated. This algorithm forms the foundation of the life simulation capability described in Chapter 8.

Variational Quantum Eigensolver (VQE)

VQE is a hybrid classical-quantum algorithm that finds minimum energy states. In banking, this is relevant for pricing complex derivatives and structured products, financial instruments whose value depends on multiple interacting variables in ways classical pricing models approximate rather than compute exactly. VQE has the theoretical potential to compute more accurate prices than classical approximation methods for certain complex derivative structures, which would reduce model risk. However, this has not yet been demonstrated at production scale on real financial instruments, and remains an open research question rather than an established result. Though more specialised than portfolio optimisation, it offers high value for trading desks and risk management at large financial institutions.

Quantum Machine Learning (QML)

QML applies quantum principles to machine learning tasks. In terms of banking relevance, quantum support vector machines can solve classification problems such as fraud detection and credit scoring, while quantum principal component analysis provides clarity when applied to high-dimensional customer data. Theoretical speedups over classical counterparts are exponential for certain highly structured and idealised problem types. It is important to be precise: These speedups have so far been demonstrated on mathematically idealised problem structures that do not fully represent the messy, high-dimensional data typical of real banking operations. Whether quantum speedups transfer to production fraud detection or credit scoring – where data is noisy and the problem structure does not fit neatly into the idealised formulations where quantum advantage has been shown – is an active research question with no confirmed answer yet. QML remains one of the most promising longer-term quantum banking applications, but demonstrable real-world advantage is more likely in the 2029–2031 window, contingent on algorithmic progress. Conservative planning should treat earlier timelines as optimistic.

Current Provider Landscape

Provider	Technology	Scale (approx.)	Access Model	Banking Relevance
IBM Quantum	Superconducting qubits	1,000+ qubits (Eagle/ Heron)	Cloud API; IBM Quantum Network membership	Most mature banking toolkit; Qiskit ecosystem; JPMorgan and Goldman Sachs pilots
Amazon Braket	Multi-provider (IonQ, Rigetti, OQC)	Varies by backend	AWS cloud; pay-per-use; integrates with AWS data stack	Easiest entry point for banks already on AWS; multiple hardware backends
Google Quantum AI	Superconducting qubits	53 qubits (Sycamore)	Research partnerships; limited commercial access	Demonstrated quantum supremacy; strong research credentials

Provider	Technology	Scale (approx.)	Access Model	Banking Relevance
Microsoft Azure Quantum	Multi-provider + topological roadmap	Varies by partner	Azure cloud; integrates with Azure ML and data services	Strong hybrid classical-quantum tooling; promising long-term topological approach
IonQ	Trapped ion qubits	36 algorithmic qubits	Cloud via AWS, Azure, Google Cloud	Higher qubit quality (lower error rates) than superconducting; growing banking pilots

The recommended starting approach is to establish accounts with IBM Quantum and AWS Braket, which provide the most mature banking-relevant toolkits and the broadest access to different hardware backends. Both offer sandbox environments for algorithm development before any commitment to production workloads.

Build Versus Partner Decision

Quantum computing's build-versus-partner question has a clear answer at this stage of the technology's maturity: Partner. Building in-house quantum capability requires that banks (or any business) hire quantum physicists and algorithm developers and maintain expertise in rapidly evolving hardware. This is an unrealistic proposition for even the very largest banks. The technology is evolving too quickly, the talent pool remains too small, and cloud vendors investing billions in the infrastructure provide the best hardware access.

Relevant in-house investment, though, occupies three areas: quantum-ready software architecture (so classical banking systems can interface cleanly with quantum cloud services); quantum literacy in technology leadership (so good decisions about where to invest can ensue); and quantum algorithm expertise (so you can access specific use cases most relevant to your business).

As for the recommended partnership model, establish relationships with one or two quantum cloud providers as anchor infrastructure partners, then engage with specialist quantum software firms that develop banking-specific quantum algorithms. Banking-specific expertise matters most in the algorithm layer. Cloud vendors provide the hardware, but the algorithms that run on it specifically need calibration for financial services applications. Specialist firms that include Quantum Basel, Quantinuum (formerly Cambridge Quantum), QC Ware, and Multiverse Computing focus on this layer and maintain banking relationships and financial services algorithm libraries. When you engage one of these firms as an algorithm development partner (and combine it with a cloud infrastructure partnership via IBM or AWS), you cover the full quantum stack without the need for in-house quantum physics expertise.

Realistic Deployment Timeline

Phase	Hardware State	Available Banking Capability	Recommended Actions
2025–2027 (Now)	NISQ: 50–1,120+ physical qubits, error rates 0.1–1% per gate	Portfolio optimisation, simplified risk modelling, basic scenario generation with reduced variable sets	• Establish cloud partnerships. • Run QAOA portfolio optimisation pilot. • Build digital twin data infrastructure in parallel. • Develop quantum literacy in technology leadership.
2027–2029 (Near-term)	Improved NISQ: Reduced error rates, longercoherence times, error mitigation techniques	More complex optimisation, expanded scenario modelling across more variables, QML pilots for fraud detection and credit scoring	• Expand pilots to limited customer-facing life scenario modelling. • Integrate quantum outputs into digital twin platform. • Begin simulation history accumulation.
2029–2031 (Fault-tolerant emergence)	Early fault-tolerant: Error-corrected logical qubits available, circuit depth no longer the primary constraint	Full life scenario simulation at meaningful complexity levels, real-time personalised guidance at scale, production quantum risk models	• Scale proven applications to full customer base. • Deploy real-time quantum simulation in customer experience. • Competitive moat begins to establish.
2031+ (Mature fault-tolerant)	Fault-tolerant at scale: Thousands of logical qubits, full theoretical quantum advantage available	Complete personalised life simulation at any complexity level, full quantum advantage across all banking applications	• Full production deployment. • Platforms with 2027 start have 4+ years of simulation history and established moats. • Late entrants face a near-impossible catch-up task.

A critical planning implication is that digital twin data infrastructure and quantum pilot programmes must begin simultaneously in 2027. Data infrastructure requires a build time of 18–24 months before it produces the quality data that makes quantum simulation useful. Starting data infrastructure tasks in 2029 means having good quantum simulation capability but mediocre data: Exactly backwards from the optimal sequence.

Key Technical Risks and Mitigations

Hardware Instability Risk: NISQ hardware remains imperfect and its error rates limit circuit complexity.

Mitigation: Use hybrid classical-quantum algorithms designed for NISQ constraints, specifically QAOA and quantum Monte Carlo variants, which degrade gracefully towards classical solutions when quantum error rates prevent reliable computation. Do not architect systems that require perfect quantum hardware to function. *Build classical fallback paths* into every quantum application from day one.

Talent Scarcity Risk: Quantum expertise is scarce and expensive.

Mitigation: Partner with specialist quantum software firms instead of building in-house algorithm development capability from scratch. Focus any internal hiring on quantum-ready software engineers (classical developers with quantum computing literacy) who can fabricate integration layers between banking systems and quantum cloud APIs. The question of whether banks need quantum physicists in-house is genuinely debated. At the current stage, a partnership model with specialist algorithm firms reduces the in-house quantum physics requirement significantly. However, as AI tools increasingly assist with algorithm development and quantum systems become more complex, the balance of required expertise will evolve. The safest approach is to maintain close partnerships with specialist firms who carry the deep physics expertise, while building sufficient internal literacy to evaluate their work and make informed investment decisions.

Regulatory Uncertainty Risk: Requirements that govern explainability (where a set of techniques and processes allow human users to understand, interpret, and trust decisions and predictions) for AI and algorithmic decision-making may create quantum systems compliance challenges.

Mitigation: Design quantum applications with explainability as a first principle. Quantum simulation is inherently explainable; it shows scenarios, their probabilities, and the reasoning that supports recommendations, without opaque outputs. This structural regulatory advantage outflanks black-box classical ML. Engage with regulators proactively as pilot programmes develop and establish frameworks for quantum transparency before officials mandate them.

Competitive Timing Risk: The risk that competitors move faster than anticipated.

Mitigation: Start. Now. Every month of delay equals a month of data, customer relationships, and simulation history that competitors can accumulate instead. Timing remains a daunting proposition but there are two ways to think about it. Move too early (employing imperfect hardware and/or suboptimal algorithms) and you'll show some wasted investment—which you could justify so long as you keep it quantifiable and bounded. Move too late and the market will consolidate around first movers with established platform moats. Laggards will confront infinite switching costs and data gaps they cannot close. Given the asymmetric risk environment, the correct response is to err towards early action.

Quantum Terms Reference

Term	Definition for Banking Practitioners
Qubit	The basic unit of quantum information. Unlike a classical bit (always 0 or 1), a qubit can be in a superposition of both states simultaneously until measured. This is the source of quantum computing's exponential parallelism for certain problem types.
Superposition	The quantum property that allows a qubit to represent 0 and 1 simultaneously. A system of n qubits in superposition represents 2^n states at once, the foundation of quantum computing's power for large-scale optimisation and simulation.
Entanglement	A quantum correlation between qubits where the state of one instantly determines information about the others, regardless of distance. Enables quantum systems to process variable interactions simultaneously rather than sequentially.
Interference	The quantum mechanism used in algorithms to amplify correct answers and suppress incorrect ones. Makes quantum computations useful rather than random by steering the system towards correct solutions.
Measurement	The process of reading the result of a quantum computation, which collapses the quantum state from superposition into a definite classical value (0 or 1). Measurement is necessary to extract usable results but also the constraint that makes quantum algorithm design challenging. Without carefully designed interference amplifying correct answers before measurement, results are random. The need for thoughtful measurement strategies is why quantum computing delivers advantages for specific problem types, not universally.
NISQ	*Noisy Intermediate-Scale Quantum.* Describes current quantum computers: Real quantum machines with real quantum capabilities, but subject to errors that limit circuit length and complexity.
Coherence time	How long a qubit maintains its quantum state before environmental interference causes errors. Longer coherence time enables more complex calculations. Improving steadily across all hardware platforms.
Gate fidelity	The accuracy of a quantum gate operation. Current NISQ machines achieve 99–99.9% fidelity per gate; errors compound over long circuits, which limits practical circuit depth.

Term	Definition for Banking Practitioners
Fault-tolerant quantum computing	A quantum computer that corrects errors in real-time using quantum error correction codes, which enables arbitrarily long and complex circuits. Expected to emerge in early form in 2029–2031.
Logical qubit	An error-corrected qubit formed from multiple physical qubits. Fault-tolerant quantum computers operate with logical qubits; current NISQ machines operate with raw physical qubits.
QAOA	*Quantum Approximate Optimisation Algorithm.* A hybrid classical-quantum algorithm for combinatorial optimisation problems. The most immediately applicable quantum algorithm for banking portfolio and risk applications today.
Quantum Monte Carlo	Quantum algorithm achieving quadratic speedup over classical Monte Carlo simulation. Enables faster probability distribution estimation for risk modelling and life scenario generation.
VQE	*Variational Quantum Eigensolver.* Hybrid classical-quantum algorithm for complex pricing problems. Used for accurate valuation of derivatives and structured products.
Hybrid algorithm	An algorithm that combines quantum and classical computation, with each handling the parts where it has the advantage. The dominant practical approach for current NISQ-era quantum applications.
Quantum advantage	The demonstration that quantum computing provides better, faster, more accurate, or previously intractable results to solve for a real-world problem compared to the best available classical approach.
Quantum supremacy	The demonstration that a quantum computer has solved a specific problem faster than any classical computer could, regardless of the problem's practical usefulness. Claimed by Google in 2019, though the result remains contested. Subsequent classical algorithms and hardware improvements have come close to or matched the specific benchmark used. The concept of quantum supremacy as a clean threshold has become less meaningful as the boundary between quantum and classical capability continues to shift. What matters for banking strategy is quantum advantage – practical, verifiable improvement on real-world problems – rather than supremacy on synthetic benchmarks.

Index

D. Mistry, L. R. Carlozo, *The Intelligent Ledger*,
https://doi.org/10.1007/978-3-032-32842-7

FSC
www.fsc.org
MIX
Papier | Fördert gute Waldnutzung
FSC® C083411

Kolibri 360 GmbH
Ferdinand-Jühlke-Straße 7
99095 Erfurt, Deutschland
produktsicherheit@kolibri360.de